Building a Sustainable Political Economy: SPERI Research & Policy

Series Editors
Colin Hay
SPERI
University of Sheffield
Sheffield, UK

Anthony Payne
SPERI
University of Sheffield
Sheffield, UK

The Sheffield Political Economy Research Institute (SPERI) is an innovation in higher education research and outreach. It brings together leading international researchers in the social sciences, policy makers, journalists and opinion formers to reassess and develop proposals in response to the political and economic issues posed by the current combination of financial crisis, shifting economic power and environmental threat. Building a Sustainable Political Economy: SPERI Research & Policy will serve as a key outlet for SPERI's published work. Each title will summarise and disseminate to an academic and postgraduate student audience, as well as directly to policy-makers and journalists, key policy-oriented research findings designed to further the development of a more sustainable future for the national, regional and world economy following the global financial crisis. It takes a holistic and interdisciplinary view of political economy in which the local, national, regional and global interact at all times and in complex ways. The SPERI research agenda, and hence the focus of the series, seeks to explore the core economic and political questions that require us to develop a new sustainable model of political economy at all times and in complex ways.

More information about this series at
http://www.palgrave.com/gp/series/14879

Colin Hay · Daniel Bailey
Editors

Diverging Capitalisms

Britain, the City of London and Europe

Editors
Colin Hay
Centre Etudes Europeennes
Universites Science Politique
Paris, France

Daniel Bailey
Political Economy Centre
University of Manchester
Manchester, UK

Building a Sustainable Political Economy: SPERI Research & Policy
ISBN 978-3-030-03414-6   ISBN 978-3-030-03415-3   (eBook)
https://doi.org/10.1007/978-3-030-03415-3

Library of Congress Control Number: 2018959878

This Palgrave Macmillan imprint is published by the registered company Springer Nature
Switzerland AG
The registered company address is: Gewerbestrasse 11, 6330 Cham, Switzerland

FOREWORD

With rising inequalities in the context of the great financial crisis, the structural power of finance and the Brexit vote, parties of the left and centre-left have an important role to play. Jeremy Corbyn's Labour Party must be congratulated for its powerful campaign in the run-up to the 2017 UK General Election, in which it was clearly able to get its message across to millions of people and many more than was expected by opposition parties and those within the progressive community itself. The message of being "for the many, not the few" resonated with close to 13 million voters and it has a truly progressive basis. But progressives must not become complacent and think that the job has been done. Now is the time to build on that success.

In fact, if we can be confident of anything, it is that the relationship between the UK and the EU will be something completely different to what was promised by the Leave campaign during the referendum. The EU must remain firm and even more importantly, must remain united. There must be no option for the UK to look for potential trade alliances in countries such as Hungary, Poland and other new member states. Not because the UK must be made to suffer. Quite the opposite. The progressive community in the UK and Europe must stick together, must use each other, to ensure the best possible deal for everyone.

Given this political challenge, FEPS (Foundation for European Progressive Studies, Brussels), Policy Network and SPERI (Sheffield Political Economy Research Institute, University of Sheffield) joined forces in 2016 to convene a series of workshops in the framework of their joint project 'Diverging Capitalisms? Britain, the City of London and Europe'. The project also benefited from the financial support of the European Parliament. The aim of the joint venture was to consider the changing nature of the British economy, its place within the European economic space and the consequences of 'Brexit'. The work undertaken fed into a number of policy briefs, and, finally, in the publication of this edited book.

The research project was designed to allow for open discussion about, the socio-economic ramifications of Brexit, the changing nature of the city of London, the global financial crisis and social and economic inequalities across Europe. One objective of this research project was also to bring together a group of scholars to reflect about these issues of profound importance to the future of Europe and the role of Britain within the European economic space—even before Brexit became a reality. The roundtable debates that took place in London and Brussels allowed the authors featured in this book to pit their ideas and hypotheses against those of other academics, policymakers and think tankers in London and Brussels. Through this publication, FEPS, Policy Network and SPERI hope to spur innovative thinking to enrich the debate about the future of progressive politics and economic restructuring in Europe.

Brussels, Belgium   Dr. Ernst Stetter
June 2018   Foundation of European
                                                    Progressive Studies

Acknowledgements

We owe a debt of gratitude to many people who were instrumental in organising the project from which this book has emerged. Tony Payne, Ernst Stetter and Roger Liddle were vital in bringing the project to fruition and it subsequently benefited from the leadership of Renault Thillaye, Lisa Kastner and Charlie Cadywould.

The research would also not have been possible without colleagues past and present at the Sheffield Political Economy Research Institute (SPERI), most notably Arianna Giovannini, Tom Hunt and Laure Astill to whom we are extremely grateful.

CONTENTS

1   Introduction: Brexit and European Capitalism—A
    Parting of the Waves?   1
    Colin Hay and Daniel Bailey

2   After Brexit: The Past and Future of the Anglo-Liberal
    Model   17
    Andrew Gamble

3   "Pragmatic Adaptation" and the Future of the City
    of London: Between Globalisation and Brexit   43
    Leila Simona Talani

4   The Limits of the City's Structural Power: The City's
    Offshore Interests and the Brexit Referendum   73
    Helen Thompson

5   European Union Financial Regulation, Banking Union,
    Capital Markets Union and the UK   99
    Lucia Quaglia

6   Integration and Disintegration: Two-Level Games
    in the EU   125
    Waltraud Schelkle

7   The UK's Growth Model, Business Strategy and Brexit   149
    Scott Lavery

8   The Bed You Made: Social Democracy and Industrial
    Policy in the EU   171
    Angela Wigger and Laura Horn

9   Unusual Bedfellows? The IMF, Tackling Inequality
    and Social Democratic Policy Renewal   195
    Ben Clift

Index   221

CONTRIBUTORS

Daniel Bailey Political Economy Centre, University of Manchester, Manchester, UK

Ben Clift Department of Politics and International Studies, University of Warwick, Coventry, UK

Andrew Gamble Sheffield Political Economy Research Institute, University of Sheffield, Sheffield, UK

Colin Hay Centre d'études européennes, Sciences Po, Paris, France

Laura Horn Roskilde University, Roskilde, Denmark

Scott Lavery Sheffield Political Economy Research Institute, University of Sheffield, Sheffield, UK

Lucia Quaglia University of Bologna, Bologna, Italy

Waltraud Schelkle European Institute, London School of Economics, London, UK

Leila Simona Talani Kennedy School of Governance, Harvard University, Cambridge, MA, USA; King's College London, London, UK

Helen Thompson University of Cambridge, Cambridge, UK

Angela Wigger Radboud University, Nijmegen, The Netherlands

LIST OF TABLES

Table 3.1   Frieden's model   56
Table 3.2   Predicted effects of expanding exposure to trade   57
Table 5.1   Overview of the UK's roles in selected financial policies
            in the EU   104
Table 6.1   Stylised two-level game representations of German
            and UK positions   131

CHAPTER 1

Introduction: Brexit and European Capitalism—A Parting of the Waves?

Colin Hay and Daniel Bailey

In the early 1990s it was *de rigueur* to argue that the challenge of competitiveness in an age of ever greater economic interdependence was likely to put pay to the institutional diversity of capitalism itself, certainly in the western world. Globalisation, in other words, was an agent of convergence like no other—driving down taxation, regulation and welfare spending. Lumped together, as it so often was, with the end of the Cold War's ideological battle, this prompted the liberal Right to herald proudly the 'end of history' with the global triumph of both Anglo-liberal capitalism and Anglo-liberal democracy (Fukuyama 1989). It political-economic terms, it was argued that the (largely) exogenous and (seemingly) agentless forces of globalisation compelled states to engage—and, ultimately, to succeed

C. Hay (✉)
Centre d'études européennes, Sciences Po, Paris, France
e-mail: colin.hay@sciencespo.fr

D. Bailey
Political Economy Centre, University of Manchester, Manchester, UK
e-mail: daniel.bailey@manchester.ac.uk

© The Author(s) 2019
C. Hay and D. Bailey (eds.), *Diverging Capitalisms*,
Building a Sustainable Political Economy: SPERI Research & Policy,
https://doi.org/10.1007/978-3-030-03415-3_1

1

in—the interstate competition for internationally-mobile capital if they were not to endure a profound loss in economic performance. In short, they had no alternative other than to adapt their political economies to the (perceived) needs of global finance. This, it was posited, would necessitate a form of state transformation characterised by fiscal restraint, supply-side rather than demand-side forms of intervention, the prioritisation of low inflation over full employment, and the re-moulding and re-purposing of existing welfare state institutions to suit the goals of national strategies for attaining and sustaining competitiveness. The 'competition state', as it was termed (by critics as well as admirers), was thus identified as the successor to the Keynesian welfare state of *les trente glorieuses*, the model around which the contemporary nation-states would henceforth crystallise (Cerny 1997).

Yet despite this claim, hypothesis, hunch or conjecture—and perhaps unremarkably to students of the *longue durée*—capitalist diversity persisted. In 2001, Peter Hall and David Soskice published their now seminal text, *Varieties of Capitalism*. Based, as it was, on a fusion of rational choice and historical variants of the new institutionalism, it sought to demonstrate that the political economies of the advanced capitalism worlds were in fact clustering around not one but *two* models. These twin Pareto optima were, in effect predicated on, and sustained by, different institutional foundations of national competitiveness. The first of these model capitalisms they termed the Liberal Market Economy (LME). It was characterised by flexible labour markets, stratified wages, and mobile capital with a typically short-term focus. LMEs, thus understood, were seen as innovative, flexible, adaptive and responsive to changing competitive circumstances, a process lubricated by a liberalised financial sector allocating resources between opportunities as they presented themselves. Hall and Soskice's exemplary LME cases were the Anglophone economies—the USA, the UK, Ireland and Australia. The liberal character of their market governance was seen to be mirrored in the more individualistic character of their cultural tendencies. The second model capitalism identified and described by Hall and Soskice was the Coordinated Market Economy (CME) model. Here we find a more densely institutionalist configuration—a corporatist model in which non-market relations take on a far more important role. This model involves by a less arms-length role for the state—a coordinator and not just a regulator. CMEs are characterised by more tightly and actively regulated labour markets, a greater degree of social protection, and a virtuous self-reinforcing cycle of patient capital, long-term investment in skills and training, and collaborative rather than conflictual industrial relations in which employer organisations and trade unions play a central role alongside the state. The CME model is most commonly used to denote the economies of Germany, Sweden, Finland, Switzerland, Norway and the Netherlands.

Hall and Soskice's approach has proved phenomenally influential. Its central premise is that the variety of capitalism to which an economy belongs shapes profoundly the types of corporate strategy to be found within it, influencing in turn levels of productivity, domestic disposable income and so forth. The theoretical and conceptual tools proffered by Hall and Soskice are a touchstone for comparative political economists seeking to understand the role of national institutional configurations in shaping economic practices and strategies of competitiveness—with their broader implications for the distributional patterns, systemic risks and political contestation pertaining to national capitalist systems (Schmidt 2002; Hay 2004, 2005; Rhodes 2005; Hall and Gingerich 2009; Hall 2014; Soskice et al. 2016).

Yet it is important to note that the analytic distinction between LMEs and CMEs is an ideal-typical one. As many scholars have argued, the theoretical categories and empirical claims posited by the framework are highly contestable (Pontusson 2005; Bruff and Horn 2012; Bruff and Ebenau 2014; Bailey and Shibata 2014; Coates 2015). As such, and as Hall and Soskice themselves made clear, no country can be expected to conform to either model in its entirety. The specificities of institutional change interact with relatively distinctive national growth models which incentivise the privileging of particular sectors in economic governance (such as the City of London or the Bavarian manufacturing industry) resulting in idiosyncratic paths of economic development (Hall and Thelen 2009; Hay and Wincott 2012). However, the categorisation did succeed in emphasising the different strategies capable of achieving competitiveness. In so doing, it came to serve as an important corrective to the expectation, typical of the literature of the time, of a globalisation-engendered process of convergence. In place of this simple convergence thesis Hall and Soskice substituted a more complex and institutionally-differentiated dual convergence thesis.

That was then. Since the 2008 financial crash the world has changed significantly—and so has how we think about it. With the benefit of the hindsight the crisis affords, some of the limits of convergence theses (whether simple or dual) are more starkly exposed. Put bluntly, to understand the developmental trajectories of contemporary capitalism it now seems rather more important to focus on sources of disequilibrium and crisis, rather than to work with equilibrium models. In a world in which it is acknowledged that crises are possible, there are limits to the value of ideal-typical reflections on stylised models of capitalism. For such approaches, however well they might describe a current situation, fail to anticipate, and lack the conceptual resources to make even retrospective sense of, crises.

Arguably, then, one of the casualties of the crisis is our current understanding of the dynamic variability of capitalism institutionally. This volume is a contribution to the debate such a reflection presages.

An initial point of departure is the acknowledgment that the political attempts to navigate low levels of economic growth since the crisis do not lend themselves readily to a story of convergence (whether simple or more variegated). The 2008 crash was followed by the European sovereign debt crisis, increasingly fractious relations between the Eurozone's creditor and debtor countries, prompting attempts at capitalist restructuring intended to instigate national economic recoveries. The 2010s have thus seen European economies implement differing levels and types of fiscal austerity, monetary activism (within and beyond the Eurozone), welfare retrenchment and labour market reform. Simultaneously, the discontent fostered by low growth and the political attempts to navigate it have contributed to the rise in popularity of right-wing and Eurosceptic populist figures and parties particularly amongst unskilled or semi-skilled workers in deindustrialised regions (the so-called 'left behind'). Although it is an identifiable trend across Europe, the most conspicuous manifestation of the populist ascendancy so far is 'Brexit' itself; the withdrawal of the UK from the European Union and (it now seems clear) the Single European Market. The exact terms of the UK's withdrawal are subject to intense on-going negotiations. It is on the outcome of these negotiations that arguably the very feasibility of the UK's existing growth model will rest.

But the uncertainty that Brexit has prompted is not contained domestically; it has certainly heightened the sense of political indeterminacy (albeit to differing degrees) within European economies. The strategic disorientation within the UK created by Brexit itself suggests further bouts of fragmentation and capitalist re-structuring in the near future, matched in all likelihood by political-economic change within the EU now that its erstwhile 'awkward partner' is set on a different course (whatever that turns out to be).

For some, particularly the Conservative Party's 'Brexiteers', Brexit represents an opportunity for a further radical liberalisation of the UK economy. No longer bound by supra-national 'red tape' and the EU's regulatory disposition, the UK in such a conception might re-fashion itself as a European Singapore, paring back still further the vestiges of its labour market regulation whilst cutting taxation and reducing further welfare eligibility and generosity. Competitiveness would be achieved in this model through the offer of a 'good business environment' to internationally mobile capital, at the expense of hard-won workers' rights, environmental protections and the scope of the state's existing welfare policies. Central to this strategy would be the swift negotiation of trade deals with the emerging economies of Asia and South America, in particular, a precondition of which is that the UK cannot remain a member of the Customs Union. In the short term, the UK would fall back to the trade terms of the WTO, or would take the advice of the group formerly known as 'Economists for Brexit' (now rebranded 'Economists for Free Trade') to declare a unilateral strategy of trade liberalisation by eliminating any and all tariff and non-tariff barriers. This would represent a drastic deepening of the Thatcherite project (or at least its neoliberal elements) in the UK. It is at present by no means widely supported. But if no trade agreement has been reached between the EU and the UK at the point of withdrawal (on March 29, 2019, two years after the triggering of Article 50) then its proponents could feasibly swell in number. This is a proposal that many card-carrying Brexiteers within the ruling Conservative Party incline towards—including, of course, both Boris Johnson and Jacob Rees-Mogg. But the opposition to it, including within the current Conservative Cabinet, should not be underestimated. At times, during what has to date been a fraught negotiation process, its value to the government has seemed to be the tacit (if perhaps rather hollow sounding) threat that it might be seen to pose. It need hardly be pointed out that this is a potentially dangerous game to play—not least as it has given a platform that it might not otherwise have had to a hyper-liberalising idea of Britain after Brexit.

A very different conception of the post-Brexit scenario is reached in the UK were it to remain a member of the Customs Union and retain access to the European Single Market (and its attendant regulatory structure). Here the potential divergence between Britain and the EU would be far less drastic. This is the so-called 'Soft Brexit' option—the scarcely veiled preference of the UK Treasury in opposition to the Department for Exiting the European Union. Philip Hammond, the Chancellor of the Exchequer and chief proponent within the Cabinet of a 'Soft Brexit', believes that such a deal is likely and that any capitalist divergence resulting from Brexit will be modest. To the dismay of the many Brexiteers in his Party, he argued at the World Economic Forum in Davos that:

> Instead of doing what we're normally doing in the trade negotiations – taking two divergent economies with low levels of trade and trying to bring them closer together to enhance that trade, we are taking two completely interconnected and aligned economies with high levels of trade between them, and selectively moving them, hopefully very modestly, apart. (Hammond 2018)

The battle lines are drawn. As this suggests, the internal politics of the Conservative Party make it extremely unclear to what degree we will witness a significant change in UK macroeconomic strategy and an associated potential bifurcation of British and EU capitalisms in the decades to come. Even the short-term trajectory is unclear. It may well be that by the end of the current Parliament, Britain will actually conform less well than it does today to the LME template. Theresa May has already professed a certain critique of financialised Anglo-liberal capitalism. In her first Conservative Party speech as Leader, in the midst of the tense political climate after the EU referendum, she chose to denounce the stateless 'international elite' and vowed to re-unite the country by making 'capitalism' operate 'more fairly for workers' (*Financial Times* 2016). In a later speech in January 2017, she refuted the principles of Thatcherism by stating that 'people who are just managing, just getting by, don't need a government that will get out of the way, they need a government that will make the system work for them' (*Financial Times* 2017). She has since proposed worker representation on corporate boards and re-introduced the language of industrial strategy (if, as yet, not with a great deal of substance) back into British politics. These are sentiments which have divided the Conservative Party and have not at the time of writing been translated into major policy changes. The difficulties of overcoming the 'lock in' effects' of existing competitive advantages and vested economic interests in order to change macroeconomic course appear to have been too great.

Yet Theresa May appears cognisant that the strategic considerations of economic re-orientation must be attuned to the broader context of the social crises precipitated by recent waves of capitalist restructuring. This is a febrile context in which to engage in macroeconomic strategising. The particular types of austerity measures and labour market reforms (chosen by ruling parties or demanded by the Troika) since the 2008 financial crash—and their impacts on the wage share, precarious work and inequality especially—have had profound political and social impacts. They have compounded deeper structural issues of socially and geographically unequal growth, the increasing importance of asset ownership in determining distributional outcomes (Piketty 2014), and the incremental dismantling of the welfare state and the concomitant rise of private debt (Soederberg 2014). These capitalist structures have contributed heavily to the spectrum of discontentment evident in Europe today. As already alluded to, one manifestation of this has been political polarisation. The precariousness in deindustrialised low-growth areas outside the major cosmopolitan cities amongst unskilled or semi-skilled workers has seemingly contributed to anti-establishment sentiment and rise of right-wing populism, as discontent has bred distributional conflicts on racialised lines and anti-immigration feeling. Meanwhile, the younger generations and the poorest (particularly but not exclusively in the UK) are looking further to the left as a result of being so deeply affected by policy decisions and being almost entirely excluded from the asset appreciation which is so central to the UK's current growth model. The decade of sluggish economic performance since 2008 has also had ramifications for geo-political fragmentation, with many in Scotland and Northern Ireland uncomfortable with their place in a 'Brexiting Britain'; reflected by separatist movements in mainland Europe under similar economic conditions. These developments seem to be, and indeed should be, of serious concern for Theresa May's government as it wrestles with strategies to improve the UK's economic performance. May has already gained the reputation of being a cautious politician, and the performance of the Labour Party in the 2016 UK General Election will only have intensified her caution further. Alternative economic thinking is not imprudent in such a context, but there is a danger that certain strategies could exacerbate rather than alleviate social instability.

This is to say nothing of the environmental threats to European prosperity, which threaten to very foundations of wealth creation. The consequences of ecological degradation to economic performance were most famously assessed by Nicholas Stern, whose findings have been seen as conservative in order to garner political support by some (Stern 2006; Anderson and Bows-Larkin 2012). Environmental degradation represents not only the threats to capitalist production still to come, but trends which are already feeding into economic performance. Pessimism about the future of economic growth itself, the levels of which have been in steady decline since the mid-1970s, suggests that the current malaise is not necessarily a punctuation of the equilibrium (Streeck 2014). This is a politically and economically tumultuous period which threatens to get even worse.

So what are the foundations of competitiveness upon which European political economies can achieve greater prosperity in the twenty-first century? What are the sectors of growth in the coming decade and what are the political strategies capable of nurturing them? And, perhaps just as significantly, what are the potential institutional means of sharing the proceeds of economic success equitably?

These are questions of profound importance for the parties of the left and centre-left, whose vote share has declined in recent years, at least in part because of their inability when in office to halt the trend towards rising inequality (Crouch 2012). As Patrick Diamond (2016) has noted, in its electoral appeal the left has tended to depoliticise economic choice since the 1980s, opting to deploy a more technocratic language vis-à-vis economic policy options. This has undermined its ability to respond to the subsequent economic crisis and created an ideational vacuum in political-economic thinking in sites of power. As a result, many progressive parties were seen as complicit in the choice for and implementation of austerity in the period since the 2008 financial crash. And they have suffered electorally as a consequence. The offerings of many traditional parties of the left are greeted with more muted enthusiasm today, with core sections of their traditional support base having become less and less enamoured by the cause and in some cases even defecting to right-wing populist parties (Mair 2011). In this context, it is crucial that the debates on developmental capitalist models return to prominence. How do social democratic parties adapt to the economic realities facing their electorates? How can progressive political-economic strategies address the economic, social and environmental issues raised by, and ultimately transform the dysfunctional capitalisms of Europe? Can socially just economic models be based on sustainable foundations of competitiveness? Is redistribution alone enough to mitigate the rise of inequality in the context of Piketty's analytical insights about the distributional patterns of capitalist societies? In short, where does progressive politics go from here (see also Coates 2018; Hay and Payne 2015)?

To respond to the failure of Europe's social democratic parties in the last decade, we must begin with a sober analysis of the character of European capitalisms, the inequalities they generate, the models of growth being nurtured, the evolving nature of the financial sector, and the UK's changing role in the European economic space in the context set by the vote for Brexit.

This edited collection brings together some of Europe's most eminent political economists to address these key questions. Its aim is to stimulate a reflection on how the financial crisis, the Eurozone crisis and Brexit have changed the political economies of the UK and Europe since 2008, and how they alter the conditions for British and European prosperity in the future. As such, the scope of the book incorporates reflection upon how recent developments have impacted upon economic instability, the City of London, inequality, economic governance, and the dynamics of the UK growth model. The authors draw upon the analytic resources of the varieties of capitalism debate (if not necessarily that of Hall and Soskice themselves), as well as their knowledge of British and European political economy, to make sense of these developments.

This analysis also serves to inform a conversation about progressive politics for the 2020s. What are the prospective progressive political strategies which are best attuned to this new economic terrain? What strategies can nurture new dynamics of prosperity and mitigate social inequality? Can Social Democracy re-invent itself to meet these challenges or should it now be considered obsolete?

The project from which this book is derived was a collaboration between the Foundation of European Progressive Studies (FEPS), the Sheffield Political Economy Research Institute (SPERI) and Policy Network. The joint mission was to reflect on the changing nature of the British economy, its place within the European economic space and the consequences of Brexit, in the context of a series of ongoing crises in the global economy and the escalation of political unrest. Our ambitious agenda sought to bring together and better articulate concerns with the particular structural imbalances characterising the British economy, the role of the City of London within it, the foundations of British and

European competitiveness, the attempts to coordinate economic govern-ance at the European level, and the implications of Brexit for each. The agenda was deliberately inclusive, a breadth justified by the importance and timeliness of the issues with which we were dealing. This volume, the final output of the project, retains that breadth and ambition. Each of the commissioned chapters offers, we feel, a provocative argument based on significant and original research.

As with any volume of this nature, the book's empirical scope is wide-ranging and its analysis multi-tonal. However, four key themes underpin the collective enterprise, marking out we hope its distinctive contribution to the existing literature. They are as follows:

- the long-term development of the UK's growth model and the potential strategies, both macroeconomic and in the UK business community, which will ensure competitiveness beyond Brexit;
- the City of London's role in the architecture of global finance, its relationship with imbalances and instability in the British and European economies, the City's evolution since the global financial crisis, and the opportunities and risks presented by a Hard Brexit;
- the role of the UK in, and the implications of Brexit for, EU eco-nomic governance;
- the prospects of social democracy in the midst of a dividing Europe.

In the opening chapter, Andrew Gamble locates the current political-economic plight of the UK in its proper historical context, charting the evolution of the UK's economic growth model and the corner-stones of its competitive advantage throughout the post-war period. He details the impact of the loss of empire, various post-war crises and the influence of successful CMEs in mainland Europe on the UK's macroeconomic strategy before contemplating potential post-Brexit re-orientations of strategic direction for the UK's LME. He argues that three political-economic scenarios are foreseeable for the UK after Brexit: a 'soft Brexit' whereby the UK would remain part of the European Single Market and capitalist divergence would be limited, the adoption of an ultra-libertarian Singaporean model entailing the dec-laration of unilateral free trade, and a protectionist turn which would profoundly re-shape the character of the UK economy. He considers the implications of each for the future of British and European capital-isms and the conditions of existence of each.

In the following chapter, Leila Simona Talani makes the case that the relationship between the City of London, the Treasury and the Bank of England (the famous 'City-Bank-Treasury nexus' first identified by Perry Anderson in the 1960s) will ensure that the City of London will continue to thrive as a global financial centre in spite of Brexit. She argues that Brexit will allow the financial institutions that together comprise the City to more credibly threaten to re-locate their operations elsewhere, and as such we are likely to see a governmental response which assuages their fears and compensates for the (still hypothetical) loss of access to the European Single Market. As such, policy-making in the UK Treasury and the Bank of England will become even more attuned to the City's needs precisely because of Brexit. The implication is that we are likely to see the protection of the square mile's competitive advantage, not its erosion. This would represent the continued privileging of financial activity over productive activity, and the privileging of capital over (unskilled or semi-skilled) labour, in UK public policy; the key characteristic of what Talani refers to as 'pragmatic adaptation'.

Helen Thompson asks herself why the City of London, given its pivotal role in the UK's growth strategy, failed to prevent the referendum on the UK's EU membership and consequently Brexit itself. The Conservative Party's decision to jeopardise the UK's historical competitive advantage in finance in such a way has been a source of consternation particularly for those who believed that the 'structural power of capital' would prohibit any political outcomes which threatened profitability. Thompson, however, puts forward a compelling three-pronged case which recasts and, in so doing, resolves this apparent paradox. Firstly, she argues the City's interests are no longer as dependent on Sterling as they were, due to the gradual development of the offshore Dollar, Euro and Renminbi markets in the 1950s, 2000s and 2010s respectively. This decreasing importance of Sterling in the City meant that the interests of the latter were not as bound up with the domestic UK economy as is commonly believed. This in turn provided David Cameron with more 'room for manoeuvre' than he would otherwise have enjoyed when it came to attempting to resolve the divide on Europe within his own party. Secondly, the City had come to fear re-regulation and the imposition of additional forms of taxation (likely a ban on short-selling, rules on bankers' bonuses and the introduction of a Financial Transactions Tax) from Brussels as part of the fall-out of the 2008 financial crisis and the subsequent Eurozone sovereign debt crisis.

These crises had exposed the City's privileged location outside the regulatory jurisdiction of the Eurozone whilst within the European Single Market. The City, despite its increasingly politicised status as Europe's offshore financial centre, had staved off punitive policies in the decade following the 2008 crash due to the UK's monetary sovereignty. Yet David Cameron during his tenure as Prime Minister was less and less able to persuade Conservative Party members that he could protect the City's interests in the face of mounting pressure from Germany and France to enforce higher regulatory standards, symbolised by his failure to ensure an agreement that protected the City when re-negotiating the terms of Britain's EU membership in February 2016. In making this case, Thompson's analysis of the City's interests not only demonstrates the City's complex relationship with Brexit but also the political difficulties of conducting EU economic governance through multiple overlapping spatial scales with divergent political inclinations.

Lucia Quaglia refocuses the discussion from the City to the UK government's role in EU economic governance since the 2008 financial crash. In so doing she examines three related policy areas specifically: financial regulation, the Banking Union and the Capital Markets Union. She argues that the UK has actually played a variety of roles in the politics of EU economic governance in recent years—foot-dragger, fence-sitter and pace-setter. Accordingly, the classic interpretation of the UK as an 'awkward partner' within the EU (a term coined by Stephen George in 1990) is in need of revision. This analysis of the political dynamics of EU policy-making contains significant insights into the prospects of capitalist re-structuring after the UK's formal withdrawal from the European Union. It suggests that in the institutions of the EU, some policy initiatives will lose political support and momentum, whilst others will profit from being shorn of its primary detractors.

Waltraud Schelkle examines the politics of three of the EU's post-2008 crisis management policies—the Fiscal Compact, the European Stability Mechanism and the Banking Union—to demonstrate the tensions which arose from such policies and to highlight their role in prompting discontent and disintegration. Utilising the concept of 'two-level games' (Putnam 1988; Bellamy and Weale 2015), her contribution not only explores the politics of disintegration in the European Union in the past decade, but also illustrates the collective action problems typical of an incomplete political union. She argues that the increasingly centrifugal nature of the EU in this period of crisis has not forged an ever closer Union, but has instead triggered the dual trends of policy coordination and fragmentation. In this sense, given the present economic backdrop, Brexit may mark the beginning rather than the end of political re-organisation and indeterminacy inside Europe, and foreshadow the increasing variegation of European capitalisms.

Scott Lavery returns to the UK growth model, its conditions of existence as such, and the strategic dilemmas for British capital created by Brexit. He describes the existing strategy of British business—acting collectively through the Confederation of British Industry—of 'extending and defending' its interests through the interactions between the British state and the institutions of the European Union. On the basis of an extensive empirical investigation, he argues that the CBI has historically tended to prohibit the development of EU social and employment policy ('defend'), whilst building coalitions to further expand trade liberalisation ('extend'). However, Brexit throws British business into a state of strategic disorientation. How do British businesses perceive, and plan to respond to, changing political-economic conditions? And what are the implications of their perceived interests for the future of the UK growth model?

In the final section of the book, Angela Wigger and Laura Horn begin the discussion of social democratic futures. They consider whether the rise of industrial policy on the political agenda of the traditional parties of social democracy could signal an upturn in their electoral fortunes; damaged so significantly in their view by their perceived complicity in the implementation of austerity measures, a backlash against the neoliberal Third Way approach, and the commitment to the European Social Model. Their analysis of EU industrial policy, however, suggests that it will be unable to generate either progressive outcomes or greater electoral success. They argue that the specific understanding of competitiveness at the heart of EU industrial strategy rationalises the depreciation of labour costs, reforms to the labour market and lower levels of taxation levied being on corporations. This policy therefore carries dire implications for inequality and fails to represent a significant change in the social contract between capital and labour. Instead, it merely represents a new phase of post-2008 neoliberal crisis management within the EU and the latest progressive policy to be co-opted by conservative actors. Progressive support for it will, thus, only further damage the electoral fortunes of social democratic parties.

Finally, Ben Clift offers a more optimistic take on the future of social democracy by changing the spatial scale of analysis. He argues that social democratic parties ought not to remain fixated on national welfare states and a Keynesianism to be delivered at the national level, but should instead renew itself though the adoption of a more transnational focus. Based on extensive primary research couched in a theoretical frame which draws on some of Keynes' less famous ideas, an argument is made for achieving the traditional aims of social democracy—in particular the curtailing of rising inequality—through new strategies and institutional means. In Clift's view, the IMF's Research department—an important but under-utilised 'subculture' within the IMF—would serve as a crucial node of this transnational renewal. This provocative argument rejuvenates discussion of the 'Mitterrand experiment' and the role of the institutions of global governance in coordinating a new wave of progressive politics.

These chapters together amount to a multifaceted analysis of Europe's evolving varieties of capitalism, the strategic dilemmas thrown up by changing economic relations, and reflections of the future of competitiveness, prosperity and progressive politics.

REFERENCES

Anderson, P. (1964, January–February). Origins of the Present Crisis. *New Left Review, 23*, 26–53.

Anderson, K., & Bows-Larkin, A. (2012). A New Paradigm for Climate Change. *Nature Climate Change, 2*, 639–640.

Bailey, D., & Shibata, S. (2014). Varieties of Contestation: The Comparative and Critical Political Economy of "Excessive" Demand. *Capital & Class, 38*(1), 239–251.

Bellamy, R., & Weale, A. (2015). Political Legitimacy and European Monetary Union: Contracts, Constitutionalism and the Normative Logic of Two-Level Games. *Journal of European Public Policy, 22*(2), 257–274.

Bruff, I., & Ebenau, M. (2014). Special Issue: Critical Political Economy and Capitalist Diversity. *Capital & Class, 38*(1), 3–251.

Bruff, I., & Horn, L. (2012). Varieties of Capitalism in Crisis? *Competition & Change, 16*(3), 161–168.

Cerny, P. G. (1997). Paradoxes of the Competition State: The Dynamics of Political Globalisation. *Government and Opposition, 32*(2), 251–274.

Coates, D. (2015). Varieties of Capitalism and "The Great Moderation". In M. Ebenau, I. Bruff, & C. May (Eds.), *New Directions in Comparative*

Capitalisms Research: Critical and Global Perspectives (pp. 11–27). London: Palgrave Macmillan.

Coates, D. (2018). *Flawed Capitalism: The Anglo-American Condition and Its Resolution.* Newcastle-upon-Tyne: Agenda Publishing.

Crouch, C. (2012). *The Strange Non-Death of Neoliberalism.* London: Polity.

Diamond, P. (2016). *Endgame for the Centre-Left: The Retreat of European Social Democracy.* London: Rowman & Littlefield.

Financial Times. (2016, October 5). Theresa May Sets Out Post-Brexit Vision for a Fairer Britain. Available at: https://www.ft.com/content/a6435046-8b93-11e6-8aa5-f79f5696c731.

Financial Times. (2017, January 9). Theresa May Blames Complacent Politicians for Rise of Populism. Available at: https://www.ft.com/content/ebcc4c56-d5b4-11e6-944b-e7eb37a6aa8e.

Fukuyama, F. (1989, Summer). The End of History? *The National Interest.* Available at: https://www.embl.de/aboutus/science_society/discussion/discussion_2006/refl-22june06.pdf.

George, S. (1990). *An Awkward Partner: Britain in the European Community.* Oxford: Oxford University Press.

Hall, P. A. (2014). Varieties of Capitalism and the Euro Crisis. *West European Politics, 37*(6), 1223–1243.

Hall, P. A., & Gingerich, D. W. (2009). Varieties of Capitalism and Institutional Complementarities in the Political Economy. *British Journal of Political Science, 39*(3), 449–482.

Hall, P. A., & Soskice, D. (Eds.). (2001). *Varieties of Capitalism: The Institutional Foundations of Comparative Advantage.* Oxford: Oxford University Press.

Hall, P. A., & Thelen, K. (2009). Institutional Change in Varieties of Capitalism. *Socio-Economic Review, 7*(1), 7–34.

Hammond, P. (2018). https://www.theguardian.com/politics/2018/jan/25/britain-cowed-brussels-jacob-rees-mogg-theresa-may-brexit-eurosceptic-mps.

Hay, C. (2004). Common Trajectories, Variable Paces, Divergent Outcomes? Models of European Capitalism Under Conditions of Complex Economic Interdependence. *Review of International Political Economy, 11*(2), 231–262.

Hay, C. (2005). Two Can Play at That Game ... or Can They? Varieties of Capitalism, Varieties of Institutionalism. In D. Coates (Ed.), *Varieties of Capitalism, Varieties of Approaches.* London: Palgrave Macmillan.

Hay, C., & Payne, A. (2015). *Civic Capitalism.* London: Polity.

Hay, C., & Wincott, D. (2012). *The Political Economy of European Welfare Capitalism.* Basingstoke: Palgrave Macmillan.

Mair, P. (2011). *Ruling the Void: The Hollowing of Western Democracy.* London: Verso.

Piketty, T. (2014). *Capital: In the Twenty-First Century*. Cambridge, MA: Harvard University Press.

Pontusson, J. (2005). Varieties and Commonalities of Capitalism. In D. Coates (Ed.), *Varieties of Capitalism, Varieties of Approaches*. London: Palgrave Macmillan.

Putnam, R. D. (1988). Diplomacy and Domestic Politics: The Logic of Two-Level Games. *International Organization, 42*(3), 427–460.

Rhodes, M. (2005). 'Varieties of Capitalism' and the Political Economy of European Welfare States. *New Political Economy, 10*(3), 363–370.

Schmidt, V. (2002). *The Futures of European Capitalism*. Oxford: Oxford University Press.

Soederberg, S. (2014). *Debtfare States and the Poverty Industry: Money, Discipline and the Surplus Population*. London: Routledge.

Soskice, D., Hope, D., & Iverson, T. (2016). The Eurozone and Political Economic Institutions. *Annual Review of Political Science, 19*, 163–185.

Stern, N. H. (2006). *The Stern Review: The Economics of Climate Change* (Vol. 30). London: HM Treasury.

Streeck, W. (2014). *Buying Time: The Delayed Crisis of Democratic Capitalism*. London: Verso.

CHAPTER 2

After Brexit: The Past and Future of the Anglo-Liberal Model

Andrew Gamble

INTRODUCTION

In the referendum held on June 23, 2016 the British people voted by a narrow margin (52–48%) to leave the European Union. Thirty seven per cent of the total electorate voted Leave. The result introduced great uncertainty into the future path of British politics and the shape of its political economy. The debate has been shaped by partisan perspectives. Some have called it the most disastrous peacetime event in British history, the greatest act of self-harm ever inflicted, (Heseltine 2017) others have described it as a liberation from a corrupt and failing organisation which allows the British people to take back control and Britain to be Britain again (Johnson 2017). The result has placed the long-term future of the UK union in doubt, since both Northern Ireland and Scotland voted to remain, and it raises question once again about the UK's place in the world, particularly the nature of its relationship with the United States and its future defence and security cooperation with its European allies.

A. Gamble (✉)
Sheffield Political Economy Research Institute,
University of Sheffield, Sheffield, UK
e-mail: a.m.gamble@sheffield.ac.uk

© The Author(s) 2019
C. Hay and D. Bailey (eds.), *Diverging Capitalisms*,
Building a Sustainable Political Economy: SPERI Research & Policy,
https://doi.org/10.1007/978-3-030-03415-3_2

17

The UK had endured three difficult decades after 1945, adjusting to the loss of empire and world power. After the Suez débacle it tried and failed twice to join the European Economic Community (EEC), finally succeeding in 1973. The decision was then ratified by a two-thirds majority in a referendum in 1975. Joining the EEC was not the economic panacea for the many ills of the British economy which some of its advocates had hoped, partly because it occurred during the major recession and prolonged crisis of the 1970s, but it did appear to many observers that it had settled Dean Acheson's concern ten years before that Britain had lost an empire and not yet found a role. Membership of the European Economic Community gave Britain a role at the heart of the European project for economic integration which complemented and supported the parallel structures of NATO for defence and security. For forty years membership of the EU was a crucial anchor of British policy, and although the UK was often reluctant to back deeper integration, it was enthusiastic in its support for the creation of the single market, and then for the enlargement of the Union after the collapse of the Soviet Union in 1991. The single market bound the UK ever more closely to its European partners and encouraged increasing convergence of the UK economy with other European economies.

The structure of this chapter is as follows. The first section examines the historical contexts which shaped the UK economy and its particular model of Anglo-liberal capitalism, and the political discourse of economic and imperial decline which took hold particularly after 1945. The second section looks at the debate on models of capitalism, and why membership of the EEC was attractive partly because of the different models of capitalism which had developed in Europe and were for a time regarded as superior to that of the UK. The third section then looks at the trajectories of the development of the UK political economy from 1942 to 2017, paying particular attention to the major shift in direction under Thatcher and Blair. The final sections analyse the tension between United States and European models of capitalism, the impact of Brexit and the different ways in which the UK might now develop.

EMPIRE AND DECLINE:
THE PECULIARITIES OF THE ANGLO-LIBERAL MODEL

The UK's political economy and the peculiarities of the Anglo-liberal model were shaped by the role Britain has played in the global economy in the last three hundred years. Britain became first a successful entrepreneurial and commercial society, an expanding colonial and naval power and then partly as a consequence the first significant industrial society. By the middle of the nineteenth century Britain had become the world's leading commercial, industrial and imperial power. Many of the peculiarities of the Anglo-liberal model became set in this period and have proved very hard to reform. Some of the features which made the UK distinctive in the nineteenth century such as Britain's industrial lead and the size of its urban working class have disappeared as other countries have caught up and industrial economies have converged. But there remain some important features of British capitalism which mark it out from development elsewhere.

One of the most important of these is the size and weight of its financial sector. One million people currently work in financial services in the UK, as many as worked in the mines in the 1920s. The City of London has an economic and political weight that is greater than in any state of equivalent size. The financial sectors of some other countries such as Switzerland are even larger in relation to their host economies, but their populations are much smaller. In the nineteenth century, the City became the leading centre for financial, shipping and insurance services for the rest of the international economy. It formed its own 'industrial district'. This cluster of expertise survived long after the disappearance of the economic and military power which made it possible. Having weathered the collapse of the gold standard and the great depression, the Second World War and the post-war social democratic settlement, the City experienced a remarkable renaissance starting in the 1960s with the development of the Eurodollar market (Green 2016). British governments allowed the City to behave as if it were an offshore financial centre, free of many of the regulations which other jurisdictions, including the United States, imposed on their financial centres. In the neo-liberal era the City became once again one of the world's leading international financial centres. One of the most significant reforms of the Thatcher Government was the deregulation of financial services in 1986, the 'Big Bang', removing restrictions on the entry of foreign banks into London.

A second distinctive feature of the British economic model is the legal framework governing its labour markets, trade unions and companies. For a time in the twentieth century, trade unions appeared powerful actors, but they were never fully incorporated as part of the governance of the economy, and their powers were granted as privileges, exemptions from the provisions of the common law. In the 1980s these privileges were revoked. Similarly UK corporate governance has always treated the company primarily as a private association rather than as a public corporation, in contrast to European law (Parkinson 1993).

A third distinctive legacy from the British Sonderweg is the size of the British state, and its relationship to civil society and the economy. This is reflected both in the relatively small size of UK public expenditure compared to those in some other European member states, and the corresponding low fiscal base, and also in the relative lack of success of the British state in recasting itself as an entrepreneurial state in the manner of Germany, France, Japan or even the United States. This liberal conception of the state is paralleled by a liberal conception of the household, reflected both in the emphasis on consumption rather than production in the Anglo-liberal growth model, and the importance placed on self-reliance and independence, which have shaped attitudes towards welfare.

In the nineteenth century, Britain became the world's most modern and advanced economy, the economy which as Marx noted, showed every other economy the image of its own future. But this was not true in every respect. Many aspects of the British model in time came to seem anachronistic and no longer modern. Britain was surpassed by other major powers. As British power waned the British model began to be questioned. Its shortcomings were exposed, and numerous prescriptions offered as to how it might be reformed. Many of the projects for reversing British decline recommended learning from the more successful models of some of the UK's competitors in Europe, East Asia and North America. The widespread perception of Britain as the 'sick man of Europe' reached a peak in the 1970s. Britain it seemed had the wrong kind of capitalism, the wrong kind of state, certainly the wrong kind of unions and was rapidly moving to the abyss. As Sir Keith Joseph, one of Margaret Thatcher's closest allies, put it (Joseph 1979):

> The visible signs of Britain's unique course - as it slides from the afflu-
> ent Western World towards the threadbare economies of the communist
> bloc - are obvious enough. We have a demotivating tax system, increasing

nationalisation, compressed differentials, low and stagnant productivity, high unemployment, many failing public services and inexorably growing central government expenditure; an obsession with equality, and with pay, price and dividend controls, and immunities for trade unions; and finally, since 1974, top of the Western league for inflation, bottom of the league for growth.

Yet within eight years these problems had been miraculously dispelled. The 1987 Conservative Party manifesto proclaimed (Conservative Party 1987):

> Remember the conventional wisdom of the day. The British people were 'ungovernable'. We were in the grip of an incurable 'British disease'. Britain was heading for 'irreversible decline'. Well, the people were *not* ungovernable, the disease was *not* incurable, the decline *has* been reversed.

This triumphalism proved slightly premature and was quickly followed by a severe recession between 1989 and 1992, which saw unemployment rise again by 1.5 million, the collapse of the housing market, plunging many houseowners into negative equity and the Exchange Rate Mechanism (ERM) débacle. But following the exit from the ERM and a substantial devaluation, growth resumed, and by the start of the new century, decline as a theme in British political discourse had almost disappeared. The condition of the economy was no longer at the centre of political debate. Triumphalism had reappeared. In his 2004 budget speech Gordon Brown declared (Brown 2004):

> For decades after 1945, Britain repeatedly relapsed into recession, moving from boom to bust...since 1997 Britain has sustained growth not just through one economic cycle but through two economic cycles, without suffering the old British disease of stop-go – with overall growth since 2000 almost twice that of Europe and higher even than that of the United States. Indeed in the Pre-Budget Report, I told the House that Britain was enjoying the longest period of sustained economic growth for more than 100 years...I have to apologise to the House. Having asked the Treasury to investigate in greater historical detail, I can now report that Britain is enjoying its longest period of sustained economic growth for more than 200 years – the longest period of sustained economic growth since the beginning of the Industrial Revolution.

Something of a sea change had taken place in Britain's economic fortunes. The pessimists had been proved wrong. Britain in 2004, the Chancellor announced, had 'the lowest inflation for 30 years, the lowest interest rates for 40 years, and the highest levels of employment in history'. The inflation peaks in the last three recessions of 27% in 1975, 22% in 1980 and 9% in 1990 were a distant memory, as were the three million unemployed of the 1980s, and high-interest rates (17% in 1980 and 15% in 1990).

Had the performance of the British economy improved? At the time many still argued that it had not, or at least that the improvement was only superficial, and that the fundamental problems of the British economy remained unresolved. The economy only appeared to improve because expectations about British economic performance had been lowered so much. As David Coates argued (Coates 2000):

> The UK had spent the first four decades of the postwar period locked in a process of cumulative economic decline caused by inadequate levels of investment in plant and equipment, and that growth trajectory remained firmly in place at century's end...[positioning] the UK as predominantly an off-shore warehouse economy, where a low-paid, underskilled and now poorly unionised workforce depended for the attraction of foreign direct investment on the economy's role as an assembly pad within the tariff boundaries of the EU for the export of medium-tech mass-consumer goods into the more prosperous heartlands of corporatist Europe. The UK economy remains disproportionately a service-based economy, internationally competitive in financial services, but otherwise centred around low-paid service provision to a slowly growing domestic market.

Others however maintained that the 1987 Conservative Manifesto had been essentially right but premature. A combination of the institutional reforms pushed through by the Thatcher Government in the 1980s and structural changes in the global economy had altered the trajectory of the British economy and created a set of conditions which had enabled first the Major Government and then the Blair/Brown Government to maintain financial stability and steady growth. A new consensus on economic policy had been established which all parties were content to work within, and which had created the conditions for addressing long-term problems of low investment and skills shortages. Typical of this point of view was Geoffrey Owen, a former editor of the *Financial Times* who argued (Owen 2000):

For the first thirty years after the war, the political climate militated against the single-minded pursuit of industrial efficiency and international competitiveness. The tide turned in the 1980s, when two powerful forces came together and reinforced each other: external economic pressure and domestic policy reform. By the end of the 1990s Britain had found a role for itself as a medium-sized industrial nation, well integrated into the world market.

From this standpoint Britain's decline from its nineteenth-century dominance had now come to an end. The adjustment had been hard, but since the 1980s a new chapter had opened, in part as a result of the changes introduced by Margaret Thatcher, consolidated and extended under John Major and Tony Blair. The policies which the Blair Government pursued were a sign that something had changed permanently in the British political economy, and UK capitalism was back in business.

MODELS OLD AND NEW

The performance of the British economy was certainly different at the beginning of the twenty-first century than it had been in the 1970s, but was it a new model, or the old model, suitably patched up? And from where did the inspiration come? In the 1960s, 1970s and 1980s, the British looked to models of capitalism from France, Germany, Sweden and Japan. But in the 1990s, the US model gained in attractiveness again as the performance of other models faltered, and the strategic choice facing Britain tended to be posed more starkly as a choice between Europe and America (Gamble 2003), which was bound up also with attitudes towards Britain's membership of the European Union and the military alliance with the United States. The rival charms of the Anglo-American shareholder model of capitalism and the European stakeholder model increasingly set the terms of this debate.

Critics of models of capitalism argue that these models presuppose a unity that does not exist. National economies are a construct of national governments; many economic relationships are transnational and cannot be neatly contained within national boundaries. Each national economy in any case is normally a hybrid, with different models in different sectors, rather than a single model throughout. Nevertheless despite these qualifications the concept of models is hard to dispense with entirely, even if as some argue the space in which such models could exist and thrive is now fast shrinking, and the logic of competition and accumulation are forcing all national models to converge (Coates 2000). On this reading it was the US model which had emerged once more in the 1990s as the leading edge model, and the European social model which was underperforming.

In their seminal analysis Peter Hall and David Soskice distinguished between two basic models of capitalism—Liberal Market Economies and Coordinated Market Economies (Hall and Soskice 2001). This distinction runs right through the political economy literature: market led/ state led; market based/trust based; bank based/credit based; individualistic/communitarian. It seeks to isolate the mechanism by which an economy is coordinated and the different ways in which successful long-term businesses are built. Hall and Soskice argue that in a Liberal Market Economy firms coordinate their activities primarily through hierarchies, competitive market arrangements and formal contracting. The exchange of goods and services is coordinated through price signals, which leads agents to adjust their behaviour. In a Coordinated Market Economy firms depend more heavily on non-market relations to coordinate with other actors. Contracting tends to be relational and incomplete. Networks are much more important for the exchange of private and privileged information, and collaborative arrangements are more common than competitive ones.

From this perspective what is important are the different national regulatory regimes, which provide the institutional foundations of comparative advantage. From an institutionalist perspective there is no reason to expect institutional foundations to merge into one best model. On the contrary the shifting circumstances and opportunities of the global economy ensure that different models will thrive at different times. The ascendancy of the Anglo-American model in the 1990s was as short-lived as the ascendancy of the French, German and East Asian in earlier decades. But that does not mean it is easily replaced in the countries where it is established. As Hall and Soskice put it (Hall and Soskice 2001: 16): 'So many of the institutional factors conditioning the behaviour of firms remain nation-specific'.

THE TRAJECTORY OF BRITISH CAPITALISM 1945–2017

In mapping the broad trajectory of British capitalism since the 1940s. Three distinct periods suggest themselves. With the vote on Brexit a new period has opened.

1942–1956, The relaunching of the UK model
1956–1992, The crisis of the UK model
1992–2016, The financial growth model

1942–1956, The Relaunching of the UK Model

In the plans for reconstruction during and after the war the priority of the British political class was to re-establish the old UK model of capitalism, based on the trading and financial links of Britain's territorial and commercial empires built up over the previous three centuries, through which so many successful British businesses had been established. At the same time there was growing acceptance that the institutional conditions of the model had to be revised to permit a political settlement with organised labour, along the lines set out in the influential 1942 Beveridge Report (Addison 1994). The report offered a compelling vision of a Britain in which the social security needs of all citizens would be met through flat rate contributions to a general fund, with additional services such as family allowances and a national health service being met by general taxation. The plan would be underpinned by government pledging to make the maintenance of full employment the prime objective of its economic policy. These proposals were implemented by the Attlee Government, in addition to a substantial enlargement of the public sector through nationalisation of core utilities, as well as the introduction of new planning powers and the restoration of legal immunities for trade unions (removed by the Conservative Government after the 1926 General Strike). By 1950 Britain had one of the most advanced welfare states in the world, one of the pioneers in combining liberal capitalism and democratic citizenship (Marshall 1950).

The enlarged state and widened conception of citizenship which the Attlee Government bequeathed to the Conservatives in 1951 survived through the 1950s and 1960s largely intact. The Conservatives concentrated their energies on assisting the networks, both industrial and financial, which British capital had built up in the nineteenth century, and which had been so badly disrupted during the war and its aftermath, to re-establish themselves (Burnham 2003). The reopening of the markets of the City of London and making Sterling convertible in 1958 were major steps on the way to re-establishing the distinctive British form of capitalism and its associated businesses that had flourished so much in the past. The liberal and global character of British capital, and the importance of Sterling and the financial networks around it were reaffirmed. In 1951 the British economy was still the third most important after the United States and the USSR, and had leading edge industrial sectors, particularly in the defence field (Edgerton 1991).

1956–1992, The Crisis of the UK Model

The crisis developed in stages, as successive programmes of modernisation were launched to overcome Britain's economic problems. The mood at first was optimistic, but the failure to improve British economic performance gradually created a mood of despondency about Britain's prospects and the intractable nature of its problems. This came to a head in the 1970s, with the discrediting of the political centre, increased polarisation between right and left and talk of ungovernability and overload (Bacon and Eltis 1976). This time of stalemate and drift was ended with the election of the Thatcher Government, which set out to reverse the collectivist and social democratic framework of policy and restore key elements of the old liberal economic model.

Fundamental to this period of crisis was the acceptance by a majority of the political class of two unpalatable facts—that the debacle of Suez meant that Britain could no longer act independently without the support of the United States, and that therefore disengagement from the Empire should be speeded up. The second was that Britain could no longer stand on the sidelines of the new European union that was in the making. 1956 was the year of both Suez and the negotiations which led to the Treaty of Rome. British governments had refused to participate in the new European institutions, believing that Britain could remain an independent power between Europe and America, linked to both but absorbed by neither. In the aftermath of Suez and the establishment of the Common Market, the British position began to seem untenable.

At the same time, it was becoming clear by the late 1950s that Britain was being outperformed by the other economies of Western Europe. The first big inquest into the failings of post-war British economic policy began (Shonfield 1958).

One of the most important features of this period which began with Suez and the setting up of the EEC in 1956 and ended with the forced exit of Britain from the ERM in 1992, was that Europe became the focus for many of the economic and social programmes of modernisation that were proposed. This was so in two senses. Membership of the European Community came to be seen as essential for Britain's future economic prosperity; at the same time European models of capitalism, particularly the French, the Swedish and the German began to be widely studied and discussed in Britain, and many of their features were incorporated in the new policies which were put forward. The French model of indicative planning in particular became highly fashionable in the early 1960s and directly inspired the setting up of the National Economic Development Council (NEDC) and the devising of a National Plan, as well as (unrealised) plans for remodelling the British civil service along French lines. Many of the interventionist agencies which the first Wilson Government established such as the Industrial Reorganisation Corporation (IRC), the forerunner of the later National Enterprise Board (NEB) were justified by the need for the state to play a much more proactive role in organising innovation and raising investment, and in re-organising British industry by arranging mergers and creating national champions which could compete with the rest of the world (Shonfield 1965).

The attraction of the French model of capitalism for the British was at its strongest in the 1960s; later the German, Swedish and Japanese models became more influential. Britain finally joined the European Community in 1973 and the emphasis shifted from establishing a more dirigiste form of state to plan the British economy, to re-organising the basic social relations of British capitalism, particularly the production process, the education system and industrial relations. But the basic premise of most of the remedies for decline in this period was that what Britain required was a developmental state which could intervene to modernise the antiquated institutions and structures of British capitalism, and make it a capitalism able to compete again with the rest of the world (Holland 1975).

The developmental state argument was further developed in the 1980s, at a time when the ascendancy of Japan was at its height and both the United States and the UK were perceived to be in decline. The Anglo-American or Anglo-Saxon model was contrasted unfavourably with European and East Asian models. Yet the decisive turn in British politics was not towards the alternative models of capitalism on offer. Instead the Thatcher Government elected in 1979 appeared to go in a quite contrary direction, aiming at the restoration of the UK model as it had existed before the entrenchment of the rights of labour and of welfare in the post-war period.

The Thatcher Government could not restore the Empire, but it did seek quite consciously to open the UK economy to international competition, through ending exchange controls, encouraging foreign direct investment both outwards and inwards, and setting its face against protectionism (at that time being strongly canvassed on the left). The consequence of this stance combined with the adoption of a strict monetary policy which pushed up Sterling was to deepen the recession into which the UK plunged in 1980 and 1981, leading to a wave of bankruptcies in manufacturing industry and a doubling of unemployment to over 3 million. This shakeout of industry was accompanied by a progressive tightening of trade union laws which removed the legal immunities trade unions had enjoyed, and hampered their freedom to call strikes by among other things outlawing secondary action.

Whether the Thatcher Government intended the shock to be as severe as it turned out to be is doubtful. But once it had occurred it was quick to seize the opportunity to argue that a watershed had been crossed and that the British economy needed to be restructured as a free market economy with a smaller public sector and much weaker trade unions. Deregulation, the reduction of taxes on high-income groups and business, privatisation of state assets, and marketisation of public services all followed. Much of this was bitterly contested in Britain, and little of it was popular at the time. Yet although many of the grandiose ambitions of the Thatcher Government were never achieved, a new framework was gradually put in place which marked a decisive change in the UK political economy and steered it in the direction it is still travelling (Heffernan 2001).

This direction pointed away from the alternative European models of capitalism that were on offer, making it less likely that Britain would participate more fully in European integration. The European social model was increasingly perceived by many Thatcherites as the model they did not wish to copy. The consequences of the Thatcher period and the type of capitalist modernisation that Britain underwent was to move Britain further away from Europe not closer to it, because during it the UK model was substantially reconstructed, and the kind of business environment the UK now sought to build owed more to the US model than the European.

1992–2016, The Financial Growth Model

The shape of the new model economy which emerged from the travails of the 1970s and 1980s was broadly neo-liberal. Its institutional foundations were open and flexible markets, including foreign exchange and labour markets, a competition state, low marginal taxation, residual welfare programmes and monetary stability. Within these constraints, however, (and contrary to many accounts of the monolithic character of neoliberalism) quite a wide variation of policies proved possible, and important political choices and emphases remained. In Britain political argument focused on such questions as membership of the Economic and Monetary Union (EMU) as against maintenance of a national currency, universalism as against selectivity in welfare, higher public expenditure as against lower taxation, employment protection as against employment flexibility, and stakeholder value as against shareholder value in corporate governance (Hutton 1995).

What was undeniable, however, was that Britain had adopted a set of institutions for its political economy which precluded certain options—including planning, industrial intervention, protectionism or corporatism. Britain after 1992 had a political economy which ensured financial stability, steady economic growth, low levels of strikes, low inflation and high employment. What was different from what went before was the removal of many of the factors which led to intractable problems, policy failure and the cycle of decline.

The post-war UK political economy had severe structural defects, both external and internal. The chief external problem was the impossibility of maintaining a value for Sterling high enough to sustain the global networks of British capital and military bases that had been built up during the British ascendancy (Blank 1977). The attempt to do so made the task of building strong competitive industries at home more difficult, and delayed effective modernisation of the industrial base, much of which eventually had to be written off in the recessions of the

1970s and 1980s. Unwinding the coils of Empire and breaking free from the straitjacket of Sterling took a long time, and many Sterling crises, but by the middle of the 1990s after a last disastrous policy choice, when entry to the ERM was made at too high a rate, the transition appeared finally to have been made.

The chief internal problems were the incompatibility of combining the voluntarist system of industrial relations, based upon the principle of free collective bargaining, with social democratic aspirations to plan all aspects of the economy, including prices and incomes. The desire of the trade unions to remain independent of the state undermined the policies of Labour and Conservative governments in the 1960s and 1970s and created the climate for the successful onslaught by the Thatcher Government on the legal immunities of trade unions. The inability to bridge this divide meant that corporatism in Britain never achieved the degree of organisation or success that was common in many other European countries, and again opened the way for the thorough-going dismantling by the Thatcher Government of corporatist structures for managing the economy. The attitude of the trade unions towards the state and towards capital in Britain also meant that the Labour movement paid little attention to the question of how companies should be governed or managed. Apart from the abandoned proposals of the Bullock Report in the 1970s there were no moves to change the institutional relationship of capital and labour except through nationalisation on the one hand and the reinforcement of free collective bargaining on the other (Clift et al. 2000).

Another internal problem was the set of principles on which the welfare state was founded. Flat rate insurance contributions to fund universal benefits, along with general taxation to fund a national health service and family allowances, failed to anticipate rising demand and rising earnings and expectations (Lowe 1999). As a result a huge chasm gradually opened up in the welfare state which came to a head in the 1960s and 1970s. Either there needed to be a move towards a much more generously funded system of welfare benefits on Scandinavian lines, to make good the original promises of the Beveridge report, or there needed to be a retreat from universalism to a residual welfare state. The first required a substantial increase in general taxation to fund the welfare state. The latter required an increasing number of citizens to take out private provision. The inability to find a political consensus for either course, coupled with the weakness of the domestic economy and the problems of Sterling, led to oscillations between sharp increases in public spending programmes, shortly followed by fiscal crises and forced public expenditure cuts. The Thatcher Government was at its least radical over the welfare state, and failed to reduce overall spending on it (Pierson 1994), but it did succeed in slowing the growth of spending by introducing a number of significant changes, such as breaking the link between benefits and earnings, and abandoning the consensus on long-term pension provision. Over twenty years this had done much to transform the British welfare state in some areas, particularly pensions and housing, into a residual welfare state (Esping-Andersen 1999).

During the Thatcher period many of the deep-seated problems in the political economy that so plagued the conduct of economic policy in the 1960s and 1970s were overcome or at least reduced. The Thatcher Government was able to pursue a strategy for smaller government, lower taxation, weaker unions, and stronger companies. It was not wholly successful, but aided by structural changes in the global economy it made sufficient institutional changes to permit the new financial growth model to emerge. This economy was not without problems, as many critics noted (Hutton 1995). Productivity and investment remained stubbornly low, there was relatively little improvement in the skill base, investment in infrastructure and science was seriously underfunded, along with most of the public services, and regional imbalances remained and were increased. But the new flexibility in many markets, along with a gradual revival of entrepreneurship marked a major change.

The Labour Government which inherited the new model economy had a ten-year period of sustained success in managing it, while shifting some of its emphases, and consolidating its achievements, for instance by giving the Bank of England operational independence. The structural changes in the global economy which took place in the 1970s and 1980s, in conjunction with the institutional changes in Britain, made the British economy much easier to manage than it had been two decades before. The global shift from manufacturing to services shifted the balance of the British economy towards those sectors where it enjoyed some comparative advantage, and removed or downsized those sectors which had been the source of so much of the instability as well as poor performance of the British economy. At the same time a new low inflation, low-interest rate international regime was established and sustained, again greatly reducing the external pressures on the British economy. Britain was not alone in enjoying low inflation, low-interest rates, high employment. It was the common experience, especially of the English-speaking countries of the Anglosphere after 1991 (Wolf 2005), and one of the chief reasons was the impact of the new emerging economies like China. It helped make British performance among the best in the OECD, whereas earlier it had regularly been among the worst. The weakness of the trade unions compared to their position in the 1960s and 1970s also helped insulate British economic policymaking from unwelcome pressures.

This good fortune did not last. The British economy was increasingly propelled by credit bubbles (in housing and equities in particular) (Watson 2003) and was running very large deficits on the balance of payments. In addition, household debt by 2007 had practically reached its limit. The economy was very vulnerable to the pricking of any of these bubbles. The sub-prime crisis in the United States provided the spark which led to a serious financial collapse, destroying Labour's reputation for economic competence. Its spending plans depended on growth continuing, and that prospect disappeared in the crash. The banking crisis precipitated a recession, and quickly became a fiscal crisis, leading to plans to cut the deficit through sharp increases in taxes and major cuts in public spending. Labour's electoral coalition fell apart and it ceded the political initiative to the Conservatives.

Before the crisis struck, the Government had persisted with its plans to expand public spending. The result was, in public expenditure terms, the most successful social democratic government Britain had ever had. Resources for the public sector were increased more substantially than under any previous Labour administration. Spending on the NHS for example which was £41 billion in 1997 was planned to reach £106 billion in 2008. From being below the European average for health spending Britain at the end of two terms of Labour Government was above and set to go higher still. Spending on the NHS which was 4% of GDP in 1950 and had risen quite slowly to 6% of GDP by 1997 had jumped to 8% of GDP in 2005 and was planned to be 9% of GDP by 2008. The same broad picture was true of education. The 2002 plans aimed to raise education spending to £69 billion per annum by 2008 (from £36 billion in 1997). Labour chose to use the growth in the economy to increase public spending rather than to reduce taxes, and it put huge emphasis on increasing investment in human capital, particularly education and skills, through schools, training programmes and the New Deal youth employment scheme. It also invested heavily in other public services such as health, but still struggled to overcome the perception of poor public services bequeathed by two decades of underfunding.

Its other main strategy was to increase the competitiveness of the British economy, partly through regulatory bodies such as the FSA, and partly through investment in science and technology to encourage innovation and an enterprise economy, focused around the industries of the new knowledge economy. There were some signs too that this had begun to pay off. A new generation of entrepreneurs and companies emerged in the UK in the 1990s, while traditional British strengths in sectors like aerospace and pharmaceuticals were retained (Bennett 2004, Ch. 6). There was no longer anything resembling an industrial strategy in the UK, and the British State no longer had the capacity, if it ever did, to manage industrial change. The shrinking of the manufacturing sector continued under Labour. Manufacturing by 2007 accounted for only 12% of total employment, compared with 28% in 1979 and 17% in 1997. There was no longer any substantial body of opinion in the UK supporting the kind of industrial strategy aimed at fostering indigenous investment, still practised in many other capitalist countries (Hay 1999). Before the crash, given the way Anglo-Saxon model countries had out-performed Germany, France, Italy and Japan since 1991 (Wolf 2005), many wondered whether it any longer mattered.

Europe and America

Many critics of New Labour acknowledged that the alternative they preferred could not be delivered within the constraints of the political economy model Labour had inherited in 1997. It required the adoption of a very different model, such as the European social model of stakeholder firms, high taxation, high welfare benefits, buttressed by high levels of trust and cooperation. The British model in the 1990s appeared much closer to the US model, particularly its policies on welfare, on deregulation, on new public management in the public sector, on public–private partnerships, on shareholder value, and on the encouragement of the knowledge economy. Gordon Brown was a strong critic of many aspects of the European model, particularly the inflexibility of its labour markets and its discouragements to business enterprise, and often contrasted Europe unfavourably with America. The very success of British domestic economic management encouraged a sceptical stance among British ministers to further European integration in the 1990s, particularly in regard to the Euro. This approach was echoed on the Conservative side. Michael Howard, the Conservative Leader, emphasised how important the US model was to Britain (Howard 2004):

> America has created the most successful form of capitalism in the free world...[but] Western nations have developed two competing models of capitalism. For several decades, the governments of mainland Europe have chosen not to emulate the more liberal economic policies of the United States. They have chosen to adopt a much more regulatory, and in some cases corporatist, approach. This has sometimes been referred to as the 'German' model, although Germany is far from unique in adopting this approach.
>
> European governments have adopted this approach with the laudable aim of seeking to protect the weakest in society. But the result of their approach has, more often than not, been quite the reverse. It has made the European economies less flexible and therefore less competitive. This has had a real cost in terms of jobs and growth. Labour costs and taxes are much higher in Europe than in the United States. Growth and job creation is much lower. There are more unemployed people in Europe and they are out of work for longer. In fact, if Europe had followed the American model, it would have created 28 million more jobs and its workers would have produced £5000 more a year in output.
>
> Europe has to wake up to what is happening in the real world. We face a challenge not just from America but also from the Pacific. The average tax burden in the Pacific region is 29.6 per cent; in America it is 28.9 per cent; and in the European Union it is 41 per cent. The EU was designed to free up our markets so that we could compete globally. But the weight of tax and regulation it has introduced has had almost exactly the opposite effect - damming the flood of enterprise that should be sweeping across Europe.

Being more like America again and less like Europe is the heart of the UK model of capitalism. For several decades modernisers toiled to make the UK more like Europe, but as the voluminous literature on models of capitalism demonstrates, they have not had much success, and the counterattack launched by the Thatcher Government swept away many of the institutional supports on which a social democratic political economy might have been built in Britain. On the other hand there are many respects in which Britain remains unlike America despite its strong appeal to the British political class (Hutton 2002; Kenny and Pearce 2018). Many of the attitudes, for example on welfare, on tax, on fairness and social justice, on public spending, and on poverty are broadly in line with those found in other European countries (Park 2003). Repeated surveys have shown that British views on welfare and taxation are not Thatcherite (Bonoli et al. 2000). The British welfare state has always been a hybrid, and quite hard to classify. Esping-Andersen sees Britain as belonging broadly to the liberal regime type of welfare state, and argues that it moved closer towards it in the Thatcher period, but at the same time acknowledges that there remain some strong social democratic aspects to the British welfare state, most notably its universalist features such as the national health service. Starting from a high base after 1950 Britain failed to move on to a full social democratic welfare state as Sweden and similar countries did in the 1960s, and since slipped back, and in that sense had come to resemble more closely the US model (Esping-Andersen 1999). The change of direction signalled by New Labour did not survive the crash.

One way of reading the history of the British political economy over the last sixty years is that after the attempt to restore Britain's lost position in the world had been abandoned, successive governments sought to transform the UK into a Coordinated Market Economy which could play its full part in the process of European integration. But these initiatives, although not as unsuccessful as sometimes suggested, nevertheless did not achieve their goal. This prepared the ground for the sharp turn of policy in the 1980s, abandoning the attempts to create either a Coordinated Market Economy or a social democratic welfare state. Instead trust was placed again in the institutions and regulatory forms of a Liberal Market Economy. By the end of the 1990s this was clearly bearing fruit, in the form of a political economy whose assumptions, including membership of the European Union, were accepted by all the leading political parties. British economic growth was not spectacular but it was steady. Critics still worried about the weakness of manufacturing, and the low wage, low skill syndrome in which Britain was caught. But the change in atmosphere and in performance from the 1970s and 1980s was marked.

THE 2008 FINANCIAL CRASH AND BREXIT

Since the crash a new phase has opened in British politics, and many of the achievements of New Labour have been rolled back. The political fall-out from the crash discredited the record of the Blair/Brown Government for economic competence, and its re-legitimation of public spending and state action, assisted the ascendancy of fiscal conservatism, and led to renewed attempts to shrink the state. Enduring features of Britain's Liberal Market Economy have been emphasised once again. With the exception of some ministers in the Coalition Government such as Vince Cable, the Business Secretary, there was little political appetite to rebalance the British economy, to shrink the financial sector, to move Britain on to a different path or embrace a different model of capitalism.

The 2008 crash also marks a watershed in the development of the international market order. This international order has been extraordinarily resilient since the financial crash in 2008. Huge efforts were made to stabilise the international economy, and a new world depression was avoided, but the recovery has been patchy and weak, the slowest recovery since 1945, and living standards for the majority have stagnated. Many incumbent governments in the western democracies lost elections after 2008, but they were replaced by governments who adhered to the broad terms of the neoliberal consensus (Gamble 2014). Events in 2016 changed that. The financial crisis started in the heartlands of Anglo-America, so it is perhaps appropriate that it is in the UK and the United States that the first serious breaches in the neo-liberal political order have been made. These breaches have still to be consummated. We do not yet know how radical either Brexit or the Trump presidency will prove to be. But they have the potential to start unravelling the western economic and political order which has been the framework of world politics for the last seventy years.

Trump's victory in the US presidential election has been compared to the vote for Brexit but there are important differences. Both were driven in part by anger and despair among sections of the white working class, and their rejection of the liberal, cosmopolitan establishment, both neoliberal and social liberal. Both are part of a wider populist rebellion against globalisation and the western international economic and political order. Populist nationalism in western democracies is a politics of *ressentiment*, fed by economic and cultural grievances. The economic grievances stem from the displacement of many workers from jobs in manufacturing. This is a process which stretches back to the 1980s and has seen the blighting of formerly prosperous industrial regions and the creation of long-term worklessness and dependency. At the same time wages have stagnated or risen only very slowly in many countries particularly since 2000, so at a time when inequality was increasing and the wealth of the top 1% was growing quite dramatically, many working class and middle-income citizens saw little if any improvement in their standard of living and were increasingly reliant upon borrowing. The social wage in the form of public services and employment protection was maintained during the boom years, but has come under sustained attack in the austerity programmes implemented since 2008. These economic grievances are often blamed on globalisation. The rapid pace of change, the introduction of new technologies, competition from immigrant labour, the outsourcing of jobs to other cheaper jurisdictions, the weakening of trade unions, have all combined to reduce labour's share in national income and weaken labour's bargaining strength. Many workers have come to feel resentful at being left behind and ignored, and they have become as a result increasingly disconnected from mainstream politics and government (Ford and Goodwin 2014).

But there are also important differences between Trump's victory and Brexit. UKIP not the British Conservatives are the natural members of the 'Global Tea Party' some of Trump's backers have been promoting. Many Conservative Brexiters like Daniel Hannan note that Trump is an economic nationalist (Hannan 2016). He wants not just to curb immigration, and deport illegal immigrants, but also wants to protect US jobs by slapping tariffs on foreign imports, ripping up trade deals and unwinding the production chains of US multinationals, ending outsourcing. Hannan insists that the vote for Brexit was instead about *increasing* free trade not limiting it. Britain is to be a global power again with greater openness than ever before. Global Brexiters like him acknowledge that immigration is still going to continue at a high level after Brexit because the UK economic model demands it. The UK Government is more ambivalent. It wants border controls *and* free trade. The Trump position is consistent—against free trade, against trade deals, and against immigration. It assumes that the United States is a large enough economy to make the costs of going protectionist bearable. That is not an option for the UK, which relies too heavily on international trade for its prosperity, and lacks a large enough internal market to be a substitute. The problem for Conservative Brexiteers is that while many of them are strong free traders, most of the people who voted for Brexit are not. They do not want a global Britain but a closed Britain or at least a protectionist Britain. They want serious controls on immigration, regardless of whether this means a contraction of trade. The May Government agrees. It has indicated both in relation to the EU and to India that controlling immigration is the priority. Trade deals come second. If that is followed through there will be serious consequences for many sectors of the British economy, lower growth, and a reduction in fiscal revenues. People in Britain will be poorer, but immigration will be lower.

Can this position hold through the negotiations on Brexit? The British Government has pursued a two-stage strategy. Falling in with the wishes of the EU Commission the Government accepted that it had first to clinch a deal over the divorce terms and then move on to discuss trade. The first was accomplished in December 2017. Although the Government was forced to make many concessions which dismayed some Leavers, it is still on course to leave the EU formally in March 2019. At that point the UK will no longer be formally bound by the European Treaties, and in that limited sense, will regain full sovereignty, control of its borders, laws and money. The Government will have delivered a Brexit which it hopes will satisfy the anti-EU wing of the Conservative Party and the right-wing tabloids. Having it hopes demonstrated that the UK is really leaving the EU, the Government will then try in the second stage of the negotiations during 2018 to negotiate a transition arrangement lasting up to two years, during which the UK will behave as though it was still a full member of the Customs Union and the European Single Market and will continue to accept the jurisdiction of the European Court. It will use this breathing space to negotiate a long-term trade arrangement with the EU. To retain access to the single market and mitigate the economic costs of leaving, the Government may be obliged to make concessions, including accepting regulatory alignment with the EU, perhaps paying for access to the single market, agreeing to the jurisdiction of the European Court for some sectors, and accepting a modified form of free movement for EU nationals. All trade deals involve some pooling of sovereignty, the acceptance of common rules and mutual dependency, The issue in the negotiations is how much the Government is prepared to concede in order to get an agreement which does not seriously disadvantage the UK economy.

If the Government makes substantial concessions in order to forestall the risk of a cliff edge or an economic collapse, then the outcome will leave Britain in a sub-optimal but broadly similar position to the one in which it is now, where it is already semi-detached from significant aspects of European integration such as Schengen and the Euro. If this occurred the EU would be confirmed as Britain's most important long-term trading partner, and that would create at least some pressure for continued convergence between the UK and the European models of capitalism. The Government intends through its EU Withdrawal Bill to incorporate all EU legislation into UK law until such time as the UK Parliament decides to replace particular measures. There will also be future pressure for the UK to adopt new regulations announced by the EU, so as to preserve its access to the single market. In this way the UK might achieve something close to an associate status with the EU, although not as complete as Switzerland and Norway, and like them with no influence over the content of new rules.

An alternative possibility, already hinted at by Ministers, is that despite the success in agreeing divorce terms, the trade talks fail to make progress or even break down altogether. If it becomes clear that the two sides are too far apart to agree on a trade deal, the UK would have to trade with the EU on WTO rules. A radical option would be to follow the advice of Economists for Brexit (Economists for Brexit 2016), and declare unilateral free trade. This would be truly global Britain. The implications for the UK model of capitalism are fairly clear. It would mean pursuing what used to be called the Hong Kong option, before that territory returned to Chinese jurisdiction. Taxes and regulation would be pared back, and welfare provision would become much less generous. One aim might be to reduce public expenditure to around 25% of GDP (still much higher than Hong Kong used to be). Reduction of employment rights, social rights and environmental protection would be required to make the UK labour market even more flexible. Such a model might not be politically sustainable. John Major among others has expressed his scepticism. It would likely hasten the departure of both Scotland and even Northern Ireland from the UK. It would represent an extreme form of the Anglo-liberal model, and the divergence between the UK and the rest of Europe would be magnified. The viability of this model would depend very much on the ability to trade freely with the rest of the world, in an era when there remain big questions over the future of economic growth and world trade.

A third possibility is protectionist Britain. This would place the primary emphasis on the national economy and the communities it supports rather than global or regional engagement. It draws on the heritage of social imperialism and protectionism from the 1930s and also on the protectionist traditions of the Left as expressed for example in the alternative economic strategy developed in the 1970s and 1980s. Such policies would have a profound effect on the UK economic model, giving priority to industry over finance, putting employment ahead of financial stability, and investment ahead of consumption. Depending on the left or right inflection of these policies, border control might become very tight. Most observers have always supposed that if there is an alternative in the form of a liberal open international order that will always command more political support than protectionism. But that assumption proved wrong over the Brexit vote. It is still true that there is not as yet a plausible political vehicle for this policy. UKIP perhaps surprisingly has not adopted the kind of economic nationalism espoused by Trump, and Labour has not tried seriously as yet to resurrect its protectionist past. There are cautious moves by the May Government to adopt a slightly more active industrial strategy, but so far it has had little substance.

In 2018, ideological and political trends in the western democracies were still running strongly against globalisation and in favour of protectionism. The populist nationalists of Steve Bannon's Global Tea Party had made significant gains in elections in Germany, France and Italy, although apart from Italy without making a decisive breakthrough. Authoritarian governments had assumed control in Poland and Hungary. On the Left anti-globalisation forces were also stronger, as the campaigns of Bernie Sanders, Jeremy Corbyn, and Jean Melenchon demonstrated, although again without any decisive breakthrough. It is possible that we are on the edge of an important shift in the ideas shaping economic governance. But although the UK is not immune to these broader trends the basic shape of the UK model is unlikely to shift very much unless there is some new cataclysm, a major trade war and depression, or the breakup of the EU and the Eurozone. In those circumstances a new protectionist and interventionist policy might emerge. But there are few signs of it at the moment. The advent of Trump has actually reminded even many Brexiters how much the UK shares in common with Europe, and how vital Europe is to the UK's economic prosperity.

REFERENCES

Addison, P. (1994). *The Road to 1945*. London: Pimlico.

Bacon, R., & Eltis, W. (1976). *Britain's Economic Problem: Too Few Producers*. London: Macmillan.

Bennett, J. C. (2004). *The Anglosphere Challenge: Why the English-Speaking Nations Will Lead the Way in the Twenty-First Century*. New York: Rowman & Littlefield.

Blank, S. (1977). The Politics of Foreign Economic Policy. *International Organisation, 31*(4), 673–722.

Bonoli, G., George, V., & Taylor-Gooby, P. (2000). *European Welfare Futures*. Cambridge: Polity.

Brown, G. (2004, March 17). *Budget Speech*. London: HM Treasury.

Burnham, P. (2003). *Remaking the Postwar World Economy: Robot and British Policy in the 1950s*. London: Palgrave Macmillan.

Clift, B., Gamble, A., & Harris, M. (2000). The Labour Party and the Company. In J. Parkinson, A. Gamble, & G. Kelly (Eds.), *The Political Economy of the Company*. London: Hart.

Coates, D. (2000). *Models of Capitalism*. Cambridge: Polity.

Economists for Free Trade. (2017, September). *New Model Economy for a Post-Brexit Britain*. Available at: https://www.economistsforfreetrade.com/publication/new-model-economy-for-a-post-brexit-britain/.

Edgerton, D. (1991). *England and the Aeroplane: An Essay on a Militant and Technological Nation*. London: Macmillan.

Esping Andersen, G. (1999). *Social Foundations of Post-industrial Economies*. Oxford: Oxford University Press.

Ford, R., & Goodwin, M. (2014). *Revolt on the Right: Explaining Support for the Radical Right in Britain*. London: Routledge.

Gamble, A. (2003). *Between Europe and America*. London: Palgrave Macmillan.

Gamble, A. (2014). *Crisis Without End?* London: Palgrave Macmillan.

Green, J. (2016). Anglo-American Development, the Euromarkets, and the Deeper Origins of Neoliberal Deregulation. *Review of International Studies, 42*(3), 425–449.

Hall, P., & Soskice, D. (Eds.). (2001). *Varieties of Capitalism: The Institutional Foundations of Comparative Advantage*. Oxford: Oxford University Press.

Hannan, D. (2016, November 10). *The Parallels Between Brexit and Trumpery Have Been Absurdly Overdone*. Conservative Home. Available at: http://www.conservativehome.com/thecolumnists/2016/11/daniel-hannan-i-got-it-wrong-the-pundits-got-it-wrong-so-what-really-lies-in-store-for-the-united-states.html.

Hay, C. (1999). *The Political Economy of New Labour: Labouring Under False Pretences?* Manchester: Manchester University Press.

Heffernan, R. (2001). *New Labour and Thatcherism: Policy Change in Britain.* London: Palgrave Macmillan.

Heseltine, M. (2017, March 8). Michael Heseltine Says Brexit Is 'Man-Sized' Task for Theresa May. *The Guardian.* Available at: https://www.theguardian.com/politics/2017/mar/08/michael-heseltine-keep-opposing-Brexit-disastrous-eu-referendum-lords.

Holland, S. (1975). *The Socialist Challenge.* London: Quartet Books.

Howard, M. (2004, March 19). *Speech to the News Corporation Conference.* Cancun, Mexico.

Hutton, W. (1995). *The State We're In.* London: Cape.

Hutton, W. (2002). *The World We're In.* London: Little, Brown.

Johnson, B. (2017, February 22). Boris Johnson Accused of Bad Taste for Calling Brexit 'Liberation'. *The Guardian.* Available at: https://www.theguardian.com/politics/2017/feb/22/boris-johnson-accused-of-bad-taste-for-calling-Brexit-liberation.

Joseph, K. (1979). *Solving the Union Problem is the Key to Britain's Recovery.* London: Centre for Policy Studies.

Kenny, M., & Pearce, N. (2018). *Shadows of Empire: The Anglosphere in British Politics.* Cambridge: Polity.

Lowe, R. (1999). *The Welfare State in Britain Since 1945.* London: Palgrave Macmillan.

Marshall, T. H. (1950). *Citizenship and Social Class.* Cambridge: Cambridge University Press.

Owen, G. (2000). *From Empire to Europe.* London: Harper Collins.

Park, A. (Ed.). (2003). *British Social Attitudes.* London: Sage.

Parkinson, J. (1993). *Corporate Power and Responsibility: Issues in the Theory of Company Law.* Oxford: Clarendon.

Party, C. (1987). *Election Manifesto.* London: Conservative Party.

Pierson, P. (1994). *Dismantling the Welfare State?* Cambridge: Cambridge University Press.

Shonfield, A. (1958). *British Economic Policy Since the War.* Harmondsworth: Penguin.

Shonfield, A. (1965). *Modern Capitalism: The Changing Balance of Public and Private Power.* London: Oxford University Press.

Watson, M. (2003). The Politics of Inflation Management. *Political Quarterly,* 74(3), 285–297.

Wolf, M. (2005, January 12). Why Are English-Speaking Nations Doing Best? *Financial Times.*

CHAPTER 3

"Pragmatic Adaptation" and the Future of the City of London: Between Globalisation and Brexit

Leila Simona Talani

Introduction

The economic, political and social domination of the City of London over any other British socio-economic actors has traditionally been at the core of the debate about "British exceptionalism". Starting from a definition of the City as the locus of merchant or commercial practices, scholars have pointed out how these activities guarantee the prosperity of the City itself as separated from the performance of British economy as a whole. In particular, the success of the City has always been detached from the risks associated with the involvement in productive enterprises, thanks to the "short-termism" stemming from its mainly commercial nature. Finally, the enduring hegemony of the City of London in the history of British capitalism

L. S. Talani (✉)
Kennedy School of Governance, Harvard University,
Cambridge, MA, USA
e-mail: leila.talani@kcl.ac.uk

L. S. Talani
King's College London, London, UK

© The Author(s) 2019
C. Hay and D. Bailey (eds.), *Diverging Capitalisms*,
Building a Sustainable Political Economy: SPERI Research & Policy,
https://doi.org/10.1007/978-3-030-03415-3_3

cannot be separated from its peculiar ties with the Treasury and the Bank of England, often considered at the roots of its "pragmatic adaptation".

This contribution will explore how this "pragmatic adaptation", relying on the friendly regulatory and economic policies enacted by the British government, will help the City of London adapt to the challenges of globalisation and the changing nature of British relation with the EU.

The chapter is structured in three parts. Pragmatic adaptation in theory; Globalisation and the future of the City of London; Brexit and pragmatic adaptation in practice.

In the first section, the theoretical foundations of the notion of pragmatic adaptation are explored and discussed with reference to the relevant literature. The second section will explore the challenges and opportunities that globalisation pose to the City of London. Here the chapter differentiates between different definitions of globalisation with the aim of identifying what is the impact of each of them on the City of London. In, particular, the author will distinguish between qualitative and quantitative definitions of globalisation and will assess the impact of each of them at the macro and the micro-level of analysis drawing on the relevant IPE literature. In the third section, the author addresses how pragmatic adaptation has already started to take place to allow the City to fully gather the benefits of a "Global City" after Brexit. In the conclusion, the author will discuss how the City of London is likely to use pragmatic adaptation to respond to the challenges of both globalisation and exit from the EU.

Pragmatic Adaptation in Theory

In the most widely accepted explanation, exceptionalism coincides with British traditionalism. As such, any aristocratic, pre-industrial elements still evident in British polity are seen as only symbolic and legitimatory in meaning and do not correspond to any effective divisions within the British capitalist class.

However, there is also an alternative, more controversial interpretation of these events; an interpretation rooted in Anderson's and Nairn's seminal works on the subject. According to this interpretation, traditionalism is still at the core of modern British ideology, not only symbolically, but also as directly impacting the structure and performance of the British economy, as it is based on the hegemony of those fractions of British capitalism which recognise it as their ideological point of reference. According to Anderson, the exceptionalism of British society is represented by the dual nature of British capitalism; that is, the separate-ness of the financial fraction of capital and the industrial one, and the dominance of the former over the latter. This is reflected in the persis-tence of aristocratic, pre-industrial forms in the organisation of the civil and political society, as the British financial and banking elite is recog-nised as the carrier of feudal, aristocratic cultural and social values.

On the other hand, the British capitalist structure is also characterised by the existence of a hegemonic position of the capitalist bloc as a whole, as opposed to the non-hegemonic though self-conscious bloc of the working class. Here the concept of hegemony is defined in Gramscian terms as the "dominance of one social bloc over another, not simply by means of force or wealth, but by a total social authority whose ultimate sanction and expression is a profound cultural supremacy".

Thus, according to this interpretation, the present equilibrium in England remains a capitalist one, but within the capitalist class itself, one economic and, consequently, social component is hegemonic. This com-ponent is the financial sector; or in other words, the City of London. The City is not only a dominant economic and social actor, but together with its political referents (the Treasury and the Bank of England), is deemed responsible for the British economic decline from the second half of the nineteenth century onward. Indeed, within this conceptualis-ation, the crisis of British industry is explained as the logical outcome of a long subordination of the needs of productive capital to the economic interests and preferences of the City of London.

The main criticisms to this interpretation are based on two points. First, the definition of the City, and consequently the nature of the relations between the City and industry; and second, the City-State connections.

The most important problem concerns the conceptualisation of City and the identification of the specific relationship between the British financial sector and industry as historically developed. For many authors interested in the subject, the City is simply the centre of British finance capital, that is, in the Marxist definition, the direct involvement of bank-ing capital in the means by which surplus value is created (Aaronvitch 1961; Overbeek 1980). A number of objections are raised by other schol-ars against this conceptualisation of the City, and an alternative definition has been proposed, which puts much more emphasis on a clear identifica-tion of the City's economic activities (Ingham 1984; Strange 1971).

Whereas many of the City's activities are "financial" in a broader sense as they make money capital available to the productive sector by means of the markets, they mainly comprise commercial practices. Thus, the role of the City's firms as intermediaries in the provision of finance indistinctly to domestic or international players should be understood as that of a commercial entrepôt, giving rise to services income.

Consequently, the City should not be simply defined as the locus of British finance capital, or in terms of the identification of its constituent companies. It should instead be conceptualised as the institutional structure of short-termism, or exchanges, in commodities, securities, money and services. This definition allows, on one hand, to link the apparently unrelated activities of investment banking, foreign exchange dealing, securities dealings and more and, on the other hand, to account for the City's uniqueness in the world. British exceptionalism is thus ontologically connected to the exceptionalism of the "City of London".

In conclusion, the main element of British exceptionalism is given not so much by the persistence of a traditional, pre-modern polity, as is the case in Britain, but by the fact that this polity is economically, politically and socially dominated by the City and its social and political allies. Moreover, the City is characterised, or defined, not as the centre of the "finance capital", but as the locus of merchant or commercial practices, ranging from insurance to brokerage activities, from trading in secondary markets to providing professional services. These activities, while on one side limit to a great extent the expansion of British productive sector, on the other side guarantee the prosperity of the City itself as separated from the performance of British economy as a whole, and in particular from the risks associated with the involvement in any productive enterprises. Finally, the explanation of British exceptionalism cannot only be related to the establishment, defense and exploitation of the Empire, but is also determined by the interactions and dialect relations between the City, the Treasury and the Bank of England, which have guaranteed, over the course of the centuries, its "pragmatic adaptation".

The interpretation of British capitalist development as proposed by Nairn and Anderson referenced above, clearly identifies the role of the City of London in explaining the historical weakness and subordination of the industrial bourgeoisie. Moreover, within this context the split between the two sectors is seen as a "basic underpinning of the state structure" (Nairn 1977: 28). However this approach has been criticised (Ingham 1984) for failing to precisely identify the economic nature of the social class dominating civil and political society, as well as neglecting the role and specific interests of the City's merchant and commercial elite and their subsequent alliance with the land-owning elite, in explaining the decline of the British industrial sector (Ingham 1984).

Longstreth (1979), on the contrary, deals more directly with the analysis of the difficult relationship between the City and industry in the UK over the past century, while also clarifying the relationship between the financial sector and the state by adopting an "instrumental" approach. This does not imply that the state is depicted as a neutral instrument in the hands of a cohesive dominant class; however, he does conceptualise the British state as a system penetrated and structured by specific class relations, though he allows for variations due to historical contingencies. Moreover, the state can be, and in Britain's case has been, dominated by a particular fraction of the dominant class, "a 'ceta dirigente', which by no means exercises power consistently in the general interest of the dominant class taken as a whole" (Longstreth 1979: 159).

More specifically, Longstreth claims that since the nineteenth century, a traditional power bloc, led by the City of London, has determined the British government's economic policy-making at the expense of the British industry (Longstreth 1979). In addition, according to Cain and Hopkins, since 1880 "no clear line could be drawn between gentlemanly governments and a united gentlemanly City over matters of fundamental importance in economic and financial policy" (Cain and Hopkins 2000: 330). Indeed, many of the political struggles over the course of the twentieth century can be interpreted as attempts to either over-turn or modify the domination of this "establishment" in the state system. Yet, this power bloc has maintained its position intact largely thanks to "pragmatic adaptation" to changing circumstances in the world economy and the domestic class struggle (Longstreth 1979: 160).

The divide within the dominant class between the City, or more generally the financial sector, and industry, or productive capital, dates back to the decline of the landed aristocracy. At the political level, the City has been able to control the economic policy-making of the British government so as to guarantee that its preferences have more or less always represented the point of reference for the determination of the economic decision making of the country. In a following section, we shall see that this is still currently the case with Brexit. Obviously, various governments and political contingencies have influenced the way in which the City has exercised its hegemonic position; however, hegemony has not been shattered by political events and has remained undisputed in the course of history (Longstreth 1979: 161).

More specifically, the City's dominant position has been reinforced within the state system for two main reasons. First, the Bank of England and its relation to the Treasury has allowed the City to directly transmit its economic preferences on the decision making level. Cain and Hopkins (2000) give a very convincing account of how Gladstonianism succeeded in boosting the power of the two gentlemanly institutions most intimately connected to the City of London and to what extent this was opposed by the British industrial sector. In their words: "The Bank remained for a time an object of suspicion outside its own circle of intimates in the City" (Cain and Hopkins 2000: 321–322). Even with nationalisation, the Bank of England remained a substantial referent of the City's interests as it kept a de facto self-governing status.

Secondly, and in line with Gramscian sociology of power,[1] the City has been able to continue dominating British political life because it was able to keep a leading role in the British economy thanks to its external success first with the empire, then with the Sterling area and now with its dominance of world financial markets. Indeed, it was the Sterling area that helped the City regain its dominance of international financial markets and thus reinforced its political and ideological superiority over industry, which was contextually experiencing its dismemberment in a multinational direction (Longstreth 1979: 161).

From the institutional point of view, the hegemonic position of the City has been guaranteed by its privileged relationship with some strategic state bureaucracies, which allowed the financial sector to control important levers of power. As previously mentioned, the most prominent among these institutions is the Bank of England, whose nationalisation did nothing to reduce its level of embeddedness into the British financial milieu from a political, economic and sociological standpoint. The Bank, by its own definition, is the trait d'union between the state and financial interests. In reality, it is even more than this, as it acts as the representative of financial interests inside state institutions. This means that the City has always been able to directly influence economic policy-making from within the state itself through the role played by the Bank

---

[1] Here it is important to point out that in a Gramscian sociology of power an economic actor can become hegemonic for two reasons: (1) economic power legitimates and renders its dominant position acceptable to the other actors; (2) only an economic actor can trigger that economic development which is considered the prerequisite to gain mass consensus (Gill 1993).

(Cain and Hopkins 2000: 320–321). The industrial sector was not afforded such a privilege, although many of the reforms of the 1960s in the industrial policy arena have been interpreted as a substantially failed attempt to redress the balance and allow industrialists to have a louder voice in the definition of the various economic strategies (Longstreth 1979: 85). Some authors (Ingham 1984, 1988, 2002) take issues with an "instrumental" definition of the class-state relationship, and in particular with the fact that the Bank of England and the Treasury are considered as "media" through which the City's interests are channelled. However, there is no doubt in the historical literature, that the City's prosperity owes much to the intervention of these two institutions (Cain and Hopkins 2000; Kynaston 1994).

With Longstreth we can conclude that: "The City has, in other words, largely set the parameters of economic policy and its interests have generally predominated since the late nineteenth century. Its dominance has been so complete that its position has often been taken as the quintessence of responsible financial policy" (Longstreth 1979: 161–162).

With regard to how the City was able to acquire such a dominant position over industry, Longstreth (1979) emphasises how the particular pattern of capitalist development in Britain served as the basis for the City's domination in the political realm. Beginning in 1870, the London capital markets experienced the expansion of foreign investment; therefore, the City developed almost entirely out of foreign trade. Susan Strange (1971) notes that due to free trade and the gold standard, the City became an international powerhouse, and, as a consequence, also the domestic locus of economic power and prestige, developing an internal outlook which corresponded to its international position. In political terms, this sealed the coincidence of interests between imperialists and the City; an alliance that persisted until the 1960s.[2]

What is difficult to understand is why there was so little opposition to this status quo from within the capitalist class itself. There is no doubt that conflict has materialised in various forms and at various times, as Longstreth (1979) analytically points out; but overall, after the Second World War the City remained the dominant actor within the British capitalist class despite substantial changes in the economic life of the country and a new reformist Labour Government, which had

[2]As he does not explain the persistent success of the City, here it is necessary to rely on Ingham (1984).

proclaimed itself highly committed to the restructuring of the industrial sector. However, the City had many powerful means to convince reluctant state institutions to follow its advice. One of the most successful was, and still is, its capacity to provoke currency crises, which, according to Longstreth (1979), is how it managed to convince the Labour Government to follow the advice of its representatives when formulating economic policy.[3]

On the contrary, trade unions did oppose the establishment but were rarely able to substantially influence the government's economic policy stances. Further, the idea of a state-planned economy in concert with the trade unions has never been particular appealing to the British industrial elite. Despite the fact that the Labour Party had, since the early 1960s, actively engaged in trying to establish corporatist practices in the UK (such as supporting a policy of greater state intervention), this alliance between "producers" never actually materialised (Longstreth 1979). Even the creation of the Federation of British Industry in 1916 and its merger with other major employers' organisations into the Confederation of British Industry (CBI) in 1965, was possible only thanks to the intervention of the Labour Government in power at that time.

One of the possible answers to this mysterious acquiescence of the industrial capitalist elite is to be found again in the specific pattern of development of the British capitalist structure as analysed above, which, while it empowered the financial sector, weakened industrial capital.

The contemporary lack of substantial opposition to the City's economic preferences from within the ranks of capital is easier to explain given the latest development in industrial production, now completely dominated by multinational corporations whose interests often coincide with those of the financial sector. As, thanks to globalisation, production is increasingly moved abroad, the British industrial sector has become increasingly involved in financial activities at home; subsequently, its economic preferences become closer to those of the City.

In the next section, therefore, we will explore how Globalisation is likely to affect the future of the City of London.

---

[3] See also Anderson's interpretation of the failures of Labour governments (Anderson 1987).

A Global City: How Does Globalisation Affect the City of London

Globalisation is one of the most hotly debated topics within the social sciences, and certainly one that has captured scholars' imagination when looking toward the future. Globalisation is not only the present, but also the future of politics and economics, and no discussion regarding future scenarios can avoid addressing it.

How does globalisation affect the future of the City of London? Does financial globalisation signal the end of the City's hegemony or does it guarantee its future success?

Questions related to how globalisation affects domestic actors cannot be disentangled from a more general and in-depth analysis of globalisation and its definitions.

The notion of globalisation is not without controversy both within the academic debate and in the wider public discourse. Despite the great success of this concept in recent decades there is still some degree of confusion about its definition, and the discussion is still open about precisely how globalisation modifies the capacity of the state to intervene in the domestic and in the global economy (Busch 2008: 5).

However, it is possible to classify positions adopted by scholars into three broad groups, alongside the three traditional approaches to International Relations/International Political Economy (IR/IPE) (Dicken 1999: 5): First, those who deny outright the very existence of the phenomenon of globalisation (Hirst and Thompson 1999; Thompson 1993); second, those who recognise it but tend to give only a quantitative definition of globalisation (Held et al. 1999; Holm and Sørensen 1995); and third, those who adopt a qualitative definition (Mittlemann 2000; Hay and Marsh 2000; Dicken 1999, 2003).

The denial of globalisation is typical of realist theory and rests on considerations about the historical recurrence of periods of increased international and cross-border interactions. In reality, those who adopt this perspective deny the "originality" of globalisation and its characterisation as a "new phenomenon". In some instances, proponents of this theory go so far as to deny the current phase of the world's economic development any "global", "globalised" or "globalising" features (Hirst and Thompson 1999).

The denial of globalisation stems from the failure to identify its distinctive characteristics due to the adoption of a quantitative definition of the phenomenon. From a quantitative point of view, globalisation is defined as:

> ...The intensification of economic, political, social and cultural relations across borders. (Holm and Sørensen 1995: 12)

An institutionalist interpretation of globalisation also exists, and is one that similarly originates from a quantitative definition of the phenomenon while stressing the "transformation" of the nation-state within globalisation and the necessity for international institutions to take over many of the responsibilities previously allocated to the state, including the regulation of global financial markets.

The traditional transnationalist approach instead adopts a distinctive qualitative definition of globalisation (Mittlemann 2000) which identifies the process of globalisation as a qualitatively new phenomenon, characterised by the dramatic increase of foreign direct investment (FDI), the transnationalisation of social groups (including labour and business), and an unprecedented interdependence of financial markets (Overbeek 2000). Technological transformation is an exogenous component of the qualitative definition of globalisation, and it is the one factor that brings about transformation in terms of financial transactions and production.

In this section, we shall deal with each of these approaches to the definition of globalisation and their consequences for the future of the City of London.

Let us start from a classical quantitative view of financial globalisation. This has been well summarised by Cohen (1996):

> Financial globalisation (or internationalisation) refers to the broad integration of national markets associated with both innovation and deregulation in the postwar era and is manifested by increasing movements of capital across national frontiers. The more alternative assets are closely regarded as substitutes for one another, the higher the degree of capital mobility. (Cohen 1996: 269)

Adopting this definition, capital mobility becomes the constituent element of financial globalisation (Obstfeld and Taylor 2004). In macroeconomic terms, the problem is called the "inconsistent quartet" (Padoa-Schioppa 1994), the "unholy trinity'" (Cohen 1996) or the "trilemma" (Obstfeld and Taylor 2004: 29), and posits that in an economic environment characterised by free capital movement, national monetary autonomy becomes an alternative to keeping stable exchange rates. The case rests on the argument that complete capital liberalisation, (as implied by the quantitative definition of financial globalisation) and exchange rate stability, (as necessary, in theory, for international trade to continue unhindered) are incompatible with divergent national monetary policies.

The economic explanation for the existence of the "inconsistent quartet" can be found in the Mundell-Fleming model, which links the monetary economic equilibrium—the equilibrium of monetarist variables given by the equilibrium between money supply and demand and summarised in the LM curve—and the real variables equilibrium, the equilibrium between investments and savings that is summarised by the IS curve. The model also includes the equilibrium of the external economic relationships in the form of the balance of payments equilibrium, summarised in the BP curve.

In short, according to this model, in a world of perfect capital mobility autonomous monetary policy is inconsistent with stable exchange rates. As a consequence, not only do national economic authorities see their capacity to implement independent monetary and fiscal policies substantially constrained, but financial markets also see their power to destabilise national economies engaging in speculative practices greatly increased.

Although in macroeconomic terms this argument is certainly sound (or, at the least I am not in a position to criticise it), the British case is particularly relevant in highlighting how financial globalisation did not particularly decrease the power of the City of London as defined here. The main point is that in the trade-off between the stability of exchange rates and autonomous monetary policy, some domestic actors (notably the City of London) might still prefer the latter, as they have demonstrated in their position toward joining the Euro area (Talani 2010). This happens for some concurring reasons.

Some sectors, like financial services, though perfectly integrated at the regional and global level might still prefer to keep autonomous monetary policy decision-making at the national level. In particular, setting the interest rates at a higher level than other financial centres represents a relevant competitive advantage in attracting short- and very short-term capital. This, of course, is harmful for industrial activity. However, here the issue becomes one of power relations between domestic economic sectors or interest groups. In the context of globalisation, the issue is also influenced by the extent to which the industrial sector is actually relying on domestic production as opposed to production abroad (Dicken 2003).

To conclude the discussion of how the British financial sector will gain from globalisation at the macro level, it is not unlikely that London will be on the winning side of speculative practices (Guth 1994; Lilley 2000). The following is just one example: In 2008, the Financial Services Authority (FSA) was compelled to pass emergency rules banning the short-selling[4] of UK bank shares in the City of London after the practice brought the HBOS share price to a collapse. Well-known City operators are believed to have profited from short-selling sub-prime mortgages and betting against HBOS. Hedge funds in the City of London are said to have made at least £1 billion in profits by shorting HBOS shares in June and July 2008, fuelled by City rumours that the bank was in financial distress. At one point in June of that year, a single fund, Harbinger Capital, traded more than three per cent of all HBOS shares. Harbinger was run by Philip Falcone, a former Barclays trader who earned £1.7 billion in 2007 alone (*The Telegraph* 2008).

It is, however, at the micro level (i.e. at the level of sectoral and domestic interest group analysis) that we see how the City of London can gain from globalisation. As Cohen correctly states, "owners of mobile capital... gain influence at the expense of less fortunate sectors including so-called national capital as well as labour" (Cohen 1996: 286).

How does this happen? To answer this question, it is necessary to adopt a domestic politics (or inside-out) approach to the international political economy. The case for a domestic politics approach has a long history.

The problem that remains, however, is explaining domestic politics. With respect to this, there are various theories. Firstly, the societal actors approach, which identifies the source of power in the preferences of societal and economic forces as shaped by their international and domestic economic situation (Rogowski 1989). Secondly, the intermediate associations explanation, which stresses the role of such organisations like

---

[4] Short-selling is selling borrowed shares in the hopes that their price will fall and that they can be bought back at a profit later on.

political parties and interest groups in linking social preferences to state institutions (Katzenstein 1977). Thirdly, state-centred theories, resting on the assumption of the central role of formal institutions, bureaucracies and rules in defining both interests and policy outcomes (Martin 1993). Fourthly, economic ideology explanations, which stress the role of economic perceptions, models and values in determining states' preferences and behaviour (Goldstein and Keohane 1993).

The societal actors approach, focusing on the role of sectoral actors and interest groups has proven most effective in proposing useful, testable hypotheses in relation to financial issues. Jeffrey Frieden greatly contributed to the development of a distributional politics approach to exchange rate policymaking from within a two-level game theoretical framework (Frieden and Stein 2001; Frieden et al. 2010; Frieden 1991, 1993, 1994a, b, 1996a, b, 1997a, b, 1998a, b, 1999, 2000, 2001, 2002, 2004, 2009). Frieden (1991) proposes a "two-step" model of national exchange rate policymaking based on domestic sectoral interests. The model identifies economic sectors' preferences vis-à-vis two interrelated dimensions of exchange rate regime (fixed or flexible) and level (appreciated or depreciated). In order to understand this approach, it is important to recall that under perfect capital mobility, adopting a fixed exchange rate, while providing currency stability, implies sacrificing domestic monetary policy autonomy.

Two groups of actors directly involved in international trade and payments who are highly sensitive to currency fluctuations and would, therefore, support fixing the exchange rate are the producers of export-oriented tradable goods and international investors. Conversely, two other groups of actors who tend to be highly concerned about domestic macroeconomic conditions and would thus favour the national monetary policy autonomy made possible by flexible exchange rates, are producers of non-tradable goods and services (mainly the public sector) and producers of import-competing tradable goods for the domestic market (Frieden 1991). The resulting cleavages would be as follows (Table 3.1).

The problem with the application of this model is that it is unclear which effects globalisation will have on exchange rates, whereas it is implicit in the quantitative definition of globalisation that it requires trade and investment liberalisation.

From this point of view, as early as 1989, Rogowski (1989) had identified which economic sectors would gain from the opening of the

Table 3.1   Frieden's model

	FLOATING EXCHANGE RATES	*FIXED EXCHANGE RATES*	
DEPRECIATION OF THE CURRENCY	Manufacturing, small companies	Export-oriented, big companies	Manufacturing, small compa-nies + export oriented, big companies
APPRECIATION OF THE CURRENCY	Public sector	Financial and bank-ing sector	Public sector + finan-cial and banking sector
	Manufacturing, small companies + public sector	Export-oriented, big companies + financial and banking sector	

markets. Based on the Heckscher-Ohlin theorem,[5] Rogowski proposes a model of factor endowments which allows the categorisation of any country according to whether it is advanced or backwards or whether its land/labour ratio is high or low (Rogowski 1989: 6). Then, applying the Stolper-Samuelson theorem,[6] he hypotheses that increasing exposure to trade will result in an urban/rural conflict in advanced economies with a low land/labour ratio and in backward economies with high land/labour ratio; on the other hand, it would result in a class cleavage in advanced economies with high land/labour ratio and in backward economies with low land/labour ratio (Table 3.2) (Rogowski 1989: 8).

Building on this model, Frieden and Rogowski were able to project the interest of socio-economic sectors with respect to globalisation (Frieden and Rogowski 1996).

Assuming that globalisation is defined in quantitative terms as "growing global trade and financial flows" (Frieden and Rogowski 1996: 26),

[5] The Heckscher-Ohlin trade model concludes that a country will tend to export goods intensive in the factor it has in abundance, and to import goods intensive in the factors in which it is scarce (Frieden and Rogowski 1996: 37).

[6] The Stolper-Samuelson theorem finds that in each country returns rise absolutely and disproportionally to owners of factors that are required intensively in the production of goods whose prices have risen; and they fall absolutely and disproportionally to factors required intensively in the production of goods whose prices have fallen (Frieden and Rogowski 1996: 37).

Table 3.2 Predicted effects of expanding exposure to trade

	Land/labour ratio	
	High	Low
Advanced economy	CLASS CLEAVAGE	URBAN-RURAL CLEAVAGE
	Land and Capital	Capital and labour
	Free trading assertive	Free trading assertive
	Labour defensive, protectionist	Land defensive, protectionist
		RADICALISM
Backward economy	URBAN-RURAL CLEAVAGE	CLASS CLEAVAGE
	Land	Labour
	Free trading assertive	Free trading assertive
	Labour and Capital	Land and Capital
	Defensive, protectionist	Defensive Protectionist
	POPULISM	SOCIALISM

Source Rogowski (1989: 8)

by applying the Heckscher-Ohlin/Stolper-Samuelson approach, the authors derive some interesting propositions about the distributional consequences of globalisation. This would imply a rise in the domestic prices of goods whose production is intensive in the given country's abundant factors and a fall in the prices of those goods intensive in scarce factors. In this context, globalisation would benefit the owners of abundant factors and disadvantage those who own scarce factors (Frieden and Rogowski 1996: 37). Therefore, as developed countries are characterised by an abundance of capital and a shortage of unskilled labour, globalisation favours capitalists and skilled labour while unskilled labour is at a disadvantage in advanced capitalist economies. (Frieden and Rogowski 1996: 40). This is relevant for our domestic politics analysis of who wins and who loses from globalisation as the City of London is composed exclusively by capitalists and skilled labour and has everything to gain from liberalisation from this perspective.

There are, however, two further dimensions that strengthen the argument that the City of London will certainly gain from globalisation. First, we must consider that on the basis of this analysis, the power of an interest group to assert its preferences is directly related to its capacity to move, which in turn depends on the mobility of its factor. If an interest group is able to credibly threaten leaving the country, its bargaining power increases. Therefore, globalisation reduces the capacity of the government to disregard the preferences of the most mobile factor, which is capital—and financial capital in particular—and increases the negotiation and political power of the owners of such capital: to wit, the City of London (Keohane et al. 1996: 19; Busch 2008: 8).

Moreover, adopting a sectoral rather than a factorial type of analysis, through the application of the specific factor approach (also known as Ricardo-Viner) the result is even more clearly supportive of the view that the British banking sector has everything to gain from globalisation (Frieden and Rogowski 1996: 38). This perspective suggests that factors like land, labour or capital are normally used for a specific activity or production, and therefore only price changes in their specific activity or production (not in all of the uses of the factors) will affect them. To apply it to the case of the UK, if capital is used specifically for banking and financial transactions when the terms of trade in banking change, only the banking sector will gain, not all capital. Overall, the application of the Ricardo-Viner variant implies:

1. That the benefits of globalisation will vary with the specificity of the relevant actors' assets.
2. That the most competitive sectors will gain more.
3. That political pressure will happen at the sectoral rather than at the factorial level.

There is no doubt that financial capital is an abundant factor in the UK. Therefore, to the extent to which the City remains competitive internationally, and a high degree of openness is guaranteed, it will improve its position not only with respect to labour but also, more importantly given the approach adopted here, with respect to industrial capital.

Let us now address the question from the perspective of a qualitative definition of globalisation. As detailed above, technological change is at the core of the qualitative definition of globalisation, bringing about changes in the productive and in the financial sphere (Dicken 2003: 85).

It is technology, therefore, that produces financial globalisation, defined here as the existence of around-the-clock access to financial transactions all over the world (Dicken 2003: 443).

Susan Strange identified the three most important technological changes that have produced financial globalisation: computers, chips and satellites (Strange 1998: 24–26):

> Computers have made money electronic...by the mid-1990s computers had not only transformed the physical form in which money worked as a medium of exchange, they were also in the process of transforming the systems by which payments of money were exchanged and recorded. (Strange 1998: 24)

Chips (microprocessors) have allowed for the credit card revolution and the "smart card" revolution as well (Cohen 2001). Finally, satellites are the basis of global electronic communication (Dicken 2003: 85–120).

It is impossible not to understand the implications on financial services in terms of increase in productivity; patterns of relationships and linkages between financial firms and clients, and within the financial community; velocity and turnover of investment capital and capacity to react to international events immediately (Dicken 2003: 443).

Even more importantly, the competitive advantage has now moved to technological infrastructure. Even the technological superiority of cable infrastructure could represent a substantial competitive advantage making physical location actually much more relevant in the globalisation era. Indeed, a study by the European Central Bank concluded that the undersea cables are a critical factor in determining the competitive strength of financial centres, especially the City of London (*Financial Times* 2017).

As a consequence, there is now consensus in the literature that financial globalisation has "made geography more, not less, important" (Dicken 2003: 59; Coleman 1996: 7).

On the one hand, some financial products contain information which is the result of long, well-established business relationships and this remains the case with financial globalisation. Equities, domestic bonds and bank loans have indeed a large amount of domestic information embedded within (Coleman 1996: 7).

On the other hand, financial technological infrastructure and financial innovation, both very location specific, have become decisive elements of competitive advantage globally.

Thus, despite the significant emphasis on financial globalisation, the location of global financial power has remained surprisingly unchanged and concentrated in a handful of urban centres, namely New York, London and, to a more limited extent, Tokyo. This concentration is unparalleled in any other kind of industry and it is also extremely stable (Dicken 2003: 462).

In fact, London is the more broadly based financial centre and its position does not seem to have changed in the last decade—the decade of globalisation. If anything, with respect to many of its main markets and services, its position has improved (Talani 2012). If globalisation is clearly benefitting the British financial sector from all points of view, how likely is the "Global City" to be put under discussion by Brexit? This is a question we will try to address in the next section of this contribution.

PRAGMATIC ADAPTATION AND BREXIT: ITS BEGINNING TO LOOK A LOT LIKE BREXIT!

There is the possibility, that, if openness is reduced, as, for example, by closing the European Single Market to the UK as a consequence of a Brexit, all the advantages of globalisation for the City of London could be off-set. This might explain why, at the outset, the City of London was against Brexit. Indeed, the City of London Corporation has openly supported Britain remaining in the EU.

A survey of 147 UK based financial services firms found 40% chose the UK over other centres because of access to the EU. 81% of 98 fintech start-up business published by Innovate Finance, voted to stay in the EU, this was comparable to the survey conducted by Tech London Advocates in 2015 (City of London 2016).

Not a single financial trade association has been favourable to Brexit in the debate leading to the 2016 referendum, and the representatives of major City institutions such as Lloyds of London, the London Stock Exchange, Aviva, Goldman Sachs, HSBC, Barclays, Prudential, RSA, Standard Life and Santander have all expressed their institutions' wish that Britain remain in the EU.

The reasons were initially very clear. If the UK stays in the Single Market, the institutions based in the City have a passport to operate everywhere else in the EU without the need to have separate businesses in other countries, with all that this means in terms of different authorisation processes, regulation as well as staffing costs (City of London 2016).

However, as a hard Brexit, i.e. an exit not only from the EU but also from the Single Market, becomes more likely, it seems that City's institutions have adapted themselves to the changing situation through their traditional "pragmatic adaptation". This will take the form of moving all EU services to another EU member states with the aim of keeping their pass-porting rights. Like in the case of the announcement made by Deutsche Bank in March 2017, if Britain were to leave the Single Market, thus losing pass-porting rights granted to EU members, Banks will probably have to turn their London branches into subsidiaries that would require capital and move their EU booking hub to an EU financial centre (*The Independent* 2017a).

Frankfurt could emerge as winner in a similar race, with Standard Chartered, Nomura, Sumitomo Mitsui and Daiwa Securities picking the city as their EU hub in the year after the Brexit vote, while Citigroup, Goldman Sachs and Morgan Stanley were considering the same location.

However, as Bill Blain, a strategist at Mint Partners in London, says, "They can move as many trading and investment assets to Frankfurt as they want, but the gravitational centre of the European financial universe will remain in London for some time - whatever Brexit we get" (*The Independent* 2017a).

Also Irish authorities claim they achieved deals with more than a dozen London-based banks and finance houses to move some of their operations to Dublin in preparation for Brexit with US bank JP Morgan buying a landmark office building in Dublin and Bank of America Merrill Lynch, which already has a presence in Dublin, speaking of expanding in the city (*The Irish Times* 2017).

Still, one year after the referendum, experts, such as Mr Donoghue, head of international financial services at Ireland's Industrial Development Authority, were convinced that the mass exodus from London that was once feared is unlikely to materialise (*The Irish Times* 2017).

In his words: "This is a sensitive event for the financial services, they don't really want to leave decades of infrastructure in London, for them to leave is a disruption to business and a cost." "We do not think that London is going to disappear, but the industry will move to a more decentralised model" (*The Irish Times* 2017).

Even more clearly: "Essentially there are going to be three or four centres in Europe that are going to grow in size, but not to the point that London becomes irrelevant" (*The Irish Times* 2017). This statement is very consistent with the analysis above on the geographical concentration effects of globalisation for financial services.

Moreover, the size of the EU market for the City of London shall not be overestimated. Indeed, the Brexit impact papers published by the European Parliament make clear how, in 2015, only 23% of the UK financial services revenues derived from activities relating to the EU (European Parliament 2016). That is to say that the remaining 77% was related to activities outside the EU.

Finally, so far London does not seem to have lost its capacity to attract especially technologically sensitive financial industry. Reuters reports that over half a billion dollars were poured into British financial technology companies in the first half of 2017. This accounts to over a third more than the same period last year, as the trade body Innovate Finance claimed in July 2017. This is a clear sign that the fast-growing fin-tech sector is betting on a post-Brexit favourable environment. UK-based fin-tech startups pulled in $564 million of venture capital investment in the first six months of the year 2017, more than half of which came from outside Britain. That was up 37% from the first half of 2016, and put Britain in third place globally for fintech investment, behind the United States and China (The Finanser blog 2017).

Fintech is a sector ranging from mobile payment apps to digital currencies like bitcoin, and one that the government considers as key for future economic growth. Therefore, the British government has identified fin-tech as a priority area, saying it provides 60,000 jobs and contributes around $9 billion to the economy. In the first six months of 2017, the global investment in fin-tech was $6.5 billion. Of this, just over half went into U.S. startups and around $1 billion into China. A third of the investment into British fintech came from venture capital firms based in the United States (The Finanser blog 2017).

The main reasons for this renewed confidence in the British economy post-Brexit, are according to Abdul Haseeb Basit, Head of Finance and Strategic Projects at Innovate Finance: "Britain's prowess in both conventional finance and technology, as well as light-touch regulation, its pro-business culture and even the fact that it is Anglophone make it difficult for other centres to compete, though many - such as Berlin and Paris - are trying" (*Reuters* 2017). He also claimed that: "while passporting rights - which give firms licenced in one EU country the right to trade freely in any other - had been a big concern for investors after Brexit, those worries had eased. Even if Britain loses passporting rights, that would affect only 20 percent of the almost 300 startups that are members of Innovate Finance" (*Reuters* 2017).

The real worry was that access to highly skilled workers would dry up when Britain leaves the EU as an estimated 30% of the sector's workers are foreigners and most of them from the EU.

In the words of Basit: "Talent is the number one concern, and has been consistently since the referendum - we test (our members on) that every three to six months. So that's been fairly consistent – it's been a worry and until we have more certainty around that, it will remain a worry" (*Reuters* 2017).

Moreover, according to Basit: "There is a lot of competition in the investment space – there's a lot of capital available and it's looking for good companies to invest in." "Were they to not invest in UK companies, they feel like they might miss an opportunity. The appetite is still strong" (*Reuters* 2017).

It seems thus that the competitive advantages secured so far by the City of London as a global financial centre, such as its technological infrastructure, financial innovation, and its high concentration of financial expertise, will be difficult to be put into question by Brexit.

It might even be argued that Brexit could enhance the competitive position of the British financial centre in the era of globalisation, as it will actually require precisely those kind of policies which further enhance the City's hegemonic potential domestically and internationally: liberalisation and deregulation.

It is indeed becoming increasingly clear that, were it to happen, a hard Brexit could actually work for the UK, providing that a specific set of policies are adopted, policies that go precisely in the direction of the kind of Thatcher-style measures strongly supported by the "ultra-liberals", the free-marketeers of the City.

Indeed, the two Chancellors, Philip Hammond, and, previously George Osborne, have already hinted at this, when they underlined the structural changes that the British economic model would need post-Brexit. Jeremy Corbyn seems very aware of the risk that Brexit poses in terms of moving towards an ultra-liberal, hyper-globalised capitalist system. Moreover, this is certainly in line with Theresa May and her cabinet's claim that Brexit will make the UK more, not less, globalised (BBC 2017).

As almost verbatim claimed in the press, in order to keep Britain competitive in the global economy after a Hard Brexit, it will need to "adapt" and the UK's economic model will need to be reset (*The Independent* 2017b). Britain will have to become a sort of Hong Kong or Singapore of Europe. It will be the completion of Mrs Thatcher City revolution, and it may be no coincidence that almost all of the Brexiteers are hard-line nostalgic Thatcherites (*The Independent* 2017b).

So what are those measures and how are they likely to shape the future of the City outside the EU? Or, put in another way, how will "pragmatic adaptation" unfold in the case of a "Hard Brexit"?

First of all, the British Government will have to declare the adoption of unilateral free trade. By reducing tariffs on all imports to the UK of both goods and services, the country can easily benefit from lower global prices, in exchange for no tariffs and no control on imported goods. According to HMRC, routine customs declarations could be made electronically and goods cleared at ports in seconds (*The Independent* 2017b).

This, of course, will undermine the productive base of the country, thus exacerbating further the divide between finance and industry already at the core of the British capitalist system, as analysed when talking about "British Exceptionalism". As during the Thatcher era, the losers will be workers, who will have to endure much higher unemployment and a reduction of the welfare system as the economy adjusted.

Contrary to expectations, migration will not necessarily decrease post-Brexit, as the competitiveness and productivity of the City of London, and of the British economy as a whole, will have to be maintained by allowing the migrants in. However, migration quotas and skills will now be controlled by the British government, with far less rights in the case of EU migrants (*The Guardian* 2017a). This more, not less, open door policy on migration, including irregular migration, will almost certainly depress domestic wages, in line with traditional supply-side neo-liberal approaches to the labour market and to increased competitiveness, but in contrast to the initial expectations of Brexit (*The Independent* 2017b).

The same aim of increasing global competitiveness in line with the imperatives of neoliberal globalisation, will produce a further liberalisation of labour and environmental laws, finally freed from the check and balances of the European Institutions, especially the European Court of Justice. An echo of this possibility is to be identified in the debate surrounding the so-called Brexit bill (*The Guardian* 2017b). Flexibility of labour markets will be facilitated by the loss of control by supranational institutions and will be justified as the only way to gain global market shares after leaving the EU trade area (*The Independent* 2017b).

This links to two further neoliberal measures which could improve the attractiveness of the UK in the global environment and which have already been advocated by leading Tory politicians: tax cuts and reduction of state intervention in the economy (*The Independent* 2017b).

In line with theories of the Competition State (Cerny 1995), attracting business in the age of globalisation, especially when capital is very mobile such as in the case of financial capital, requires low taxes, a light-touch regulatory environment, the rule of law and political stability. The UK will need to be able to offer all this once outside the EU because it will not be able any more to be the gateway to the largest regional trade-block. It will therefore need to re-orientate the incentives it needs to offer foreign investors in a much more liberal way. However, lower taxes will reduce public spending and more spending for infrastructure will further decrease the share of public expenditure going to the welfare state, including the NHS, education and benefits. Again the lower strata of society will be the main losers of such a move, whereas the City of London will benefit not only from the new, more favourable regulatory environment, but also from the increase in the use of insurance services to substitute for the demise of the welfare state.

The direction of British economic structure change as a consequence of Brexit seems, therefore, unlikely to be towards social democracy, and even less, socialism. Instead, it will conform more to an exasperated form of neoliberal globalisation, the only one that, it is claimed, could guarantee some prosperity to the country outside the EU, and also the one that the City of London always favoured to maintain its global competitiveness and domestic hegemony (*The Independent* 2017b).

Indeed, the City is already positioning itself in this debate. The CityUK report published in July 2017 suggests that: "Britain will lose its status as Europe's top financial centre unless it keeps borders open to specialist staff, improves infrastructure and expands links with emerging economies" (CityUK 2017).

Conclusion: The Future of the City of London Between Globalisation and Brexit

Concluding, globalisation does not seem to be a real challenge for the City of London. The analysis thus far proves that its role and bargaining power inside the national polity will increase, as its economic position is very likely to improve in the future thanks precisely to globalisation. This will be the case no matter which definition of globalisation we take into account, and regardless of whether the analysis is carried on at the macro or at the micro level.

Starting from a quantitative definition of globalisation, at the macro level this implies a trade-off between national monetary autonomy and stable exchange rates. As exchange rate stability is necessary for trade liberalisation, countries will need to renounce their macro-economic autonomy and integrate their monetary policy-making through global agreements and institutions.

However, the decision by the UK government not to join the EMU demonstrates that, in the trade-off between the stability of the exchange rates and autonomous monetary policy, some countries, and especially some domestic actors (notably the City of London), might still prefer the latter. The reasons are many. Primarily, financial services have everything to gain from being able to set the interest rates at a higher level than the other financial centres and to keep the level of domestic regulation under control as this represents a relevant competitive advantage in attracting short-term and very short-term capital. Moreover, unstable exchange rates may and do actually signify a substantial source of revenues for the City of London. Finally, the City of London is most likely to be one of the main winners of financial speculative practices.

From the micro point of view, when adopting a factorial approach, globalisation favours capitalists and skilled labour and therefore, undoubtedly, the City of London. Furthermore, if an interest group is able to credibly threaten to leave the country, its bargaining power increases. As a consequence, globalisation reduces the capacity of the government to disregard the preferences of the most mobile factor, which is capital and financial capital in particular, increasing the negotiation and political power of the owners of such capital: the City of London.

Finally, adopting a sectoral instead of a factorial kind of analysis, to the extent to which the City remains competitive internationally, with a high degree of openness of the markets, it will improve its position not only with respect to labour but also with respect to industrial capital.

From the qualitative point of view, around-the-clock access to financial markets all over the globe does not threaten the geographical allocation of financial power. This remains surprisingly stable and concentrated in three centres: New York, London and, to a more limited extent, Tokyo. This concentration is unparalleled in any other kind of industry and it is also extremely durable. London is the most successful of these centres and its position does not seem to have been affected by globalisation. If anything, and with respect to many of its main markets and services, it has improved.

Summing up, what really counts for the prosperity of the City within globalisation is a relaxed regulatory environment. This is very likely to be of guaranteed by a friendly government post-Brexit.

However, this is a necessary but not sufficient condition for the City to maintain its hegemony both domestically and internationally in the globalisation era.

The second, vital condition is open access to markets globally. This could be jeopardised by a Brexit as it is highly unlikely the EU will grant the UK similar conditions of access to its markets as if it were still a member of the club. However, Brexit could also represent the catalyst for the adoption of ultra-liberal policies, ranging from a liberalisation of labour and environmental laws, import tariffs and controls and low taxes, to the diversion of public funds from the welfare state to infrastructures.

This would enhance the capacity of the City to attract investment globally at the expense of the living and working conditions of the lower strata of society. Will this be the future of the UK? Will the revenge of the ultra-liberals happen? It will all depend on whether the City-state nexus will hold post-Brexit. It seems, though, that the City's pragmatic adaptation strategy has already started.

REFERENCES

Aaronvitch, S. (1961). *The Ruling Class.* London: Lawrence and Wishart.

Anderson, P. (1987, January–February). The Figures of Descent. *New Left Review, 161,* 20–77.

BBC. (2017, July 31). *Brexit: UK Will Not Cut Taxes, Says Philip Hammond.* Available at: http://www.bbc.com/news/uk-politics-40771900. Accessed August 1, 2017.

Busch, A. (2008). *Banking Regulation and Globalization.* Oxford: Oxford University Press.

Cain, P. J., & Hopkins, A. G. (2000). Gentlemanly Capitalism and Economic Policy: City, Government and the "National interest", 1850–1914. In C. Michie (Ed.), *The Development of London as a Financial Centre* (Vol. 2, pp. 319–356). London and New York: I.B.Tauris Publishers.

Cerny, P. (1995). Globalization and the Changing Logic of Collective Action. *International Organization, 49*(4), 595–625.

City of London. (2016). *How We Make Decisions.* Available at: https://www.cityoflondon.gov.uk/about-the-city/how-we-make-decisions/Documents/implementing-markets-union.pdf. Accessed April 28, 2016.

CityUK. (2017, July 6). *A Vision for a Transformed, World-Leading Industry.* Available at: https://www.thecityuk.com/research/a-vision-for-a-transformed-world-leading-industry/. Accessed August 1, 2017.

Cohen, B. J. (1996). Phoenix Risen: The Resurrection of Global Finance. *World Politics, 48*(2), 268–296.

Cohen, B. J. (2001). Electronic Money: New Day or False Dawn? *Review of International Political Economy, 8*(2), 197–225.

Coleman, W. D. (1996). *Financial Services, Globalization and Domestic Policy Change*. London: Palgrave Macmillan.

Dicken, P. (1999). *Global Shift, Transforming the World Economy*. London: Paul Chapman Publishing.

Dicken, P. (2003). *Global Shift: Reshaping the Global Economic Map in the 21st Century*. Thousand Oaks, CA: Sage.

European Parliament. (2016, December 9). *Brexit: The United-Kingdom and EU Financial Services*. Available at: http://www.europarl.europa.eu/RegData/etudes/BRIE/2016/587384/IPOL_BRI%282016%29587384_EN.pdf. Accessed December 21, 2017.

Financial Times. (2017, July 5). EU Hopes of Winning London's Euro Trading Sunk by Undersea Cables. Available at: https://www.ft.com/content/56ad41e6-617a-11e7-8814-0ac7eb84e5f1. Accessed July 26, 2017.

Frieden, J. (1991). Invested Interests: The Politics of National Economic Policies in a World of Global Finance. *International Organization, 45*(4), 425–451.

Frieden, J. (1993). The Dynamics of International Monetary Systems: International and Domestic Factors in the Rise, Reign, and Demise of the Classical Gold Standard. In J. Snyder & R. Jervis (Eds.), *Coping with Complexity in the International System*. Westview: Westview Press.

Frieden, J. (1994a). Exchange Rate Politics: Contemporary Lessons from American History. *Review of International Political Economy, 1*(1) (Spring).

Frieden, J. (1994b). International Investment and Colonial Control: A New Interpretation. *International Organization, 48*(4) (Autumn).

Frieden, J. (1996a). Economic Integration and the Politics of Monetary Policy in the United States. In R. O. Keohane & H. V. Milner (Eds.), *Internationalization and Domestic Politics*. Cambridge: Cambridge University Press.

Frieden, J. (1996b). The Impact of Goods and Capital Market Integration on European Monetary Politics. *Comparative Political Studies, 29*(2), 193–222.

Frieden, J. (1997a). Monetary Populism in Nineteenth-Century America: An Open Economy Interpretation. *Journal of Economic History, 57*(2), 367–395.

Frieden, J. (1997b). The Politics of Exchange Rates. In S. Edwards & M. Naim (Eds.), *Mexico, 1994: Anatomy of an Emerging Market Crash*. Washington, DC: Carnegie Endowment for International Peace.

Frieden, J. (1998a, September). The Euro: Who Wins? Who Loses?. *Foreign Policy, 112*, 24–40.

Frieden, J. (1998b). *The New Political Economy of EMU*. Oxford: Rowman & Littlefield.

Frieden, J. (1999). Actors and Preferences in International Relations. In D. A. Lake & R. Powell (Eds.), *Strategic Choice and International Relations*. Princeton: Princeton University Press.

Frieden, J. (2000). The Political Economy of the Euro as an International Currency. In R. Mundell & A. Clesse (Eds.), *The Euro as a Stabilizer in the International Economic System*. Boston: Kluwer Academic.

Frieden, J. (2001). Making Commitments: France and Italy in the European Monetary System, 1979–1985. In B. Eichengreen & J. Frieden (Eds.), *The Political Economy of European Monetary Integration*. Westview: Westview Press.

Frieden, J. (2002). Real Sources of European Currency Policy: Sectoral Interests and European Monetary Integration. *International Organization, 56*(4), 831–860.

Frieden, J. (2004). One Europe, One Vote? The Political Economy of European Union Representation in International Organizations. *European Union Politics, 5*(2), 261–276.

Frieden, J. (2009, March). Global Governance of Global Monetary Relations: Rationale and Feasibility. *Economics E-Journal, 3*, 2009-6.

Frieden, J., & Rogowski, R. (1996). The Impact of the International Economy on National Policies: An Analytical Overview. In R. O. Keohane & H. V. Milner (Eds.), *Internationalization and Domestic Politics* (pp. 25–47). New York: Cambridge University Press.

Frieden, J., & Stein, E. (2001). The Political Economy of Exchange Rate Policy in Latin America: An Analytical Overview. In J. Frieden & E. Stein (Eds.), *The Currency Game: Exchange Rate Politics in Latin America*. Baltimore: Johns Hopkins University Press.

Frieden, J., Leblang, D., & Valev, N. (2010). The Political Economy of Exchange Rate Regimes in Transition Economies. *Review of International Organizations, 5*(1), 1–25.

Gill, S. (1993). *Gramsci, Historical Materialism and International Relations*. Cambridge: Cambridge University Press.

Goldstein, J., & Keohane, R. O. (1993). *Ideas in Foreign Policy*. Ithaca: Cornell University Press.

Guth, M. A. (1994). *Speculative Behavior and the Operation of Competitive Markets Under Uncertainty*. Aldershot: Avebury Ashgate.

Hay, C., & Marsh, D. (2000). *Demystifying Globalization*. London: Palgrave Macmillan.

Held, D., & McGrew, A. (2000). *The Global Transformations Reader*. Cambridge: Polity Press.

Held, D., McGrew, A., Goldblatt, D., & Perraton, J. (1999). *Global Transformation*. Cambridge: Polity Press.
Hirst, P., & Thompson, G. (1999). *Globalization in Question* (2nd ed.). Cambridge: Polity Press.
Holm, H. H., & Sørensen, G. (1995). *Whose World Order? Uneven Globalization and the End of the Cold War*. Boulder: Westview Press.
Ingham, G. (1984). *Capitalism Divided*. Hampshire: Macmillan.
Ingham, G. (1988, November–December). Commercial Capital and British Development: A Reply to Michael Barratt Brown. *New Left Review, I/172*, 45–65.
Ingham, G. (2002, March–April). Shock Therapy in the City. *New Left Review, 14*, 152–158.
Katzenstein, P. J. (Ed.). (1977). *Between Power and Plenty: Foreign Economic Policies of Advanced Industrial States*. Madison: University of Wisconsins Press.
Keohane, R. O., & Milner, H. V. (Eds.). (1996). *Internationalization and Domestic Politics*. Cambridge: Cambridge University Press.
Kynaston, D. (1994). *The City of London. A World of its Own, Vol. I and II*. London, Pimlico.
Lilley, P. (2000). *Dirty Dealing: The Untold Truth About Global Money Laundering*. London: Kogan Page.
Longstreth, F. (1979). The City, Industry and the State. In C. Crouch (Ed.), *State and Economy in Contemporary Capitalism* (pp. 157–191). London: Croom Helm.
Martin, L. (1993). International and Domestic Institutions in the EMU Process. In *Economics and Politics, 5*(2).
Mittleman, J. H. (2000). *The Globalization Syndrome: Transformation and Resistance*. Princeton: Princeton University Press.
Nairn, T. (1977, February–April). The Twilight of the British State. *New Left Review, 101–102*, 3–61.
Obstfeld, M., & Taylor, A. M. (2004). *Global Capital Markets. Integration, Crisis and Growth*. Cambridge: Cambridge University Press.
Overbeek, H. (1980). Finance Capital and the Crisis in Britain. *Capital and Class, 11*(Summer), 99–120.
Overbeek, H. (2000). Globalisation, Sovereignty and Transnational Regulation: Reshaping the Governance of International Migration. In B. Gosh (Ed.), *Managing Migration: Time for a New International Regime*. Oxford: Oxford University Press.
Padoa-Schioppa, T. (1994). *The Road to Monetary Union in Europe: The Emperor, the Kings and the Genies*. Oxford: Clarendon Press.
Rogowski, R. (1989). *Commerce and Coalitions: How Trade Affects Domestic Political Alignments*. Princeton: Princeton University Press.

Reuters. (2017, July 26). Exclusive: Banks Dealing EU Sovereign Debt May Be Dragged Out of London. Available at: http://uk.reuters.com/article/us-britain-eu-primary-dealers-idUKKBN1AB10U. Accessed July 26, 2017.

Strange, S. (1971). *Sterling and British Policy*. London: Oxford University Press.

Strange, S. (1998). *Mad Money*. Manchester: Manchester University Press.

Talani, L. S. (2010). *The Global Crash*. London: Palgrave Macmillan.

Talani, L. S. (2012). *Globalization, Hegemony and the Future of the City of London*. London: Palgrave.

The Finanser blog. (2017, July). *FinTech: $6.5 Billion Invested in First Half of 2017*. Available at: https://thefinanser.com/2017/07/fintech-6-5-billion-invested-first-half-2017.html/. Accessed August 1, 2017.

The Guardian. (2017a, September 6). Stupid or Duplicitous, This 'Leak' Tells EU Nationals Their Status in Britain Is Perilous. Available at: https://www.theguardian.com/commentisfree/2017/sep/06/leak-eu-nationals-status-britain-brexit. Accessed September 11, 2017.

The Guardian. (2017b, September 5). The Brexit Bill Is Cataclysmic. Only a Swerve Will Save Us. Polly Toynbee. Available at: https://www.theguardian.com/commentisfree/2017/sep/05/brexit-bill-government-negotiations-labour. Accessed September 11, 2017.

The Independent. (2017a, July 6). Brexit: Deutsche Bank Said to Be Switching from London to Frankfurt. Available at: http://www.independent.co.uk/news/business/news/brexit-latest-news-deutsche-bank-london-frankfurt-uk-leave-eu-switch-a7826361.html. Accessed July 26, 2017.

The Independent. (2017b, July 17). Surviving Hard Brexit Will Require Sacrifices Not Seen Since the Second World War. Sean O'Grady. Available at: http://www.independent.co.uk/voices/brexit-david-davis-free-trade-migration-labour-laws-low-taxes-a7845421.html. Accessed August 1, 2017.

The Irish Times. (2017, June 30). Brexit: A Dozen London Firms, Banks Moving to Dublin, IDA Says. Available at: https://www.irishtimes.com/business/financial-services/brexit-a-dozen-london-firms-banks-moving-to-dublin-ida-says-1.3138874?mode=amp. Accessed July 26, 2017.

The Telegraph. (2008, September 17). Protect Bank Shares from Short-Selling, Ministers Told. James Kirkup. Available at: http://www.telegraph.co.uk/news/uknews/2977387/Protect-bank-shares-from-short-selling-ministers-told.html. Accessed June 28 2010.

Thompson, G. (1993). *The Economic Emergence of a New Europe?* Broadheath: Edward Elgar.

CHAPTER 4

The Limits of the City's Structural Power: The City's Offshore Interests and the Brexit Referendum

Helen Thompson

Introduction

In terms of Britain's historical political economy there is an apparent paradox at the centre of the Cameron government's decision in 2015 to legislate for a referendum on Britain's membership of the European Union (EU). Why, one might ask, would a British government operating with a finance-led growth model and subject to the long-standing political influence of the City of London hold a referendum that threw into existential question Britain's participation in the Single European Market in which the dominant firms in the City have a long-standing substantial interest? Beyond reasonable doubt, the City matters to the British economy even if the City also brings problems. It is Britain's one palpably world-class business sector. It also brings particular benefits to an economy that carries a number of external weaknesses. Financial services

H. Thompson (✉)
University of Cambridge, Cambridge, UK
e-mail: het20@cam.ac.uk

C. Hay and D. Bailey (eds.), *Diverging Capitalisms*,
Building a Sustainable Political Economy: SPERI Research & Policy,
https://doi.org/10.1007/978-3-030-03415-3_4

run a substantial trade surplus with the EU—a surplus that more than doubled between 2005 and 2015 (Howarth and Quaglia 2017: 9)—in an economy that has long run an overall trade deficit. Furthermore, in terms of EU membership itself, the direction of travel within the EU on financial matters was in at least one respect, namely the emergence of the capital markets union (CMU) agenda from 2014, of particular benefit to the City (Quaglia et al. 2016: 192–193). Indeed, considering what was apparently at stake for the City, and taking seriously the view that the City has long exercised structural power over British governments, one might push the initial question further and ask: how was it possible that the City was unable to prevent the Cameron Government pursuing the referendum?

Of course, it is possible to reject immediately the apparent paradox from within its own terms. One could argue that if there was any significant chance that the City could not eventually adapt to Britain's exit from the EU, whatever the immediate commercial fallout, then there would have been no referendum. In this sense the question posed here might become: what in terms of interests was actually at stake for whom in the City during the referendum and what does that tell us about the ways in which the City's structural power works? Seen this way there certainly were divisions within the City. During the run-up to the referendum the loudest case for Britain's ongoing membership of the EU from within the City came from the international banks located in London. For example, Jamie Dimon, the chief executive of JP Morgan, warned in February 2016 that British-based banks would no longer be able to sell services across the EU and as a consequence JP Morgan would leave London: 'If we can't passport out of London, we'll have to set up different operations in Europe' (quoted in Jenkins and Agnew 2016). By contrast, many hedge funds, private equity funds and venture capital groups saw the greater risk in ongoing EU membership and the threat of greater regulation driven by the Eurozone group of EU states. As the chairman of one investment firm, Shore Capital Group, said, outside the EU 'we wouldn't suffer European regulation' (quoted in Jenkins and Agnew 2016). For their part, British banks were more sanguine about a possible Brexit than the international banks in the first half of 2016, but less convinced that they would be net beneficiaries than the hedge funds and their allies. Representatives from Barclays and HSBC told the House of Commons Treasury Select Committee in January 2016 that whilst Brexit would be a 'very big disruption' the City would still thrive outside the EU.

One Barclays representative said: 'Do I think there is a risk that if we were to leave the union that the UK would not be the leading financial centre in Europe? I do not' (quoted in Arnold 2017). In this respect there was indeed no collective City interest in Britain's ongoing membership of the EU.

Moreover, even in terms of the majority City interest in membership, the issue may be more marginal than the most strident opponents of Brexit from within the City declared it to be in advocating their position. For example, on the issue of passporting, on which Dimon was so insistent and which has often been presented as central to the City's objections to Brexit, it is not actually clear that the City's interests are that uniform or that deep. As the House of Lords' select committee on the EU discovered in its inquiry into the impact of Brexit on the financial services, even after the referendum result, quite a number of City firms were unaware of what their own passporting requirements were (House of Lords 2016: 13–14). Moreover, Jamie Dimon himself in his 2016 report to shareholders, which was published nine months after the referendum in April 2017, did not mention the passporting issue and said that the prospect of hard Brexit did 'not entail moving many people in the next two years' (JP Morgan Chase & Co 2017: 11). For all the rhetorical bluster in some quarters, it is not unreasonable to suppose the City will eventually adapt to the post-Brexit world. Indeed, in some quarters it was already re-orienting before June 2016.

The apparent paradox at work could also be rejected on the grounds that the outcome of the referendum was unexpected and that the decision made by the Cameron Government to legislate for the referendum was premised upon the assumption that Remain would easily win. Here, whilst we are left to explain the outcome of the vote, there is no puzzle in regard to Cameron's judgement in relation to the City's interests. Seen this way the referendum represents a spectacular misjudgement by Cameron about possible outcomes because it would appear not to have occurred to him that a Leave outcome was a possibility. The referendum then becomes a political gamble to try to solve the internal divisions about the EU within the Conservative Party that went wrong. Looked at this way, the Conservative Government risked the future of Britain's financial sector because the Prime Minister privileged dealing with short-term party political problems over understanding the long-term politics required to sustain the British economy's growth prospects in its present form. From this perspective what needs to be explained, as Jensen and

Snaith (2016) argue, is the relative autonomy of domestic party politics in the face of what otherwise appears like the structural power of business including that influence generated by economic interdependence.

A third rejection of the apparent paradox can be made by pushing such an argument about the inevitable primacy of politics further. Obviously, the EU is much more than a set of economic arrangements in which different sectors of the economy, like financial services, can prosper or struggle. It is fundamentally a political and legal order in which the laws of the EU, including the de facto constitutional law generated by the Union's treaties, have primacy over domestic law. Consequently, whatever the economic arguments at stake in the referendum, the British electorate was asked to decide on the constitutional and political order under which Britain should be governed. Of course, this reality does not in itself preclude either the government or the electorate deciding that treating membership of the EU primarily as a constitutional question was a luxury that the country could not economically afford. Nonetheless, the constitutional question from the onset of the British political debate about participating in the European Economic Community (EEC) has been a particularly vexed question, raising particular problems that have not been there for other member states. Britain joined the European Community (EC) without the British parliament accepting the principle, asserted by the European Court of Justice (ECJ) in 1962, that the European treaties created their own legal system existing independently of any legislation passed by the legislatures of member states (Thompson 2017c: 63–64). This constitutional tension was undoubtedly accentuated by the absence of referendums in Britain on any of the Maastricht treaty, the 2005 constitutional treaty, or the Lisbon treaty, despite promises of referendums on the latter two treaties made at different times by the two principal British political parties. Consequently, it might be argued that the Cameron Government had little room for manoeuvre in its decision-making over holding a referendum on membership from its first months in office, not least given the legacy of Cameron's guarantee to hold a referendum on the Lisbon treaty (Thompson 2017a).

Nonetheless, none of these objections can be quite decisive in rejecting the paradox. Even if the City ultimately can thrive outside the EU, the majority of City firms had a clear interest in the retention of membership and expressed that preference strongly both in public and in private. As for Cameron's decision-making in regard to the referendum, its context, including in regard to the legacy of his promise on the Lisbon treaty, was very much shaped by the interaction of the Eurozone crisis and Britain's position in regard to financial services within the European Single Market (Thompson 2017a). Put differently, the City itself was part of the path taken to the referendum. In understanding that path there is something to be learned about the City's historical relationship to British governments. Indeed, the City's apparent weakness over the referendum may well cast doubt on interpretations of the City's historical political influence that present its structural power as decisive on economic questions.

In this chapter I offer an explanation of the City's relative weakness in relation to the politics of the Brexit referendum situated in the historical relationship between the City and the British state from the time of the City's development of an offshore dollar market that took the City's commercial currency interests away from Sterling. The chapter is divided into four sections. The first section argues that the City's structural power has often been misconceived, especially in relation to issues generated by the emergence from the 1950s of the City's offshore currency operations. The second section considers the political impact of the 2008 crash and the Coalition Government's approach to the City in the aftermath of the crisis as part of the broad context in which City firms came to engage with the issue of Britain's membership of the EU. It argues that although the Coalition Government did engage in significant reform of the banking sector, it eventually strengthened the long-standing commitment of British governments to encourage growth in the City's international commerce and offshore trading, especially in regard to China. The third section explains how the Eurozone crisis politicised the City's position as the offshore financial centre of the Eurozone, causing serious difficulties for the two Cameron Governments' ability to manage Britain's membership of the EU both inside the EU and in regard to domestic politics. Once these difficulties were in play they led Cameron, I argue, to his referendum decision. Crucially, however, in trying to deal with these difficulties Cameron let loose a more general problem of domestic consent to EU membership generated in good part by freedom of movement issues. The final section draws some conclusions.

THE STRUCTURAL POWER OF THE CITY AND THE CITY'S OFFSHORE CURRENCY INTERESTS: A HISTORY

The view that the City enjoys structural power in regard to the British state is common and long-standing. In particular scholars over several generations have stressed the existence of a City-Bank of England-Treasury axis through which the preferences of the City are materialised in British economic decision-making (Ingham 1984; Moran 1990; Burn 1999; Cain and Hopkins 2001). These scholars have frequently stressed the importance of the City to understanding the decision-making of British governments about Sterling under stressed economic and political conditions going back to the interwar years (Ingham 1984; Cain and Hopkins, Chs. 20 and 26; Davies 2017).

This institutional foundation of structural power also looks like it was reinforced by the emergence of a finance-based growth model from the mid-1980s, what Colin Hay (2011, 2013b) has called the 'Anglo-liberal' model. Regardless of the institutional relationship between the City and the Treasury and the Bank of England, this growth model created incentives for successive governments to prioritise financial sector growth because of the relative weakness of the manufacturing side of the economy. After the difficulties around Sterling that led to Britain's short-lived membership of the Exchange Rate Mechanism (ERM) from 1990 to 1992, this growth model led until 2008 to a relatively strong currency that in its consequences for much of the manufacturing sector only made finance even more crucial to growth (Thompson 1996, 2009). The consequence of the dependency of growth on finance became a simultaneously fiscal dependency. For example, the financial sector is around 7% of British GDP but contributes 12% of PAYE and national insurance revenue and 15% of onshore corporation tax (House of Lords 2016: 5).

In recent years some scholars have argued that the 2008 crisis and its aftermath have demonstrated the limits of general claims about the structural power of business (Culpepper 2015) and about the City in particular (Bell and Hindmoor 2014; Talani 2011). These arguments are in themselves persuasive. However, in regard to the City they have for their own purposes generally started from a conception of the City's structural power before 2008 that does not clearly distinguish between areas where the City was politically influential and where it was less so. In particular, these arguments are engaged with different matters than the particular questions posed by the relationship between the City's international commercial activities around currency operations and the interests of British governments in the external economic and political environment that preoccupied earlier scholars.

Certainly, there are good reasons to see the City's structural power at work in relation to the City's own offshore currency interests. Most significantly, British governments in the 1950s and the 1960s facilitated the development of the eurodollar market in London, by which foreign currency deposits that were exempt from the British state's capital and exchange controls could be lent through banks' offices in London (Baker and Collins 2005). These governments allowed London to turn itself into an offshore dollar centre by taking advantage of the contrast between the informal supervision deployed by the Bank of England and the post Glass-Steagall regulatory environment in the United States (Cottrell 2005: 177; Moran 1990: 56, 85).

Yet the very position of London as an offshore dollar centre makes it difficult to see the British state after the late 1950s as subservient to the City on Sterling matters as those matters affected the British economy and domestic economic management. Certainly, the political support given to the Eurodollar market compounded the difficulties of exchange rate management for British governments because British capital controls could be evaded in the eurodollar market. Yet as Sterling became increasingly less important to the City, the fact that British governments remained unwilling to adapt to Sterling's weakness by devaluing the currency was the consequence of other strategic considerations, starting with the conjunction of Britain's financial dependency on the United States and its ongoing imperial and oil interests in the Middle East (Thompson 2017b: 14–15). Nonetheless, so long as British governments remained committed to an exchange rate policy that appeared to hurt the manufacturing sector, the City risked being made the political scapegoat for the problem.

By the early 1970s, there was a clear disjuncture between the preoccupation of British governments with endless Sterling problems and a City focused on offshore dollar business. In this context, Britain's access to the then EC in 1973 represented a significant change. EC membership offered the British state a new opportunity to pursue a higher level of economic growth and the City the eventual prospect of participating in an integrated financial services market that it would be in a strong position to dominate. This possibility was accentuated after the first Thatcher Government abolished capital and exchange controls, making Britain the first state after the US to embrace financial liberalisation and giving London significant commercial advantages over other European competitors.

Yet this realignment of the interests of the City with those of the British state became strained again from the late 1980s by the arrival of monetary union on the EC agenda. With its decision to keep Britain permanently out of the euro in the aftermath of Sterling's exit from the ERM on Black Wednesday, the Major Government appeared to ignore the concerns of some in the City that once monetary union began London would lose out to Frankfurt as the primary centre of cross-border European financial activity. Non-membership of the euro, at least in principle, also put at risk Britain's long-term influence within the Single Market with potentially deleterious consequences for the City.

In practice, of course, the first of these threats did not materialise. Indeed, within two years of the euro's introduction large financial corporations had concentrated their euro foreign exchange dealing and non-sovereign euro-denominated business in London, making London the centre for euro-denominated trading (Roberts 2005: 309). In this sense monetary union eventually became another offshore currency opportunity for the City. But the development of the City as the offshore financial centre of the euro also added another potential complication to Britain's membership of the EU that British governments would eventually have to navigate. As well as creating another divergence between the British economy and the economies of other EU member states, the issue had the potential to leave Britain in a political minority of one when it came to decision-making about financial services within the Single Market.

Seen from this historical perspective, it is clear both that by the first decade of the twenty-first century the City had acquired a dual set of offshore currency interests and that these stood in a complex relation to the British state. In regard to the City's offshore dollar interests, City firms did exercise structural power in procuring the support of the British state in developing the Eurodollar market. Yet in turning itself towards dollar trading the City separated its currency interests from the fate of Sterling. When the ongoing existence of Sterling as a national currency became an issue in the late 1980s and 1990s the commercial interests of the City in regard to the development of the euro were ultimately a secondary consideration for successive British governments. Although the exclusion of Britain from the Eurozone did not hurt the City in the first years of the new currency, the potential for conflict between the City's interests in euro trading and those of any British government that could not contemplate joining the single currency remained in place, buffered only by the rules of non-discrimination within the Single Market.

AFTER THE CRASH: WHERE NEXT?

Within Britain the City's position came under considerable political scrutiny in the wake of the 2007–2008 financial crisis. In the domestic political arena, the recklessness and excess that had characterised the behaviour of many financial firms during the bubble years fuelled deep political anger among many voters when banks had to be rescued from pending insolvency. This anger was then in many ways legitimised by the Bank of England's response to the crisis, with a number of senior officials at the Bank using extremely strong language to condemn the banks (Baker 2010). For example, Andy Haldane (2010: 2), the executive director for financial stability, published an official Bank paper in 2010 describing the banking industry as a 'pollutant' that 'endanger[ed] innocent bystanders'. Meanwhile a number of critics resurrected the long-standing critique that the City distorts both the British national economy through its weak provision of capital to productive sectors and British politics by reinforcing an essentially oligarchic power structure centred around London and the south east (Engelen et al. 2011).

In this post-crisis environment there emerged a domestic political narrative that could be heard as much on the centre-right of British politics as on the left that at least on the surface made the City an economic and political problem (Berry and Hay 2016). Most consequentially, the then Conservative Shadow Chancellor, George Osborne developed a critique of the British economy in which the place of the financial sector was dysfunctional to the overall national economy. The 2010 Conservative Party manifesto committed the Party to achieving a 'more balanced economy' (Conservative Party 2010: 3). Including a graphic contrasting the rapid growth in the financial sector from 1997 to 2009 with the dismal growth in the manufacturing sector, it proclaimed 'Britain needs a new economic model' that 'does not depend so heavily on the success of financial services' and in which 'a safer banking system ... serves the needs of the economy' (Conservative Party 2010: 3). This aspiration reappeared in the Coalition Government's 2011 'Plan for Growth', tying the problems of low investment and poor export performance to the weakness of the manufacturing sector in contrast to the strength of the City (Berry and Hay 2016: 6).

In part, this post-crisis political backlash represented a genuine problem for the City. This problem, however, was first and foremost a problem for the banking sector rather than other parts of the City. Reforming the banks was in the first instance practically viable. By contrast, rebalancing the economy away from the financial sector as whole to manufacturing was not, not least in the context when manufacturing sectors were in steady decline across advanced economies. Moreover, reforming the banks was also a medium-term fiscal imperative for any government if another crisis in which banks that were both 'too big to fail' and 'too big to bail' was to be avoided.

In this context, the Coalition Government did engage in significant reform of the banking sector In June 2010 it announced that it would abolish the Financial Services Authority and transfer responsibility for banking regulation to a new Prudential Regulation Authority located within the Bank of England. In October 2010 the Coalition Government published draft legislation to turn its predecessor's one-off tax on bankers' bonuses into a permanent levy on the global balance sheets of British banks and British operations of foreign banks. Meanwhile, it took a comparatively hard line on international regulatory change. In implementing Basle III when most EU member states looked to dilute some requirements, the Coalition Government secured the right within the EU framework to implement the reform measures in full. The Coalition Government also acted on the separation of retail and investment banking, ordering the Royal Bank of Scotland in 2011 to shrink radically its investment activities, and setting up an Independent Commission on Banking under the Chairmanship of John Vickers that recommended, among other things, that banks ring-fence their retail operations from their investment activities. It then accepted Vickers' recommendations and committed to pass legislation by 2015 to force change upon the banks with a transition period up to 2019.

Nonetheless, the rhetoric of the Coalition Government in embracing the Vickers Report revealed quite clearly that the Chancellor and the Treasury drew a clear distinction between the overall place of the City in the British economy and need to reform the banking sector. The government was, the Treasury said, 'committed to ensuring that the UK continues to be at the heart of the international banking and finance sector'. But this was best achieved, it continued, 'by establishing a stable financial system in the UK', not by 'providing implicit taxpayer subsidies to *a small proportion of the financial institutions that constitute the City*' (HM Treasury 2011) (italics added). Whatever the ambitions with which the Conservative Party had re-entered office, the difficulties of achieving an economic recovery let alone of rebuilding the manufacturing sector rendered a fantasy an alternative growth strategy in which Britain forsook its comparative advantages in international financial trading and commercial services. In this context, the Coalition Government wished to strengthen the City at what it had been historically successful by reform of the part of it that had created economic and political problems for British governments since the massive expansion of the banking sector in general, and investment banking in particular, from the late 1990s.

In good part, the Coalition Government and its majority-and-minority Conservative successors have had little choice in pursuing this strategy. The crisis and its aftermath have not changed the balance of the economy nor was there much reason to think in view of the structural problems besetting the British economy that they readily could have done (Berry and Hay 2016; Hay 2013a: 33–36). Betting on the manufacturing sector when not a single G7 economy had returned manufacturing production to its pre-recession output by 2016 would have been foolhardy (Cadman and Bounds 2016). Moreover, Britain's financial services have become increasingly important to Britain's increasingly dismal trade performance. In 2015 Britain's trade deficit in goods reached a record high, whilst financial services continued to achieve a considerable surplus (Cadman 2016). Given that Britain has by some distance the worst current account balance of any G7 economy, financial services exports have become effectively the last bulwark against a balance-of-payments generated currency crisis.

Nonetheless, the post-2010 governments also actively chose to double-down on the City's advantages in international commerce and offshore trading. This strategy can be seen most clearly in the encouragement given by these governments to the City's growing relationship with China. For the City, the internationalisation of the renminbi represents another offshore opportunity, one that in effect gives London a third international currency in which to do major business. Since 2012 the City of London Corporation has driven at attempt to make London the centre of offshore renminbi business (Green 2017: 12). In this project, it has received systematic support from both the Treasury and the Bank of England. Over the past few years a number of significant agreements have, among other things, facilitated a currency swap between Britain and China, the right of London-based assets managers to invest directly in renminbi-denominated assets, the issuing of British sovereign bonds in renminbi, and the sale of Chinese sovereign renminbi-denominated bonds in London (Green 2017: 12; Moore and Wildau 2015). The government and Mayor of London have also encouraged direct Chinese investment in the City. Most significantly, the largest Chinese investment fund, China Minsheng Investment, announced in 2015 that it would invest £1 billion in the project begun by a Chinese construction company in 2013 to build a third financial district for London in the Royal Albert Dock. In announcing the deal, the investment fund's President, Li Huaizhen, said that the project was 'the international platform and foundation for Chinese companies and capital to enter the European market' (quoted in Wong 2015).

This political effort to make London the centre of offshore renminbi business and enhance the City's geographical scope as an international financial centre has been part of a broader government strategy to use Chinese capital to drive investment in infrastructure and construction. Chinese companies and the Chinese sovereign wealth fund have invested in a number of high profile transport and infrastructure sites and projects, most visibly the Hinckley nuclear power station, making the British economy the top site of Chinese investment in Europe since 2014. Trumpeting this new British–Chinese economic relationship, David Cameron said on a visit to Beijing in November 2013 that he wanted to see much more Chinese investment in Britain and declared that he was 'not embarrassed that China is investing in British nuclear power, or has shares in Heathrow airport, or Manchester airport' (quoted in Le Corre 2015). Indeed, in an article for *The Guardian* newspaper before his visit, he declared that 'there is no country in the western world more open to Chinese investment, more able to meet the demands of Chinese consumers, or more willing to make the case for economic openness in the G8, or the EU'. Britain was, he continued, 'uniquely placed to make the case for deepening the EU's trade and investment relationship with China' and in particular to achieve 'an ambitious and comprehensive EU-China Free Trade Agreement' (Cameron 2013).

The British government's embrace of this economic relationship with China and the City's part in it has created some undoubted political problems at home and abroad. Externally, the Chancellor's decision in early 2015 to pursue British membership of the Asian Infrastructure Investment Bank independently of any consultation with other EU states or the Obama administration caused consternation in Washington. What the Cameron Government saw as an economic relationship in which Britain could procure comparative advantages not least for the City, the Obama administration saw as indulgence of China in a deteriorating security situation in the Pacific (Rachman 2015). Domestically, it left the government open to the charge that once again the City was being privileged over other sectors of the economy. This accusation was particularly pertinent during the crisis in early 2016 over Britain's remaining steel works. When Tata Steel announced its intention—later rescinded—to withdraw from its British operations, citing, among other reasons, the burden of large-scale cheap Chinese imports, the Conservative Government's unwillingness over the previous three years to support EU anti-dumping action against China that might have saved Britain's steel plants incurred wrath across the political spectrum. As the *Daily Telegraph* columnist, Ambrose Evans-Pritchard (2016) charged, 'Britain's special relationship with China is becoming more expensive by the day. It now threatens to destroy the British steel industry, a foundation pillar of our manufacturing economy'.

These political problems reflect the long-standing historical patterns in the relationship of the City's international orientation to the rest of the British economy outlined earlier. In this sense, the 2007–2008 financial crisis changed very little. There proved no realistic alternative to a growth model based on financial services that focused on London's comparative commercial and offshore advantages, and at least for the medium term the particular problems generated by the banking sector were contained by reform. The encouragement of Chinese business into the City also made it possible to strengthen Britain's economic relationship with China more generally, which brought investment capital to a number of large infrastructure projects. In this respect, the interests of the City in developing another offshore market and those of the government were complementary.

Nonetheless, at the same time as the historical relationship reasserted itself, other aspects of the fallout of the 2008 crash soon came to undermine it, most significantly as a result of the Eurozone crisis.

The Eurozone Crisis and the Path
to the Referendum

The relationship of the City to the international dynamics of both the 2007–2008 financial crisis and the Eurozone crisis were from the onset politically charged. Politicians in both the US and other EU states were on occasion keen to turn London into the symbol of feckless financial capitalism where rules did not apply and their own countries' financial corporations came to grief. As one Democrat member of the House of Representatives said in a congressional hearing in 2012 on the financial crisis: 'It seems to be that every big trading disaster happens in London' (quoted in Jones 2012). In France, meanwhile, President Sarkozy, claimed after an agreement reached on financial regulation at the G20 summit in April 2009 that the world had 'turned the page' on 'Anglo-Saxon capitalism' (Hall et al. 2009). Later the same year, when Michel Barnier, a French politician, was appointed EU Commissioner for Internal Market and Services, Sarkozy declared it 'a defeat for Anglo-Saxon capitalism' (quoted in Waterfield 2009) and said 'the English are the big losers in this business' (quoted in Munchau 2009).

In a number of ways, reality was much more complex. The experiences of British banks during the financial crises were more similar to those of German and French banks than they were to US banks because large banks in the three European countries had much more internationalised bank sheets and were dependent on foreign currency funding. In this sense the much-vaunted Anglo-Saxon, or Anglo-American, financial model was an erroneous construction when applied to the banking sector (Thompson 2016). After the crisis hit, on a number of issues, not least capital standards, deleveraging, and the separation of retail and investment banking, the British government took a tougher stance than the other large-economy EU states including France and Germany (Howarth and Quaglia 2015).

Yet underneath French rhetorical posturing lay a fundamental problem that the City posed for other large EU states in a political context in which financial sectors invited domestic political hostility and the

Eurozone required reform. London was the premier European financial centre and its predominance included euro trading. Consequently, as the Eurozone descended into crisis from late 2009, its financial centre was offshore, beyond the direct grasp of the Eurozone regulatory authorities under their existing remits. In this context, the Eurozone authorities and the French and German governments acquired considerable incentives either to try to find ways, including through the EU's institutions, to secure some leverage over euro activity in London, or to push euro business away from London.

In more specific terms the Coalition Government from 2011 to 2013 found itself at odds with other EU member states over a series of financial service issues including the ECB's 'locational' policy, whereby clearing houses handling more than five percent of euro-denominated product would have to be located within the Eurozone, the proposed Financial Transactions' Tax, a ban on short-selling in emergencies, and bank bonuses. In almost all respects the Coalition Government found its influence over proceedings weak. On the Financial Transactions Tax, eleven EU states, led by France and Germany, agreed in principle to move ahead with the tax under the EU's procedure of 'enhanced co-operation', a process rarely used before and in recent years only in relation to divorce and patent law (PWC 2012). When David Cameron in December 2011 then tried to use the prospect of a new EU treaty to secure an opt-out for the City from future financial services regulation, he discovered there was no new treaty to leverage and his veto of the Fiscal Compact led only to the other EU states constructing an intergovernmental treaty that still used, despite his attempt to block it, the EU's institutions for its implementation (Schelke 2016).

In response to its overt political weakness within the EU over the City the British government was left to mount a series of legal challenges in the ECJ. Yet only on the ECB's locational policy did the British government secure a legal win. In this case, the ECJ ruled in March 2015 that the ECB did not have the authority to regulate clearing house activities. Even here, however, the victory was only partial. In accepting the British government's technical case, the Court refused to rule on the British government's legal claim that the ECB had violated the freedoms enshrined in the Single Market and was attempting to practice discrimination against non-euro members (Barker and Stafford 2015).

These developments sorely exposed the difficulties the EU had come to pose for the City in the post-2008 environment. Whilst prior to 2008 the City could take very considerable benefit from Britain being inside the Single Market and outside the euro, the change of stance in Berlin and Paris towards London's offshore euro position risked reducing the advantages to be had from the Single Market, not least in the absence of any clear legal principle that the Single Market forbids discrimination against non-euro members. Meanwhile the British government could no longer use the rules of decision-making around the Single Market to advance its agenda for financial services, and was struggling either to stop the Eurozone becoming a winning majority coalition within the EU on matters beyond the single currency or to prevent a site of new competencies that could reduce the possibilities for financial trading in euros outside euro borders.

These difficulties also created domestic political trouble for the Coalition Government that would through Cameron's management of the issue ensure further problems for the City. The political and legal failures around defending the City's external interests politically strengthened euro-scepticism within the Conservative Party at a time when UKIP discovered the ability to exploit the disaffection of a growing number of voters with the free movement of labour within the EU and rising migration to Britain in particular from countries in the periphery of the Eurozone. After his failure to secure a new opt-out for the City and his subsequent exercise of the British veto over the Fiscal Compact treaty in December 2011 yielded substantively nothing, Cameron struggled to present himself and his ministerial allies as sufficiently Euro-sceptic for the fault-lines within the EU that had taken political shape around Britain's position as the offshore financial centre of the Eurozone.

This difficulty was manifested most obviously in the position taken by the then Mayor of London, Boris Johnson, who, prior to the 2015 general election and his return to the House of Commons, positioned himself as willing to speak and act more robustly for the City than his Party rival. Johnson starkly sought to present the strategic difficulty that had emerged as a direct attack from other EU states on British interests requiring a hard line British defence. For example, in March 2013, Johnson gave an interview in France where he said: 'In my view, Europe's problem is that at the moment it is attacking London's bankers. That is a diversion, a distraction. The problem remains the euro' (BBC News 2013). In August 2014, he gave a speech to launch the publication of a report he had commissioned from his chief economic advisor on Britain's EU membership. On this occasion, he said that Britain should leave the EU unless it could reform the EU, including in matters of financial services decision-making to 'end pointless attacks on the City' (Johnson 2014). In this sense, the City's offshore euro position rendered Britain's entire EU membership a much more vexed question for the British government than it was prior to the Eurozone crisis. For nearly four decades British governments had dealt with the problem of Britain's relative political weakness within the EU by looking for opt-outs on any issue that posed particular difficulties. But in linking the Eurozone to financial services regulation, the other EU states in good part bankrupted this strategy.

In January 2013 Cameron decided to deal with the political problems EU membership was creating by vowing that a future Conservative government would renegotiate the terms of Britain's membership and then hold an in-out referendum no later than the end of 2017. His decision has been much criticised. But it was a political moment with a clear history going back to the Conservatives' return to office in May 2010 at the time of the first Greek bailout (Thompson 2017a). In terms of the substance of renegotiation Cameron promised in his Bloomberg speech, Cameron initially appeared to have made the City his priority, demanding what he called 'cast-iron' legal protections for the City against the Eurozone members acting as a caucus to impose financial services legislation on Britain (Watt 2014). During 2014 and 2015, however, the centre of Euro-sceptic gravity in the parliamentary Conservative Party appeared to move away from City issues towards freedom-of-movement matters. In this political context, Cameron became less and less focused on financial services and the issue of how to protect the principle of non-discrimination within the Single Market between euro and non-euro members. Indeed, when, in November 2015, Cameron announced his new majority-Conservative Government's priorities for the renegotiation he explicitly ruled out in his letter to European Council President Donald Tusk asking for any new opt-out covering financial services (Parker et al. 2015).

In several ways the City's difficulties intensified after Cameron switched the Conservative's policy towards holding an in-out referendum. On the one side, the immediate regulatory risks remained in place. In March 2014 the main financial services sector lobby group, The City UK, published a report calling for the government to be more 'muscular' in its defence of the City's interests and warned that there was a 'credible threat' that the new Eurozone banking authorities would damage London's ability to serve its non-domestic client base (Jenkins and Jones 2014). Yet highlighting the political difficulties Britain faced within the EU as a permanent member of the minority group of non-euro states had to raise awkward questions when Britain's membership of the EU was becoming increasingly politically contested. Moreover, as noted at the beginning of this chapter, the City was far from internally united on whether London needed membership of the EU to retain its position as Europe's premier international financial centre.

Nonetheless, the referendum also offered some at least temporary respite to the fundamental problem for the City generated by Britain's membership of the EU and non-membership of the Eurozone in the post-crisis environment. The prospect of the referendum at a time when the EU was facing a number of existential crises, not least in regard to the migration and the Schengen rules, did create some incentives for the other large EU states and the Commission to compromise with the British government. Moreover, the area of financial services was a more propitious matter for accommodating British preferences than the free movement of labour because of the effective side payments that would almost certainly have been required to secure the acquiescence of the eastern European member states to any significant change.

Certainly, these incentives were far from straightforward. The final agreement on renegotiated terms for Britain's membership of the EU agreed in February 2016 was at most a qualified means of protecting the City from Eurozone-generated regulation. It stated that 'legal acts … directly linked to the functioning of the euro area shall respect the internal market … and shall not constitute a barrier to or discrimination in trade between Member states' (European Union 2016). But no robust political mechanism for guaranteeing this principle was identified. Whilst the agreement allowed Britain unilaterally to escalate any issue pertaining to the principle to the European Council, it clearly did not grant Britain a veto. As the *Financial Times* described it, 'the emergency brake [wa]s a political threat, rather than a legal shield' (Barker 2016). Nonetheless, in the period between Cameron's announcement of the referendum in January 2013 and the new agreement on Britain's EU membership in February 2016 the pressure on the City from within the EU significantly lessened. Although Jean Claude Juncker's appointment to the Presidency of the Commission in 2014 was fiercely opposed by the British government, Juncker's allocation of Commission jobs produced the unexpected boon of the British Commissioner, Lord Jonathan Hill, taking the portfolio for Financial Stability, Financial Services, and CMU. By September 2015, the Commission was talking about eliminating 'unnecessary regulatory burdens' and other 'unintended consequences' of the EU's banking and financial markets legislation (quoted in Brunsden 2015). Most significantly, under Lord Hill's tenure, the Commission's push for a CMU occurred on essentially British terms. Since the CMU aimed to increase financial market funding for firms across the EU and London is home more than half of capital market activity in the EU, the proposal in good part sought to make the rest of the EU more like the British economy whilst creating no new sites of regulatory authority.

Seen from David Cameron's perspective the shift in the Commission's policy agenda on financial services matters since late 2014 could in principle have been seen as the kind of political victory he could have used to argue that EU decision-making did not leave Britain in a permanent minority and that the rest of the EU was moving economically closer to Britain. Yet in the context of the post-crisis political environment this political claim would have had limited resonance, however useful it would have been for the majority City interests that opposed Brexit. Apparent success in defending the City's interests might have helped in managing Euro-scepticism within parts of the Conservative Party prior to the referendum promise in 2013, but it would never win over voters concerned about freedom of movement. Indeed, given the extremely weak concessions the Conservative Government gained on the free movement of labour issues during the 2016 renegotiations, presenting the deal as securing something for the City would have been a positive liability. Put more schematically, the majority interest in the City became at the mercy of the domestic politics of a referendum which occurred at a time when the claim of finance to economic primacy was already increasingly contested in democratic politics.

CONCLUSIONS

The comfortable status quo that allowed the City to thrive as an international financial centre with offshore dollar and euro interests without causing the British government domestic political problems ended with the 2008 crash and the Eurozone crisis. Indeed, these developments exposed the whole tension between Britain's membership of the EU and non-membership of the euro that had previously threatened problems that had not in practice materialised.

Given the near political impossibility of Britain ever joining the euro, Brexit in one sense is a more straightforward long-term solution to that dilemma than ongoing membership, whatever the scale of short to medium-term problems it is generating including for a good part of the City. Yet it is in this political space around currency matters that we can see the relative political weakness of the City. From the perspective of those international banks in the City with the most to lose from Brexit, Britain's entry to the euro would have been largely inconsequential. But from the point of view of any British government, ending monetary sovereignty to have dealt with the post-2008 EU problem would have been a massively difficult proposition and one that certainly could not have been politically pursued for the sake of the City. In the late 1980s and 1990s when the first version of this divergence between the EU calculus facing the majority of the City and that confronting a Conservative government emerged the problem was solved by the 'events' of the ERM crisis and the City's latent strengths as an international financial centre. But it is very difficult to see how the difficulty could have been traversed so readily this time round, precisely because London did become the offshore financial centre of the Eurozone. London, because of the strength of its operations, may well be able outside the EU to fend off what will continue to be pressure to move more euro-denominated financial activity inside the Eurozone. But the British government inside the EU could only have kept politically isolating itself by attempting to fight the battle for the City and in so doing have added political fuel to the argument that British influence inside the EU was too weak to justify ongoing membership. Certainly, the CMU was a significant change in direction by the Commission in its approach to the integration of financial and capital markets. But in itself it could not have possibly defused the political issue of London's offshore euro status for the national governments of the large Eurozone states.

London's ability to serve and profit from offshore business has been crucial to London's re-invention as an international financial centre since the late 1950s. For much of this time the City has received considerable support from British governments in maintaining this offshore position even when, as in the 1960s, the consequences of the currency flows generated fuelled significant macro-economic problems, or when, as recently with the offshore renminbi market, encouraging that activity has significant consequences for other sectors of the British economy and Britain's relations with its security allies. In this sense, British governments have encouraged a distinctive form of capitalism in the British economy and been willing to act externally in ways that prioritised its success over other foreign policy considerations. However, British governments cannot ultimately escape either from the political difficulties national democratic politics create, especially at times of economic weakness, or the international political problems generated by the absence of allies who share common economic and political interests. More particularly, the long-standing weaknesses of the British economy outside financial services created a fierce incentive for British governments to retain as much macro-economic discretion as possible. That incentive has been fuelled further by the absence of any belief that British governments have been strong enough inside the EU in relation to national economic performance, and for a long time Sterling's vulnerability to crisis, to exercise any meaningful influence over German economic decision-making. As a consequence, the Cameron government became unable to protect the City's majority's interest in retaining Britain's membership of the EU even as during the same time period it had encouraged the City's efforts to become the centre of offshore renminbi trading in Europe. In this sense, the referendum exposed the limits of the City's structural power arising from the divergence between the City's offshore currency interests and the political need of British governments to think about Sterling in terms of managing the domestic economy and politics.

REFERENCES

Arnold, M. (2017, January 6). Bankers Sound Alarm over Brexit Consequences. *Financial Times.* Retrieved from: https://www.ft.com/content/d0af25ac-b49e-11e5-b147-e5e5bba42e51.

Baker, A. (2010). Restraining Regulatory Capture? Anglo-America, Crisis Politics and Trajectories of Change in Global Financial Governance. *International Affairs, 86*(3), 647–663.

Baker, M., & Collins, M. (2005). London as an International Banking Centre 1958–1980. In Y. Cassis & E. Bussière (Eds.), *London and Paris as International Financial Centres in the Twentieth Century* (pp. 247–264). Oxford: Oxford University Press.

Barker, A. (2016, February 20). Britain's EU Deal: The Results and the Verdict. *Financial Times.* Retrieved from: https://next.ft.com/content/7c90bfec-d76e-11e5-829b-8564e7528e54.

Barker, A., & Stafford, P. (2015, March 4). Victory for UK over Eurozone Clearing Houses. *Financial Times.* Retrieved from: http://www.ft.com/cms/s/0/425aeee0-c24f-11e4-bd9f-00144feab7de.html#axzz3v32O1XRn.

BBC News. (2013, March 15). *Boris Johnson Defends City Bankers on French Radio.* Retrieved from: http://www.bbc.co.uk/news/uk-politics-21800089.

Bell, S., & Hindmoor, A. (2014). The Ideational Shaping pf State Power and Capacity: Winning Battles But Losing the War over Bank Reform in the UK and the US. *Government and Opposition, 49*(3), 342–368.

Berry, C., & Hay, C. (2016). The Great British 'Rebalancing' Act: The Construction and Implementation of an Economic Imperative for Exceptional Times. *British Journal of Politics and International Relations, 18*(1), 3–25.

Brunsden, J. (2015, September 30). European Commission Changes Tone over Financial Regulation. *Financial Times.* Retrieved from: https://next.ft.com/content/a20b200c-6787-11e5-97d0-1456a776a4f5.

Burn, G. (1999). The State, the City and the Euromarkets. *Review of International Political Economy, 6*(2), 225–261.

Cadman, E. (2016, February 9). UK Exports Failures Highlights Difficulties in Rebalancing the Economy. *Financial Times.* Retrieved from: https://next.ft.com/content/ee6a8c1a-cf17-11e5-831d-09f7778e7377.

Cadman, E., & Bounds, A. (2016, January 28). UK Manufacturing Retains Bright Spots Despite Overall Gloom. *Financial Times.* Retrieved from: https://next.ft.com/content/ff19bb16-c4fa-11e5-b3b1-7b2481276e45.

Cain, P. J., & Hopkins, A. G. (2001). *British Imperialism: 1688–2000* (2nd ed.). London: Routledge.

Cameron, D. (2013, December 2). My Visit Can Begin a Relationship to Benefit, Britain and the World. *The Guardian.* Retrieved from: http://www.theguardian.com/commentisfree/2013/dec/02/david-cameron-my-visit-to-china.

Conservative Party. (2010). *Invitation to Join the Government of Britain*. London: Conservative Party.

Cottrell, P. (2005). Established Connections and New Opportunities: London as a Financial Centre 1919–1958. In Y. Cassis & E. Bussière (Eds.), *London and Paris as International Financial Centres in the Twentieth Century* (pp. 153–182). Oxford: Oxford University Press.

Culpepper, P. D. (2015). Structural Power and Political Science in the Post-crisis Era. *Business and Politics, 17*(3), 391–409.

Davies, A. (2017). *The City of London and Social Democracy: The Political Economy of Finance in Britain, 1959–1979*. Oxford: Oxford University Press.

Engelen, E., Ertürk, I., Froud, J., Johal, S., Leaver, A., Moran, M., et al. (2011). *After The Great Complacence: Financial Crisis and the Politics of Reform*. Oxford: Oxford University Press.

European Union. (2016). *Draft Decision of the Heads of State or Government, Meeting Within the European Council, Concerning a New Settlement for the United Kingdom Within the European Union*. Retrieved from: http://www.politico.eu/article/full-text-of-deal-changing-britain-eu-membership-brexit-referendum/.

Evans-Pritchard, A. (2016, March 31). Britain Sacrifices Steel Industry to Curry Favour with China. *Daily Telegraph*. Retrieved from: http://www.telegraph.co.uk/business/2016/03/30/britain-sacrifices-steel-industry-to-curry-favour-with-china/.

Green, J. (2017). The Offshore City, Chinese Finance, and British Capitalism: Geo-Economic Rebalancing Under the Coalition Government. *British Journal of Politics and International Relations*. https://doi.org/10.1177/1369148117737263.

Haldane, A. (2010, March 30). *The $100 Billion Question*. Speech at the Institution of Regulation and Risk, Hong Kong.

Hall, B., Barker, A., & Bryant, C. (2009, April 9). Sarkozy Claims Credit on Tighter Regulation. *Financial Times*. Retrieved from: https://next.ft.com/content/10b0bbee-1fb3-11de-a1df-00144feabdc0.

Hay, C. (2011). Pathology Without Crisis? The Strange Demise of the Anglo-Liberal Growth Model. *Government and Opposition, 46*(1), 1–31.

Hay, C. (2013a). Treating the Symptom Not the Condition: Crisis Definition, Deficit Reduction and the Search for a New British Growth Model. *British Journal of Politics and International Relations, 15*(1), 23–37.

Hay, C. (2013b). *The Failure of Anglo-Liberal Capitalism*. London: Palgrave Macmillan.

HM Treasury. (2011, December 19). Government Sets Out Plans to Reform the Structure of Banking in the UK. Press Release.

House of Lords. (2016). *Brexit: Financial Services', European Union Committee, 9th Report of Session 2016–17* (HL Paper 81). London: House of Lords.

Howarth, D., & Quaglia, L. (2015). *The Comparative Political Economy of Basle III* (Working Paper). Retrieved from: http://speri.dept.shef.ac.uk/wp-content/uploads/2013/06/The-Comparative-Political-Economy-of-Basel-III-in-Europe-PDF-265KB.pdf.

Howarth, D., & Quaglia, L. (2017). Brexit and the Single Financial Market. *Journal of Common Market Studies Annual Review, 55*(S1), 149–164.

Ingham, G. K. (1984). *Capitalism Divided? City and Industry in British Social Development.* London: Macmillan.

Jenkins, P., & Agnew, H. (2016, February 23). What Would Brexit Mean for the City of London? *Financial Times.* Retrieved from: https://next.ft.com/content/e90885d8-d3db-11e5-829b-8564e7528e54.

Jenkins, P., & Jones, C. (2014, March 18). City of London Urges 'Muscular Defence' Against Eu Regulation. *Financial Times.* Retrieved from: http://www.ft.com/cms/s/0/6c540dd8-ae84-11e3-aaa6-00144feab7de.html#axzz3v32O1XRn.

Jenson, M. D., & Snaith, H. (2016). When Politics Prevails: The Political Economy of Brexit. *Journal of European Public Policy, 23*(9), 1302–1310.

Johnson, B. (2014). *Transcript of a Speech on 6 August 2014 at Bloomberg, London in Response to Receipt of Dr Gerard Lyon's Publication of 'The Europe Report: A Win-Win Situation'.* Retrieved from: http://www.london.gov.uk/sites/default/files/bj-europe-speech_0.pdf.

Jones, H. (2012, June 20). London Stung by Us Attack on Bank Regulation Record. *Reuters.* Retrieved from: http://uk.reuters.com/article/uk-britain-usa-regulation-idUKBRE85J0WV20120620.

JP Morgan Chase & Co. (2017). *Annual Report 2016.* https://www.jpmorgan-chase.com/corporate/investor-relations/document/2016-annualreport.pdf.

Le Corre, P. (2015). What the Budding UK-China Romance Means for the Global Economy. *Brookings Blog.* Retrieved from: http://www.brookings.edu/blogs/order-from-chaos/posts/2015/10/22-china-uk-relations-lecorre.

Moore, E., & Wildau, G. (2015, October 20). China Completes First London Debt Sale. *Financial Times.* Retrieved from: https://next.ft.com/content/01bfe6aa-76e1-11e5-8564-b4bb9a521c63.

Moran, M. (1990). *The Politics of the Financial Services Revolution: The USA, UK and Japan.* Basingstoke: Palgrave Macmillan.

Munchau, W. (2009, December 9). Barnier Is No Threat but Shame About His Job. *Financial Times.* Retrieved from: http://www.ft.com/cms/s/0/5d14af9e-e29b-11de-b028-00144feab49a.html#axzz3uxsq6e5D.

Parker, G., Pickard, J., Noble, J., & Barker, A. (2015, November 10). Cameron Sets Out Formal Demands to the EU. *Financial Times.* Retrieved from: http://www.ft.com/cms/s/0/50fc868a-8788-11e5-90de-f44762bf9896.html#axzz3v32O1XRn.

PWC. (2012, July). The EU Financial Transactions Tax: Unprecedented Steps. *Global FS Tax Newsflash.* Retrieved from: http://www.pwc.com/sg/en/tax-newsflash/assets/taxnewsflash-201207.pdf.

Quaglia, L., Howarth, D., & Liebe, M. (2016). The Political Economy of European Capital Markets Union. *Journal of Common Market Studies Annual Review, 54*(S1), 185–203.

Rachman, G. (2015, March 13). Transatlantic Spat Exposes Deeper Cracks. *Financial Times*. Retrieved from: https://next.ft.com/content/4c3195da-c971-11e4-a2d9-00144feab7de.

Roberts, R. (2005). London as an International Financial Centre 1980–2000: Global Powerhouse or Wimbledon EC2? In Y. Cassis & E. Bussière (Eds.), *London and Paris as International Financial Centres in the Twentieth Century* (pp. 287–312). Oxford: Oxford University Press.

Schelke, W. (2016). Financial Centre and Monetary Outsider: How Precarious Is the UK's Position in the EU? *Political Quarterly, 87*(2), 157–165.

Talani, L. S. (2011). The Impact of the Global Financial Crisis on the City of London: Towards the End of Hegemony? *Competition and Change, 15*(1), 11–30.

Thompson, H. (1996). *The British Conservative Government and the European Exchange Rate Mechanism*. London: Pinter.

Thompson, H. (2009). National Economic Policy. In M. Flinders, A. Gamble, C. Hay, & M. Kenny (Eds.), *The Oxford Handbook of British Politics* (pp. 897–911). Oxford: Oxford University Press.

Thompson, H. (2016). Enduring Capital Flow Constraints and the 2007–8 Financial and Eurozone Crises. *The British Journal of Politics and International Relations, 18*(1), 216–233.

Thompson, H. (2017a). Inevitability and Contingency: The Political Economy of Brexit. *British Journal of Politics and International Relations, 19*(3), 434–449.

Thompson, H. (2017b). How the City Lost at Brexit: A Historical Perspective. *Economy and Society, 46*(2), 211–228.

Thompson, H. (2017c). Returning to Democracy: The British Left and the Constitutional Temptation of the European Union. In R. Ekins & G. Gee (Eds.), *Judicial Power and the Left: Notes on a Sceptical Tradition* (pp. 62–66). London: Policy Exchange.

Waterfield, B. (2009, December 21). Sarkozy 'Will Use Michel Barnier to Advance French Interests'. *Daily Telegraph*. Retrieved from: http://www.telegraph.co.uk/finance/newsbysector/banksandfinance/6861065/Sarkozy-will-use-Michel-Barnier-to-advance-French-interests.html.

Watt, N. (2014, January 15). David Cameron to Demand EU Treaty Reform to 'Save' City of London. *The Guardian*. Retrieved from: http://www.the-guardian.com/world/2014/jan/15/cameron-to-demand-eu-treaty-reform.

Wong, S.-L. (2015, February). China's Minsheng to Invest 1 Billion Pounds in New London Financial District. *Reuters*. Retrieved from: http://uk.reuters.com/article/uk-china-britain-property-idUKKBN0LI04X20150215.

CHAPTER 5

European Union Financial Regulation, Banking Union, Capital Markets Union and the UK

Lucia Quaglia

INTRODUCTION

The European Union (EU) undertook major reforms of its economic and financial governance framework after the international financial crisis and the sovereign debt crisis. Three financial policy areas stand out: financial regulation, which was significantly revised in the wake of the international financial crisis; Banking Union (BU), which was the EU

Part of the material on Banking Union is informed by my joint work with David Howarth (University of Luxembourg) and was funded by a fellowship awarded by the Fonds National de la Recherche in Luxembourg. Part of the material on Brexit and finance was informed by my joint work with Scott James (King's College, London) and was funded by a fellowship awarded by the Hanse Wissenschafts-Kolleg in Germany. Usual disclaimers apply.

L. Quaglia (✉)
University of Bologna, Bologna, Italy
e-mail: lucia.quaglia@unibo.it

© The Author(s) 2019
C. Hay and D. Bailey (eds.), *Diverging Capitalisms*,
Building a Sustainable Political Economy: SPERI Research & Policy,
https://doi.org/10.1007/978-3-030-03415-3_5

(to be precise, the euro area)'s response to the sovereign debt crisis; and Capital Markets Union (CMU), which was the EU's attempt to revamp financial activities and the real economy after two consecutive crises. These reforms were complex and intertwined. They built on the existing EU framework, notably the Single Financial Market in the case of financial regulation and CMU. The reforms enacted also substantially modified the existing framework, as in the case of BU, which was designed to complete Economic and Monetary Union (EMU).

This chapter examines the dynamics of EU reforms in these policy areas by focusing on the preferences and influence of the United Kingdom (UK). The UK has often been considered as an 'awkward partner' in the EU. Stephen George's classic book, *An Awkward Partner: Britain in the European Community* (1990), points out the troubled relationship of the UK with the process of European integration since its inception. This chapter argues that this view is somewhat unwarranted, especially in the case of financial policies. In these policies the UK has been a foot-dragger, a fence-sitter and a pace-setter, depending on the circumstances. The chapter does not discuss in-depth the (often complex) intra-EU negotiations in these policy areas. At the same time, the domestic politics and political economy of these issues in the UK are not investigated in details. The aim of the chapter is to explore how the EU policy process and the domestic arena in the UK interacted and with what outcome. The material is organised as follows. Section "Member States in the EU Policy Process" discusses some concepts that can be useful in order to examine the preferences and the influence of the member states in the EU policy process. The empirical sections follow by and large a chronological order, discussing EU financial regulation first (Sect. "Post-crisis EU Financial Regulation"), then BU (Sect. "Banking Union") and CMU (Sect. "The Building of CMU"). The Final Section briefly discusses Brexit and finance.

MEMBER STATES IN THE EU POLICY PROCESS

This section discusses some concepts that can be useful in order to examine the role of the member states in the EU policy process. It first outlines a typology of roles and then examines the domestic process of national preference formation and the sources of influence for the member states in the EU.

A Typology of Roles

In her seminal work, Börzel (2002) distinguishes three roles that member states can perform in the EU policy process: foot-draggers, fence-sitters and pace-setters. *Foot-dragging* takes place when a member state seeks to block, delay or substantially water down a policy measure at the EU-level because it does not reflect the preferences of that member state. Foot-dragging comes in two shades: opposition to the EU policy measure *tout court*; and partial foot-dragging by seeking to substantially reshape the proposed EU measure. Partial foot-dragging is something that goes beyond the traditional processes of negotiation whereby member states seek, for example, to fine-tune specific provisions of EU legislation. The foot-draggers are sometimes 'late-movers' if they do not have domestic templates already in place in a given policy area, as in the case of Southern European countries and environmental policy (Börzel 2002). Post-financial crisis the UK was at times a foot-dragger in the reform of EU financial regulation, albeit in different ways, sometimes calling for stricter EU regulation, other times calling for less strict EU rules, as elaborated in (Sect. "Post-crisis EU Financial Regulation"). In other cases the UK was a foot-dragger *tout court*, seeking to prevent the setting in place of an EU measure, as in the case of the Financial Transaction Tax (Gabor 2016; Wasserfallen 2014), which, however, was controversial also for other member states.

Fence-sitting coincides with passive policy-taking, rather than active policy-making. It takes place if a member state does not have strong preferences on the EU measure under discussion or does not have the capacity to substantially engage in negotiations. Hence, the fence-sitter can build tactical coalitions with pace-setters and foot-draggers (Börzel 2002). Often fence-sitters adopt a 'wait and see approach'. The Nordic countries in EMU are examples of this dynamic. At the time of the Maastricht Treaty, the UK sought to block EMU (Dyson and Featherstone 1999), hence it was a foot-dragger, rather than a fence-sitter. Member states can also be 'constructive' fence-sitters by supporting in principle a given EU measure, but opting-out (*de jure* or de facto) and letting others go ahead, as in the case of the UK in BU, which is discussed in Sect. "Banking Union".

Pace-setting takes place when a member state actively pushes for a certain policy measure at the EU level in a way that reflects its preferences. It often presupposes the presence of domestic policy templates to upload (in which case, the pace-setter is also a 'first-mover') and the capacity to do so, which in turn is based on the resources that a member state can mobilise. A typical example of pace-setting are the Nordic countries and Germany in environmental policy (Börzel 2002); Germany in macroeconomic policies (Dyson 2000); the UK in pre-crisis financial services regulation, especially the completion of the single financial market (Mügge 2010; Posner and Véron 2010; Quaglia 2010a). Post-crisis, the UK was a pace-setter in the building-up of CMU, as elaborated in Sect. "Banking Union". Other examples of the UK's pace-setting role that are not examined in this chapter due to space constraints were the UK's immediate response to the international financial crisis and the negotiations on the Transatlantic Trade and Investment Partnership (TTIP). In the midst of the financial crisis, the so-called 'British plan' provided a 'template' for the policy response of the EU and its member states (see Quaglia 2009). In external economic (trade) relations of the EU, the UK supported the Commission in the TTIP negotiations with a view to promoting the inclusion of financial services into the agreement (Jones and Macartney 2016).

It is noteworthy that the adoption of one of these roles by a member state varies over time: the 1980s and 1990s were the 'golden age' for the pace-setters on the Single Market and EMU (see Armstrong and Bulmer 1998; Egan 2001; Jabko 2006; Dyson and Featherstone 1999). There is variation across policy areas: for example, the UK is more likely to be a pace-setter in areas related to the Single Market than, for example, in social policy, from which it temporarily opted-out. There is also variation within a policy area: the UK was very supportive of CMU, it opposed certain pieces of EU post-crisis financial legislation, such as hedge funds rules, but supported other measures, such as a new framework for bank resolution. Moreover, the UK was a Single Market pace-setter in the 1980s under the Conservative Government (Moravcsik 1998), but was a foot-dragger on EMU in the same period (Dyson and Featherstone 1999). In the 1990s, the UK was a pace-setter in the completion of the single financial market (Mügge 2010; Posner and Véron 2010; Quaglia 2010a) under the Labour Government. With a Conservative Government, the UK was a pace-setter in the making of CMU and the TTIP negotiations (Quaglia et al. 2016), a fence-sitter on BU (Howarth and Quaglia 2016) and a foot-dragger on certain pieces of EU financial services legislation (Pagliari 2013; Quaglia 2012; Woll 2013).

The Domestic Process of National Preference Formation

In order to explain why member states adopt one of the roles outlined above it is crucial to understand the domestic process of *national preference formation* with reference to specific EU policy areas. Domestic politics and domestic political economy interact in the formation of national preferences (e.g. Moravcsik 1997, 1998), which are the aggregated preferences of the public authorities and private actors at the domestic level. The preferences of the public authorities are affected by the economic and political costs of the proposed measure for their country, and the lobbying efforts of specific interest groups in the domestic arena. National policy-makers might also be sensitive to the allocation of new powers to EU bodies, which might be a contested move in domestic politics, especially in some member states, such as the UK.

The preferences of interest groups depend of the expected economic costs and benefits of the proposed EU measure, particularly financial policies, which have clear-cut costs and benefits. The groups most affected by the measure are likely to mobilise the most, albeit subject to resource constraints (Mahoney 2007). Particularly important in the UK are the preferences of the financial sector, the City of London, given the large size of the financial sector in the national economy. Moreover, the financial industry has the economic and human resources to be an effective lobbyist (Baker 2010). The British financial industry follows closely and systematically contributes to the policy discussions on these matters at the national and EU levels. On the one hand, different part of the financial industry sometimes have different preferences (Pagliari and Young 2014) or certain issues carry greater salience for some (e.g. hedge funds) but not for others (e.g. collective investment funds, see Woll 2013). On the other hand, one often speaks of national financial 'system' (rather than just 'sector') because the various parts of the national financial industry are generally interlinked. Indeed, the literature on varieties of financial capitalism seeks to tease out typologies or common features of national financial *systems* (Allen and Gale 2000; Hardie and Howarth 2013).

The Sources of Member States Influence

The *influence* of a member state in the EU is affected by a variety of sources: economic and political power (such as GDP, votes in the Council); the size of the specific sector under discussion; subject-specific expertise and general negotiating skills (for a review, see Bailer 2010).

Table 5.1   Overview of the UK's roles in selected financial policies in the EU

Pace-setter

Pre-crisis: Financial Services Action Plan, most EU financial legislation (e.g. Solvency II, Lamfalussy directives in securities markets)

Post-crisis: British (Brown) plan, CMU, TTIP (finance), some EU legislation (BRRD)

Fence-sitter

Pre-crisis: Stability and Growth Pact

Post-crisis: BU, some EU financial legislation (e.g. EMIR)

Foot-dragger

Pre-crisis: EMU-TEU

Post-crisis: Most EU financial legislation (e.g. AIFM, FTT)

The UK is the third largest member states in the EU in terms of GDP. Under the current QMV voting rules in the Council, the four largest member states (Germany, France, the UK, and Italy), together with any other EU member state, have sufficient votes to block any proposed piece of legislation. The UK financial sector is by far the largest in the EU and London is the largest financial centre in Europe and the second largest in the world. Given the size of the financial sector, the British authorities have considerable subject-specific expertise on matters related to finance. The influence of the UK in financial policies has been considerable, given the conspicuous resources it can mobilise.

The following empirical sections examine EU post-crisis financial regulation, BU and CMU, explaining the dynamics of the EU policy process with a particular focus on the preferences and influence of the UK, explaining why it was a foot-dragger, fence-sitter, and pace-setter depending on the circumstances (for an overview, see Table 5.1).

Post-crisis EU Financial Regulation

A host of new financial legislation was issued by the EU in the aftermath of the international financial crisis. The vast majority of these measures regulated activities or entities that were previously unregulated (or subject to self-regulation) in the EU and its member states (such as credit rating agencies, CRAs); or at the EU level (such as hedge funds and bank resolution); or at the national, EU and international levels (OTCDs). In

other instances, they imposed heavier, more prescriptive and more burdensome requirements on financial entities that were already regulated
prior to the crisis, as in the case of higher capital requirements for banks
and new liquidity management rules (the Capital Requirements Directive
IV, CRD IV), or they set in place more substantial protection for depositors (the revised Deposit Guarantee Scheme Directive). Some of the
post-crisis EU rules had potential protectionist effects due to the conten-
tious provisions concerning the access of third-countries entities or products to the EU market, for example in the legislation concerning credit
rating agencies (CRAs), hedge funds, OTCDs (Quaglia 2015). The
reform of the financial services architecture following the De Larosière
Report (2009) was designed to strengthen financial supervision at the
EU level and to foster macro-prudential supervision in the EU (Buckley
and Howarth 2011; Hennessy 2014).

By looking at the entirety of EU post-crisis legislation, the UK was
often a foot-dragger, and less frequently a fence-sitter and a pace-setter.
First, the UK was a *foot-dragger* concerning the legislation on hedge
funds, rating agencies (Quaglia 2012) and the Financial Transaction Tax
(Gabor 2016). These pieces of legislation were resisted by the UK on the
ground that they would impose unnecessary costs, damaging the competitiveness of the financial industry in Europe and reducing the attractiveness of European financial centres as a result of regulatory arbitrage. The
UK stressed that EU financial regulation should support the development of 'open, global markets' (Darling 2009). The concern about international 'regulatory arbitrage' has traditionally been at the forefront of
policy-makers' minds in Britain, given the fact that London hosts many
non-British-owned financial institutions and successfully competes with
other financial centres worldwide to attract business (Quaglia 2010a).

A combination of domestic politics and domestic political economy
account for British preferences on the regulation of hedge funds, rating
agencies and the Financial Transaction Tax. The UK hosts 4/5 of all the
EU hedge fund managers and several non-EU hedge funds operate in
London (Woll 2013). The main CRAs that are based in North America
use their subsidiaries in London in order to issue ratings across the EU.
Moreover, financial products traded in London have ratings issued within
and without the EU. Hence, EU legislation on hedge funds and CRAs
de facto mainly 'hit' the UK. Lord Myners, a UK Treasury minister, suggested that it was easy for other European countries to make political

capital out of demanding 'intrusive regulation of an industry of which they have little or no direct experience' (*Financial Times*, 1 July 2009).

Similarly, the Financial Transaction Tax would be detrimental to international financial centres, such as the City of London and Wall Street, which mostly operate in the wholesale market (*Financial Times*, 23 September 2011; *Reuters*, 4 November 2011). Indeed, several reports (House of Lords 2012; London Economics 2014) indicated that up to 80% of the Financial Transaction Tax in the EU would be collected in the UK. Moreover, there was the possibility that part of the taxes collected in the UK would be transferred to the EU and/or shared with other EU countries, which hosted firms that were party to financial transactions taking place in the UK (House of Lords 2012). Chancellor Osborne went so far as arguing that the 'financial transaction tax is not a tax on banks or bankers; it is a tax on pensioners and people with savings and investments' (*BBC*, 20 April 2013). Eventually, the UK brought the case before the European Court of Justice, which dismissed the challenge as premature because the details of the tax had not been finalised (*Financial Times*, 6 May 2014).

Finally, the UK was a *partial foot-dragger* in the negotiation of the CRD IV legislative package designed to implement the Basel III accord in the EU by replacing the 'old' CRD III with a directive that governs the access to deposit-taking activities and a regulation that establishes prudential requirements for credit institutions. However, in this case, unlike in the case of CRAs and hedge funds, the UK authorities resisted EU rules because they were regarded as *not strict enough* and not in line with Basel III (James 2016). Speaking at a meeting of the Economic and Finance ministers held to discuss the CRD IV, the British Treasury minister complained that 'We are not implementing the Basel agreement, as anyone who will look at this text will be able to tell you' (*Financial Times*, 2 May 2012). Indeed, the BCBS subsequently found the EU materially non-compliant with Basel III (BCBS 2014). Moreover, the British authorities and those who argued in favour of EU standards that exceed the Basel minimum successfully opposed the initial proposed for maximum capital ratio, which meant that national regulators would not have been able to impose higher capital requirements on domestic banks should they have deemed it necessary to do so (James 2016). By contrast, an issue on which the British authorities lost their battle in Brussels and that differentiate the CRD IV package from the

Basel accord was the legally binding cap imposed on banker bonuses. This had been an amendment introduced and strongly advocated by the EP with some support from continental countries (Greenwood and Roederer-Rynning 2014).

A combination of domestic politics and domestic political economy account for British preferences on the CRD IV (and Basel III) (see James 2016). At the time of the CRD IV negotiations, the main British banks were relatively well capitalised in part as a result of the state-led recapitalisation in the wake of the crisis, whereas the banks in many continental European countries were under-capitalised. The impact of stricter capital requirements on lending to the real economy was less of a concern for the UK because the City is mostly 'disconnected' from the real economy in the UK. By contrast, continental European countries have a bank-based financial system, where banks provide funding to small and medium enterprises. Finally, during the crisis, the UK authorities had engaged in massive bailout of banks using taxpayer money. Hence, banking regulation became politically salient for politicians and the public opinion in the UK (James and Quaglia 2017b).

British policy-makers were also *partial foot-draggers* concerning the setting up of the European Supervisory Authorities, given the British reluctance to transfer powers away from national supervisors to bodies outside their borders (*Financial Times*, 20 March 2009), granting decision-making powers to EU-level authorities, while public funds to tackle banking crises came from national budgets. To this effect, Gordon Brown, the British Prime Minister, secured a guarantee that the new supervisory system would not include powers to force national governments to bail out banks (Buckley and Howarth 2011).

UK policy-makers were (*constructive*) *fence-sitters* on other EU legislative measures, such as the European Market Infrastructure regulation (EMIR) (James 2015). On this piece of legislation, UK preferences were mostly in line with those of the other member states and the measures proposed by the Commission. The EMIR prescribed the shifting of OTCDs trading to central counterparties (CCPs) and the mandatory reporting of transactions to trade repositories. It also set harmonised rules for CCPs and trade repositories, which would be subject to EU supervision. There were two controversial issues for the UK in the negotiations of the EMIR. First, there was the complex third country regime for CCPs and trade repositories. Without going into much detail, the British authorities were keen to ensure open markets by setting 'broad' criteria to ascertain the equivalence of the regulatory framework of third countries. They also objected to the concept of reciprocity proposed by the Commission and were supported by France (see Pagliari 2013; Quaglia 2015).

The second controversial issue for the UK were the provisions concerning the location of CCPs and their access to central bank liquidity. Some regulators—notably the French—believed that CCPs clearing OTCDs should have access to central bank liquidity in the same currency as the product being cleared. In other words, a CCP would have to be located in the euro area and clear euro-denominated products in order to access European Central Bank (ECB) liquidity. The British authorities successfully opposed this view because London is one of the main locations for derivatives trading and clearing worldwide, also for euro-denominated assets. The measures initially proposed would have be detrimental to the clearing houses located outside the euro area—first and foremost, those currently operating in the London OTCD markets (*Risk Magazine*, 10 January 2011).

On bank resolution, the UK was a *pace-setter*. The BRRD was controversial in the EU and was therefore issued with considerable delay: it was agreed in 2014, even though the Commission began consulting on cross-border bank resolution as early as 2009 (Commission 2009) and held two successive consultations (Commission 2011, 2013). It was a matter that touched upon politically sensitive issues and had potential fiscal implications. The UK authorities actively contributed to the policy debate by developing the concept of the bail-in and loss-absorbing capacity that were new resolution tools devised post-crisis. The idea of bail-in was initially put forward by two senior economists of Credit Suisse, Calello and Ervin, in an article in *The Economist* in January 2010. It immediately gained traction at the Bank of England because the 'traditional' way to resolve banks was seen as unsuitable for large cross-border banks, especially G-SIBs.

As early as July 2010, Andrew Bailey (2010), who later became the director responsible for financial stability, argued that 'an alternative worth exploring, drawing on the tools used to restructure non-banks, is creditor recapitalisation or 'bail-in'. In September 2010, Paul Tucker reiterated that the bail-in should be considered as a resolution tool. In December 2010, well before the FSB included the bail-in in the *Key Attributes*, and well before the BRRD (2014) the Financial Stability Report of the Bank of England (Bank of England 2010), stated that the bail-in should be extended to other potentially systemic institutions, including investment banks and market infrastructures. The Independent Commission on Banking (the so-called Vickers Commission) (2011a, b) recommended statutory bail-in powers and a loss-absorbing capacity of at least 17–20%, which was broadly in line with the standard subsequently on loss absorbency capacity set by the FSB in 2015.

Banking Union

BU was the main (and delayed) response of the euro area to the sovereign debt crisis that began in Greece in 2010 and subsequently extended to Ireland, Portugal and Spain. When the crisis threatened to extend to Italy, BU was proposed, even though the final version of BU agreed is less ambitious of what was initially planned (on the politics of BU, see Donnelly 2014; Epstein and Rhodes 2016; Schäfer 2016). In June 2012, the President of the European Council, the President of the Eurogroup, the President of the Commission and the President of the ECB, presented an interim report entitled 'Towards a Genuine Economic and Monetary Union', that laid the foundations for BU. Afterward, the various components of BU were set in place, with one important exception.

The Regulation for the establishment of a Single Supervisory Mechanism (SSM) was adopted in October 2013. The SSM applies only to the euro area member states and to the non-euro area member states that decide to join BU. In the SSM, responsibility for banking supervision was assigned to the ECB in cooperation with national competent authorities. This was followed by the adoption of the BRRD in June 2014 (discussed in the previous section) and the Regulation on the Single Resolution Mechanism (SRM) in July 2014. The SRM, which was to complement the SSM, was responsible for the planning and resolution phases of cross-border banks and those directly supervised by the ECB, while national resolution authorities would be responsible for all other banks.

The revised DSG directive was finalised in June 2014, but a common EU deposit guarantee scheme did not materialise mainly because of German opposition. In November 2015, the Commission launched a proposed regulation for the creation of a European DGS. The European Stability Mechanism (ESM)—which was established by an intergovernmental treaty finalised in 2012 to replace the temporary European Financial Stability Facility—began operation in September 2012. It was envisaged that, subject to certain conditions, the ESM could provide financial support to ailing banks as well as to the governments of countries experiencing severe financial difficulties.

BU was designed to rebuild financial market confidence in both banks and sovereigns—especially in the euro area periphery—by stabilising the national banking systems exposed directly to a vicious circle. In fact, the sovereign debt crisis created a 'doom-loop' between the instability of the banking sector—which had to be bailed out in the majority of euro area countries— and the fragility of public finances, which were becoming unsustainable in some countries (Howarth and Quaglia 2015). BU was also to reverse the fragmentation of European financial markets that had begun with the international financial crisis and was worsened by the sovereign debt crisis. BU transferred powers from the national to the EU (to be precise, the BU) level. It was also significant because not all EU member states joined: it included only euro area member states even if other EU member states were able to opt-in. Hence, BU increased the trend towards differentiated integration in the EU (Dyson and Sepos 2010; Schimmelfennig 2016; Schimmelfennig et al. 2015), which posed a major challenge to the EU as a whole and to the opt-out countries— first and foremost the UK, given the size of its financial sector and its interconnection to the euro area. Non-euro area countries had a choice about joining (or not) the SSM and faced incentives and disincentives.

The UK was a *constructive fence-sitter* on BU: it was by and large supportive of BU and specifically the SSM for euro area member states, notably as a way to tackle the sovereign debt crisis distressing the euro area periphery and to ensure financial stability therein (see, for example, *The Telegraph*, 13, 19 December 2012). However, the UK did not want to be part of BU because of domestic politics and domestic political economy considerations. BU implied a considerable pooling of power at the EU/BU level, first and foremost the supranationalisation of banking supervision, which was politically unacceptable in the UK. Moreover, the institutional and decision-making framework of BU were primarily designed for euro area members—and in fact none of non-euro area countries joined it.

As for domestic political economy, the British banking system was not only the most 'Europeanised' of the largest six EU member state banking systems in terms of the holdings of other EU-headquartered banks in the UK (as both a percentage and in total terms) and British bank holdings elsewhere in the EU (in total terms), it was also very internationalised in terms of non-EU-headquartered banks active in the UK and the activities of British banks abroad. The UK was most exposed to the potential instability of globally systemic banks, which affected the British banking system more in relative terms than others in Europe (Howarth and Quaglia 2016). British banks by and large supported the creation of the SSM, but none sought British participation (British Bankers Association 2012).

During the negotiations on Banking Union, British policy-makers feared that a euro area majority would be able to impose its rules on non-euro area members in the European Banking Authority (EBA) (*Financial Times*, 13 December 2012). Hence, they demanded an EBA voting reform, whereby any decision by the Authority should be approved by a minimum number of member states outside BU and thus effectively by a 'double majority' of member states inside and outside the BU. Some euro area member states, first and foremost France and Germany, resisted British requests and eventually an agreement was reached on the creation of a double majority system until the number of non-BU member states dwindled to less than four. However, the safeguard in EBA will end once the number of non-BU member states is less than four (Howarth and Quaglia 2016). All in all, the UK was a constructive fence-sitter on BU, and carefully negotiated specific issues that were significant for non-euro area countries.

BU will have significant implications for the single financial market. First, it will increase financial integration in the euro area, hence creating a 'market within a market'. Second, BU will promote the formation of a coalition of member states with similar interests and hence potentially voting as a block on several issues concerning EU financial (banking) regulation. The 'double majority' safeguard in EBA that euro area outsiders, first and foremost the UK, obtain will end once the number of non-BU member states is less than four and there is not such a safeguard in the Council of Ministers. Third, and related to the previous point, there is a potentially uneasy relation between the European Banking Authority, which remains responsible for developing regulatory policy and technical standards for the single rulebook in banking across Europe, and the SSM, which has the ECB at its centre and was given regulatory powers in addition to its supervisory powers.

The Building of CMU

The idea of CMU was first mentioned in the 'Political Guidelines' of the (then) newly appointed President of the European Commission Jean-Claude Juncker in October 2014. The project of CMU was fully in line with the 'Investment Plan for Europe' (aka the Juncker plan 2014 European Commission) of November 2014, which set out to remove obstacles to investment, providing funding and technical assistance to investment projects. According to the Commission, CMU would 'improve the financing of the economy... cut the cost of raising capital, notably for SMEs, and help reduce the very high dependence on bank funding. This would also increase the attractiveness of Europe as a place to invest' (2014: 8).

In February 2015, the Commission (2015a) published the Green Paper 'Building a Capital Markets Union', which was subject to a public consultation. At this stage, CMU was a 'mixed bag'—it was a 'long shopping list' of things to do in order to complete the single financial market and boost EU's capital markets. In September 2015, the Commission (2015b) put forward an Action Plan for CMU, together with a package of two legislative proposals to promote securitisation. Furthermore, the Commission began preparing a proposal for the revision of the Prospectus directive and the Solvency II directive. Finally, it opened a consultation on venture capital and social entrepreneurship funds, a consultation on covered bonds in the EU, and a call for evidence on EU regulatory framework for financial services. The member states reached an agreement on the securitisation proposals in a matter of weeks, but the EP refused to fast-track the proposals mainly because left-leaning MEPs called for a thorough review in order not to revive pre-crisis excesses (*Financial Times*, 3 March 2016).

The European Commission was the main policy entrepreneur on CMU, which was enthusiastically supported by the UK, joined by those member states with the most well-developed and diversified financial sectors, including Ireland, the Netherlands, Sweden and Luxembourg. These member states unequivocally supported the market liberalisation agenda in CMU. The main continental countries—notably France and Germany (Schäuble and Sapin 2015)—expressed their reservations on CMU and so did some of their domestic players (e.g. domestic banks and investment firms). By contrast, the most competitive parts of the financial industry, the main transnational players, such as large banks engaged in securitisation, insurance companies and the international financial centres in the EU, first and foremost the City of London. The new measures designed to promote securitisation would benefits the large banks based in the UK, but also in France, Germany, the Benelux countries, Italy and Spain. Small banks would benefit from the new proposed legislation on securitisation, but the large banks would benefit the most, as they are the most engaged in shadow banking (Gabor and Vestergaard 2015).

The proposed revision of the Solvency II directive, de facto reducing solvency requirements for insurers that invest in long-term infrastructural projects, would benefit insures, in particular the large ones that are more likely to invest in these sort of activities—large insurers are mainly based in the UK, but also Germany, France and Italy. The revision of the Prospectus directive and future legislative and non-legislative measures designed to harmonise securities market legislation and ease cross-border activities would be particularly advantageous for the largest, most competitive financial centres, first and foremost the City of London, that would be able to attract business from the periphery of the EU, but also potentially from Paris and Frankfurt (Quaglia et al. 2016).

British policy-makers were *pace-setters* on CMU, at least compared to other member states. First, a British national, Jonathan Hill was chosen to lead the CMU project at the European Commission and as was appointed as Commissioner 'for Financial Stability, Financial Services and Capital Markets Union', one of the few examples in European Union history where a Commissioner's job title matched that of a specific project. Second, UK policy-makers and stakeholders engaged extensively in the agenda-setting process. For example, almost a quarter of the Commission's responses to consultation were from the UK, 16% from Belgium (EU-level financial associations are located in Brussels), 13% each from France and Germany and 4% each from Italy and the Netherlands. The House of Lords (2015) produced a timely report on CMU, urging the 'the UK, where capital markets are better established than in other Member States, to take the lead in spearheading this Capital Markets Union'. Third, the areas prioritised for action, namely securitisation (banking), Solvency II (insurance) and Prospectus (securities markets) were those that would benefit the most the UK and indeed were indicated by the UK government as the three tops priorities for action on CMU (UK Response to Green Paper 2015). The call for a call for evidence on EU regulatory framework for financial services also chimed well with British concerns about EU's over-regulation following the international financial crisis. Furthermore, the strong UK government opposition to further centralisation helps to explain the absence of institutional measures in both the February 2015 Green Paper and the September 2015 Action Plan.

Of all EU Member States, the UK had the most potentially to benefit from the financial liberalisation and diversification promised in the CMU project, given the diversity of its financial sector and, in particular, the high concentration of wholesale market activity, private equity and hedge funds. As noted by Dawson (2015) 'If a single capital market is established, demand for funding will be Europe-wide, but supply will by dominated by the City. The policy plays precisely to Britain's area of expertise. UK financial services could provide the funding for businesses and investment projects across £10 trillion market—a move potentially as transformational as the Big Bang in 1986. This is not something that can be replicated outside the EU. What would give capital markets union its power is the sheer scale of the European market'. In a speech made to the City of London Corporation Policy Committee, Commissioner Hill noted that 'From here investment flows out across the continent: UK banks lend more than $2 trillion into other European countries.... More than a third of UK private equity funds' investments go to companies elsewhere in the EU. So the success of the City is tied to a successful Europe'.

In the UK, given the fact that CMU would also involve new EU regulation and further centralisation, there was some reluctance on the basis of national sovereignty. In its responses to the Commission's consultation on CMU the UK Government (2015) opposed: the transfer of direct supervisory responsibilities to European institutions; tax and solvency law harmonisation. This might also explain the somewhat different views of Commissioner Hill and Commission President Juncker as to the institutional content of CMU. Commissioner Hill and DG FISMA officials did not discuss institutional reform in their presentations on CMU. By contrast, President Juncker in the Five Presidents Report (2015) argued that CMU 'should lead ultimately to a single European capital markets supervisor'. Hence, domestic political economy and domestic politics in the UK pulled in somewhat different directions with reference to CMU.

Given the implications of BU for the single financial market (see Sect. "Banking Union"), CMU was deliberately framed as an initiative to complement BU and ultimately to complete EMU (see Juncker 2015), even though CMU involves all the 28 member states. Some commentators (for example, Ringe 2015: 5) interpret CMU, in part, as an attempt to repair the strained relations between the UK and the EU/euro area by giving 'a political signal to strengthen the Single Market as a project of all 28 Member States', not only to the euro area countries, and in an area where the UK had a clear competitive advantage. Hence, CMU was designed to attract the support of those member states that had not joined BU and/or EMU (first and foremost, the UK). Hence, it was a way to address the concerns of the repercussions of 'differentiated integration'—linked to EMU first and BU—on the single financial market.

Brexit and Finance

As explained in the previous sections, the UK financial industry benefitted greatly from EU financial integration over recent decades with over 30% of financial services exports destined for the EU27. The EU27 was the biggest market for UK exports of financial services: UK exports to the EU amounted to £26 billion per annum whilst UK imports from the EU were £3 billion. Consequently, the outcome of the British referendum on continuing membership of the EU in June 2016 was a major shock for the British financial sector. The priority for the bulk of British finance was to preserve membership of, and full access to, the single financial market. It soon became clear that a European Economic Area (EEA) style arrangement post-Brexit was highly unlikely given the politics of the Conservative Party and the perception of the result as being a backlash against the free movement of labour. As its main alternative, the City favoured a special deal for finance, which will likely be rejected by the EU Commission and member states which insist on maintaining all four freedoms of the internal market or none. Hence, the British financial industry called for the preservation of as much market access as possible (The CityUK 2016a, b). However, the City was surprisingly ineffective at shaping the UK's Brexit policy (see James and Quaglia 2017a).

In February 2017, Prime Minister Theresa May announced her intention to negotiate a so-called 'hard' Brexit that will leave the UK outside the single market and the Customs Union, as outlined in the Conservative Government's 'Brexit White Paper' (UK Government 2017). Nonetheless, the White Paper also highlighted 'a legitimate interest in mutual cooperation arrangements that recognise the interconnectedness of markets' (p. 42) in finance. Although the outcome of the June 2017 General Election led to a change of tone regarding Brexit and improved relations with business, the government's official position remained unchanged. With reference to financial services, three qualifications should be made. First, the negotiations on finance were part of a broader set of negotiations, whereby it would have been politically difficult for the UK government to grant finance a special status. Second, there were divisions within the UK government, whereby the Chancellor of the Exchequer was more sympathetic than other parts of the government of the concerns of the financial industry (for example, *Bloomberg*, 11 October 2017). Third, the UK financial industry, albeit it was mostly against a hard Brexit, was not united on this issue. Different parts of the financial industry would be impacted by Brexit in different ways, and the parts most likely to be badly affected were those that mobilised the most against a hard Brexit. The UK-based financial services most potentially affected were wholesale—not retail—because wholesale business is international and cross-border in nature, and its services depended upon EU passporting agreements (see James and Quaglia 2017a).

British authorities and the UK financial sector faced a 'dilemma' in the Brexit negotiations. On the one hand, if the UK lost unrestricted access to the single financial market, UK-based financial entities and activities would need to relocate to the continent in order to continue to benefit from passporting across the EU (that applies to the full range of financial services). Moreover, the UK would no longer serve as the main point of entry into the EU for third country financial entities and products, which would therefore choose to place a range of operations in other EU member states to secure access to the passport. Finally, the UK would no longer be able to legally challenge the efforts of the ECB and a number of other member states to transfer euro clearing to the euro area.

On the other hand, if unrestricted access to the single financial market were retained, the UK would have to continue to comply with EU financial regulation. In the past, the UK financial sector frequently complained about excessively burdensome EU financial regulation. As this chapter has argued, in several financial policy areas, the UK yielded considerable influence in 'calibrating' (at times, toning down) EU financial rules. Hence, EU financial regulation is likely to be different in the future without the UK's 'market-making' approach—this will make EU rules less suitable for the financial industry based in the City. Moreover, euro area member states will tend to develop specific preferences on financial regulation and supervision through their cooperation in BU.

The EU also faced a Brexit dilemma (Howarth and Quaglia 2017). Any 'special deal' for the financial services sector in the UK would be politically unpalatable for the EU because it represents exactly the type of 'pick and choose' approach (or 'bespoke deal' in the rhetoric of UK government officials) which the EU has historically resisted. A bespoke deal would give the UK important benefits of EU membership, namely, unrestricted access to the single financial market, including passporting. However, whilst political unpalatable, the City of London was by far the main financial centre in Europe—the home of many continental banks, insurers, securities dealers, etc.—and so there were incentives to retain it in the single market.

Conclusion

The UK has been a key player in the post-crisis reforms of European economic and financial governance, albeit in different ways and with varying intensity. The (at times considerable) British influence was geared towards the attainment of preferences that were shaped by domestic politics and political economy, first and foremost the interests of the financial services industry and the City of London. The UK was mostly a foot-dragger (with important exceptions) on the 'market-shaping' post-crisis EU financial services regulation, unlike in the previous period when the UK had been a pace-setter in the completion of the single financial market, notably the so-called Lamfalussy directives on securities markets and Solvency II in insurance. The UK was a (constructive) fence-sitter on BU, unlike in the making of EMU, which the UK had tried to block, acting as a foot-dragger. Finally, the UK was a pace-setter on CMU in the same way it had been in the completion of the single financial market in the previous decades. Thus, the UK supported EU financial policy measures whenever they reflected the British 'market-making' approach (see Quaglia 2010a, b, 2015) and had economic benefits for the City of London. The main exception was the BRRD, which had a considerable British 'input' but no direct benefit for the financial industry. The UK opposed EU policy measures that were excessively market-shaping and were therefore very burdensome for the financial industry, especially the City. The main exception was the CRD IV, whereby the UK was in favour of stricter EU rules (see James 2015, 2016). The UK was a fence-sitter on issues that mainly concerned the euro area, albeit paying attention to the implications of those measures for non-euro area members (see Howarth and Quaglia 2016).

The result of the British referendum on continuing membership of the EU represented a turning point in the relationship between the UK and the EU. The economic and political effects of Brexit will be far-reaching for both. Although events are still unfolding, Brexit raises a set of important questions to address with reference to the financial policies discussed in this chapter: what will be the implications of Brexit for the UK and the EU? Since the UK opted-out of EMU, declined to join BU but was a full member of the Single Financial Market, the impact of Brexit will be felt principally on access to the single financial market and on issues related to financial regulation. Much will depend on the new relationship put in place between the UK and the EU, as negotiators try to solve the UK and EU27 'dilemmas' highlighted in the previous section.

Brexit will have a major impact on the British variety of capitalism, albeit the magnitude of change will depend on the new relationship that will be agreed between the EU and the UK. Specifically, the implications of Brexit for the UK finance-based liberal market capitalism will depend on: (a) the terms of reciprocal market access, but especially the terms of access for British financial entities and products to single market in finance (including passporting); and (b) the degree of financial regulatory alignment between the UK and the EU. In a nutshell, the greater the market access and the regulatory alignment, the lesser the impact of Brexit on the UK financial sector and on the key role that finance has on the UK liberal market economy. Vice versa, the more restrictive the terms of single market access and the greater the regulatory divergence between the two jurisdictions, the greater the negative impact of Brexit on the UK financial sector, and the greater the incentive for UK to forge closer financial relations with jurisdictions outside the EU.

Brexit will also have an impact on finance in the EU and potentially on the funding available to the real economy on the continent. Here again, the implications of Brexit will depend on the future relationship between the EU and the UK, and specifically on the terms of market access and the degree of financial regulatory alignment. In case of considerable market access and regulatory alignment, the UK would continue to be 'Europe's investment banker' (Carney 2017) and to serve as the main financial centre of (albeit not in) the EU. This situation would have some economic advantages for the EU, notably to maintain access to the UK's deep and liquid financial markets and its efficient market infrastructures. However, it would also have political disadvantages, as it would look like a bespoke deal favourable to the UK. Furthermore, it would represent an acceptance on the part of the EU that its primary financial centre would be outside the direct regulatory and supervisory reach of the EU authorities. Vice versa, in case of limited market access and regulatory divergence, the EU might end up with a competing international (offshore) financial centre on its doorstep. This could have negative implications for regulatory arbitrage, potentially leading to a regulatory clash, or at the very least, regulatory disputes, between the two jurisdictions. It would also be detrimental to the UK's role as 'Europe's investment banker'. Yet, it might enable the main financial centres based in the EU (first and foremost, Paris and Frankfurt) to thrive by luring business away from the UK.

REFERENCES

Allen, F., & Gale, D. (2000). *Comparing Financial Systems.* Cambridge, MA: MIT Press.

Armstrong, K., & Bulmer, S. (1998). *The Governance of the Single European Market.* Manchester: Manchester University Press.

Baker, A. (2010). Restraining Regulatory Capture? Anglo-America, Crisis Politics and Trajectories of Change in Global Financial Governance. *International Affairs, 86*(3), 647–663.

Bailer, S. (2010). What Factors Determine Bargaining Power and Success in EU Negotiations? *Journal of European Public Policy, 17*(5), 743–775.

Bailey, A. (2010, July 13). *Speech: The Financial Crisis Reform Agenda.* London: Bank of England.

Bank of England. (2010, December). *Financial Stability Report.* London.

Basel Committee on Banking Supervision (BCBS). (2014, December). *Regulatory Consistency Assessment Programme Assessment of Basel III Regulations European Union.* Basel.

Bloomberg Politics. (2017, October 11). *U.K. Accepts EU's Need to Share Clearing Oversight, Hammond Says.* https://www.bloomberg.com/news/articles/2017-10-11/u-k-accepts-eu-s-need-to-share-clearing-oversight-hammond-says.

Börzel, T. (2002). Member State Responses to Europeanization. *Journal of Common Market Studies, 40*(2), 193–214.

British Bankers Association (BBA). (2012, September 12). *BBA Statement on European Commission Banking Union Proposals.* https://www.bba.org.uk/news/press-releases. Accessed July 14, 2013.

Buckley, J., & Howarth, D. (2011). Regulating the So-Called "Vultures of Capitalism". *Journal of Common Market Studies, 49*(s1), 123–143.

Carney, M. (2017, April 7). *Speech: The High Road to a Responsible, Open Financial System.* Bank of England.

Darling, A. (2009, March 3). Letter to Miroslav Kalousek, Czech Finance Minister. [Letter] (Personal Communication).

Dawson, G. (2015, February 19). It's Time the City—And the UK—Show Support for a Capital Markets Union. *City AM.*

De Larosière, J., et al. (2009). *Report of the High-Level Group on Financial Supervision in the EU.* Brussels. Available at: http://ec.europa.eu/internal_market/finances/docs/de_larosiere_report_en.pdf.

Donnelly, S. (2014). Power Politics and the Undersupply of Financial Stability in Europe. *Review of International Political Economy, 21*(4), 980–1005.

Dyson, K. H. (2000). *The Politics of the Eurozone.* Oxford: Oxford University Press.

Dyson, K. H., & Featherstone, K. (1999). *The Road to Maastricht.* Oxford: Oxford University Press.

Dyson, K. H., & Sepos, A. (2010). *Which Europe? The Politics of Differentiated Integration.* Basingstoke: Palgrave Macmillan.

Egan, M. (2001). *Constructing a European Market: Standards, Regulation, and Governance.* Oxford: Oxford University Press.

European Commission. (2015a, February 18). *Green Paper: Building a Capital Markets Union.* Brussels. http://ec.europa.eu/finance/capital-markets-union/index_en.htm. Accessed February 8, 2016.

European Commission. (2015b, September 30). *Action Plan for CMU.* Brussels. Available at: http://ec.europa.eu/finance/capital-markets-union/index_en.htm. Accessed March 3, 2016.

Epstein, R. A., & Rhodes, M. (2016). The Political Dynamics Behind Europe's New Banking Union. *West European Politics, 39*(30), 415–437.

Five Presidents Report. (2015). *Completing Europe's Economic and Monetary Union.* Brussels: European Commission.

Gabor, D. (2016). A Step Too Far? The European Financial Transactions Tax on Shadow Banking. *Journal of European Public Policy, 23*(6), 925–945.

Gabor, D., & Vestergaard, J. (2015, April). *Capital Markets Union: The Systemic Issues Buried Deep in the Markets Infrastructure Plan* (FEPS Policy Brief).

George, S. (1990). *An Awkward Partner: Britain in the European Community.* Oxford: Oxford University Press.

Greenwood, J., & Roederer-Rynning, C. (2014). The "Europeanization" of the Basel Process: Financial Harmonisation Between Globalization and Parliamentarization. *Regulation and Governance, 9*(4), 325–338.

HM Government. (2017, February 2). *The United Kingdom's Exit from, and New Partnership with, the European Union* (White Paper, CM 9417). London: HM Stationery.

House of Lords. (2012, March 20). *Towards a Financial Transaction Tax?* London.

House of Lords. (2015, March 20). *Capital Markets Union: A Welcome Start.*

Hardie, I., & Howarth, D. (Eds.). (2013). *Market-Based Banking, Varieties of Financial Capitalism and the Financial Crisis.* Oxford: Oxford University Press.

Hennessy, A. (2014). Redesigning Financial Supervision in the European Union (2009–2013). *Journal of European Public Policy, 21*(2), 151–168.

Howarth, D., & Quaglia, L. (2015). The Political Economy of the Euroarea's Sovereign Debt Crisis. *Review of International Political Economy, 22*(3), 457–484.

Howarth, D., & Quaglia, L. (2016). *The Political Economy of Banking Union.* Oxford: Oxford University Press.

Howarth, D., & Quaglia, L. (2017). Brexit and the Single European Financial Market. *Journal of Common Market Studies Annual Review, 55*(1), 149–164.

Independent Commission on Banking. (2011a, September). *Final Report Recommendations.* London.

Independent Commission on Banking. (2011b, April). *Interim Report.* London.

Jabko, N. (2006). *Playing the Market: A Political Strategy for Uniting Europe, 1985–2005.* Ithaca, NY: Cornell University Press.

James, S. (2015). The UK in the Multilevel Process of Financial Market Regulation: Global Pace-setter or National Outlier? In R. Maynz (Ed.), *Multilevel Governance of Financial Market Reform* (pp. 121–137). Cologne: Campus Verlag.

James, S. (2016). The Domestic Politics of Financial Regulation: Informal Ratification Games and the EU Capital Requirement Negotiations. *New Political Economy, 21*(2), 187–203.

James, S., & Quaglia, L. (2017a). *Brexit and the Limits of Financial Power in the UK* (Working Paper). University of Oxford. https://www.geg.ox.ac.uk/brexit-and-limits-financial-power-uk.

James, S., & Quaglia, L. (2017b). Why Does the UK Have Inconsistent Preferences on Financial Regulation? The Case of Banking and Capital Markets. *Journal of Public Policy.* Available at: https://www.cambridge.org/core/journals/journal-of-public-policy/article/why-does-the-united-kingdom-uk-have-inconsistent-preferences-on-financial-regulation-the-case-of-banking-and-capital-markets/C1A7FB0138C2C8A87D3EB07C2BDBAA02/core-reader.

Jones, E., & Macartney, H. (2016). TTIP and the 'Finance Exception': Venue-Shopping and the Breakdown of Financial Regulatory Coordination. *Journal of Banking Regulation, 17,* 4–20.

Juncker, J.-C. (2014, July 15). *Political Guidelines for the Next Commission*. Brussels. Available at: http://www.eesc.europa.eu/resources/docs/jean-claude-juncker—political-guidelines.pdf. Accessed January 15, 2016.

London Economics. (2014). *The Effects of a Financial Transaction Tax on European Households' Savings*. London.

Mahoney, C. (2007). Networking vs. Allying: The Decision of Interest Groups to Join Coalitions in the US and the EU. *Journal of European Public Policy, 14*(3), 366–383.

Moravcsik, A. (1997). Taking Preferences Seriously: A Liberal Theory of International Politics. *International Organization, 51*(4), 513–553.

Moravcsik, A. (1998). *The Choice for Europe*. London: UCL Press.

Mügge, D. (2010). *Widen the Market, Narrow the Competition: Banker Interests and the Making of a European Capital Market*. Colchester: ECPR.

Pagliari, S. (2013). A Wall Around Europe? The European Regulatory Response to the Global Financial Crisis and the Turn in Transatlantic Relations. *Journal of European Integration, 35*(4), 391–408.

Pagliari, S., & Young, K. L. (2014). Leveraged Interests: Financial Industry Power and the Role of Private Sector Coalitions. *Review of International Political Economy, 21*(3), 575–610.

Posner, E., & Véron, N. (2010). The EU and Financial Regulation: Power Without Purpose? *Journal of European Public Policy, 17*(3), 400–415.

President of the European Council, the President of the Eurogroup, the President of the Commission and the President of the ECB. (2012). *Towards a Genuine Economic and Monetary Union*.

Quaglia, L. (2009). The 'British Plan' as a Pace-setter: The Europeanisation of Banking Rescue Plans in the EU? *Journal of Common Market Studies, 47*(5), 1059–1079.

Quaglia, L. (2010a). *Governing Financial Services in the European Union*. London: Routledge.

Quaglia, L. (2010b). Completing the Single Market in Financial services: The Politics of Competing Advocacy Coalitions. *Journal of European Public Policy, 17*(7), 1007–1022.

Quaglia, L. (2012). The "Old" and "New" Politics of Financial Services Regulation in the European Union. *New Political Economy, 17*(4), 515–535.

Quaglia, L. (2015). The Politics of 'Third Country Equivalence' in Post-crisis Financial Services Regulation in the European Union. *West European Politics, 38*(1), 167–184.

Quaglia, L., Howarth, D., & Liebe, M. (2016). The Political Economy of European Capital Markets Union. *Journal of Common Market Studies Annual Review, 54*(s1), 195–203.

Ringe, W. G. (2015, March). *Capital Markets Union for Europe—A Political Message to the UK* (Oxford Legal Studies Research Paper No. 26/2015).

Schäfer, D. (2016). A Banking Union of Ideas? The Impact of Ordoliberalism and the Vicious Circle on the EU Banking Union. *Journal of Common Market Studies, 54*(4), 961–980.

Schäuble, W., & Sapin, M. (2015). *Letter*. http://www.economie.gouv.fr/files/files/PDF/2015-07-06_letter-about_capital-markets-union_6-july-2015.pdf. Accessed September 10, 2015.

Schimmelfennig, F. (2016). A Differentiated Leap Forward: Spillover, Path-Dependency, and Graded Membership in European Banking Regulation. *West European Politics, 39*(30), 483–502.

Schimmelfennig, F., Leuffen, D., & Rittberger, D. (2015). The European Union as a System of Differentiated Integration: Interdependence, Politicization, and Differentiation. *Journal of European Public Policy, 22*(6), 764–782.

The CityUK. (2016a, August 15). *UK Financial and Related Professional Services: Meeting the Challenges and Delivering Opportunities*. Available at: https://www.thecityuk.com/research/uk-frps-challenges-and-opportunities/.

The CityUK. (2016b, September 7). *Brexit and the Industry*. Available at: https://www.thecityuk.com/research/brexit-and-the-industry/.

UK Government. (2015). *UK Response to the Commission Green Paper on Capital Markets Union: Building a Strong Capital Markets Union*. Available at: https://ec.europa.eu/eusurvey/files/634a485d-8dd9-41e6-af91-030013307436. Accessed December 12, 2015.

Wasserfallen, F. (2014). Political and Economic Integration in the EU: The Case of Failed Tax Harmonization. *Journal of Common Market Studies, 52*(2), 420–435.

Woll, C. (2013). Lobbying Under Pressure: The Effect of Salience on European Hedge Fund Regulation. *Journal of Common Market Studies, 51*(3), 555–572.

CHAPTER 6

Integration and Disintegration: Two-Level Games in the EU

Waltraud Schelkle

INTEGRATION AND DISINTEGRATION IN POST-CRISIS EUROPE

The prolonged crisis of the euro area has strengthened centrifugal forces in the EU. For the first time in the union's history, a member state has decided to leave the EU, following an in-out referendum. EU-sceptic parties have become a vocal presence and have taken about a third of all seats in the European Parliament, although their ideological differences and/or nationalistic stance makes them an ineffective opposition to further integration. Governments in Greece and Hungary have used referenda to challenge collective decisions of the EU, challenging the norm that the EU is a union of representative democracies. Inside the Eurozone area, a perception has taken hold, supported by academic research, that Southern and Northern European political economies cannot coexist using the same currency. Johnston and Regan (2016: 333) argue that even permanent fiscal transfers from the North to the South would not change this verdict. The Balkanisation of financial markets, in

W. Schelkle (✉)
European Institute, London School of Economics, London, UK
e-mail: w.schelkle@lse.ac.uk

© The Author(s) 2019
C. Hay and D. Bailey (eds.), *Diverging Capitalisms,*
Building a Sustainable Political Economy: SPERI Research & Policy,
https://doi.org/10.1007/978-3-030-03415-3_6

particular for government bonds, has become a manifest legacy of the crisis that undermines the traction of monetary policy in stimulating the economy (ECB 2015).

But this is not the whole story. At the same time, we have witnessed a series of sovereign bailouts in the EU that make all IMF bailouts pale in comparison, among them the biggest in history for Greece. The emergency funds, above all the permanent European Stability Mechanism (ESM) but also the European Financial Stabilisation Mechanism (ESFM) operated by the Commission, have generated a lending capacity of the EU that surpasses that of the IMF. The banking union, created within a few years, made the ECB then the world's biggest financial supervisor and prudential authority in terms of bank assets under its purview.

Hence, the story is one of astonishingly rapid and far-reaching steps of institutional integration, at the same time as centrifugal political-economic forces are on the rise. Still, most observers either stress the centrifugal tendencies and the incompleteness of the steps towards integration that were taken (De Grauwe 2013; Stiglitz 2016), or they revive the Whig history of European integration that, according to one of its founding fathers, Jean Monnet, will be forged in crises, so every crisis is good news of further progress.[1]

This chapter suggests that integration and disintegration tend to be the outcome of the same process. Integration is always subject to limits and boundaries; disintegration is never complete but leaves elements of integration in place. To study this simultaneity, I choose the most extreme case of a country apparently promoting disintegration and seeking deliberate outsider status, the UK, on the one hand, and the country with an unwanted leadership role in the EU, Germany, on the other.

Our theories of integration were not formulated to analyse processes of disintegration. The main post-war theory of European integration, supranationalism, predicts ratchet effects that make every step of integration to some degree irreversible. In its *neo*-functionalist guise, supranationalism allows for more contestation and agency in bringing ever closer union about but this does not change the fundamental claim that European integration is a one-way street (Rosamund 2000: 65, 72).

Intergovernmentalism can provide a more plausible account of the reverse of ever closer union: it can explain why certain steps towards

---

[1] For references and a critique of this Whig history, see Parsons and Matthijs (2015).

integration may come to a halt or even go backwards, if they do not suit a sufficiently large or influential number of member states. But its liberal version, formulated by Moravcsik (1998), has opened the black box of member state interests and would predict that the main sources of such a backlash should be particular economic interests (Rosamund 2000: 138–139). This is at odds with the overwhelming impression that the opposition to further integration has electoral, ideological and outright populist origins.

The new intergovernmentalism responded to precisely this state of affairs (Bickerton et al. 2015a, b). Contributors to this literature observe a fundamental 'integration paradox: Member States pursue more integration but stubbornly resist further supranationalism' (Bickerton et al. 2015a: 705). Their argument expresses a kind of disappointed supranationalism because they demonstrate how dysfunctional this paradoxical integration is. For instance, the emergence of a Fiscal Compact outside the Treaty framework is taken as evidence for politically counter-productive intergovernmentalism, because it circumvents the Commission as guardian of the Treaty and conforms only with the priorities of more powerful member states (read: Germany).

This is a timely update of intergovernmentalism and can make sense of manifestations of differentiated integration instead of merely elaborating various descriptive metaphors (variable geometry, concentric circles, integration à la carte, etc.). It synthesises an impressive number of insights about the malaise of capitalist democracies in Europe. But like all integration theories, the new intergovernmentalism treats these manifestations of power asymmetry and collective action failure as an idiosyncratic European problem.[2] Yet, the populist backlash against integration and the difficulties of interstate cooperation can be seen elsewhere. The antagonistic politics of the United States is a prime example: none of the mainstream Presidential candidates has been supported by grass-root movements and the eventual Republican nominee excelled in insults against immigrants and Mexico, a NAFTA member state. The long-awaited bilateral trade agreement between the EU and the United States, the Transatlantic Trade and Investment Partnership (TTIP), has stalled, in line with previous attempts at reviving multilateral trade negotiations. An even more important example is the utter failure of leading nations to cooperate on the restoration of

---

[2] Although, to be fair, neo-functionalism has tried to overcome this theorising of one case early on (Rosamund 2000: 68–72).

some kind of order in failed states in the Middle East and Africa, notwith-standing their shared interest in containing the associated refugee flows.

This chapter analyses recent EU institution-building amidst signs of re-nationalisation and EU-scepticism by applying the concept of two-level games, both in the classic instrumental version of Putnam (1988) and in a more recent normative version developed by Bellamy and Weale (2015). Understanding the new economic governance of the EU, in particular fiscal governance, as the result of two-level games can grasp both the specific collective action problems of an incomplete and diverse union as well as the general problems of interstate cooperation. It also allows us to see the dilemma of EU-ins and euro area-outs more sharply: choosing to be in or out is a way of dealing with the inherent tensions between honouring international commitments and responding to demands of domestic constituencies. The two-level game concept high-lights not only this political dilemma but also the strategic opportunities open to policymakers.

The next section spells out the conceptual basis of the chapter in more detail. It then proceeds to analyse the new economic governance of the EU, which saw a shift from the sole emphasis on fiscal surveil-lance to emergency lending and financial supervision; the latter two have an important fiscal component. The chapter tries to make sense of the impression that the EU has become politically extremely divided, while relentless institution-building nonetheless progresses. The outs of the euro area, in particular the UK, are taken as a suitable lens to capture the tensions underlying this contradictory impression. The conclusions summarise.

INSTRUMENTAL AND NORMATIVE TWO-LEVEL GAMES

The original concept of two-level games is based on an instrumental understanding of international agreements between nationally account-able administrations (Putnam 1988). It starts from the simple fact that all international agreements between democracies have to be ratified at home. From this flows a powerful hypothesis about the distribution of gains and losses whenever international cooperation is successful (Putnam 1988: 452–453): governments that face strong domestic oppo-sition to an international agreement have a strong position in getting their way when negotiating this agreement with other governments. The other parties know that the international agreement will not be ratified in this member state unless they make considerable concessions. This is a variant of the paradox of weakness (Schelling 1960). The keenest supporters of an international agreement, with large win-sets, typically get a raw deal while those not particularly interested in cooperation (small win-sets) will reap the gains.

In contrast to integration theories, the framing of integration as a series of two-level games is not biased towards assuming that international agreements and cooperation will always succeed. Even when there is room for agreement (overlapping win-sets), the paradox of weakness gives each party an incentive to exaggerate domestic constraints to get an upper hand at the international level. This strategic behaviour can easily lead to collective action failure if too many participants pretend that their hands are tied. Negotiations break down because everybody bluffed, foregoing the benefits from finding a solution.

Anticipating this strategic behaviour, those with a strong interest in an agreement may think of devices that deter it. For instance, they may allow for degrees of membership or ratification by a qualified majority, calling the bluff of those who merely pretend to be weak. This is a central element in explaining the byzantine institution-building that has been going on in the EU regardless of growing resistance, in particular the abandonment of the Community method noted by the new intergovernmentalism in favour of 'de novo institutions' (Bickerton et al. 2015a: 705).

The game can also be played the other way round or 'vice versa' (Putnam 1988: 460). Administrations involved in international negotiations may collude with other governments to achieve a reform that they could not achieve at home without the international hands-tying. This is using the international agreement as a lever to overcome the domestic constraint. Obviously, this works only if opposing domestic interests can be disciplined by the prospect of not being party to the international agreement. Sectoral interests, such as a financial industry interested in cross-border business, can be more easily disciplined in this way than the sceptical electorate at large.

The instrumental version of two-level games grasps the rise in Euroscepticism at the member state level only as a constraint on negotiating executives. Bellamy and Weale (2015) have recently presented a normative variant of the two-level game logic, so as to bring the political crisis of the EU into much sharper focus. Their starting point is the irreducible diversity of sovereign peoples (*demoi*) represented in international negotiations. This diversity must be respected and reflected in any legitimate agreement. Instead of analysing the strategic interaction and instrumentalisation of each level for the negotiator's own purposes, they stress the political constraint that the two levels impose: 'when governments make commitments to one another about their future behaviour, they simultaneously need to be responsible and accountable to their domestic populations in order to retain their political legitimacy' (Bellamy and Weale 2015: 259). This normative logic of two-level games resonates with Mair (2009) who saw an increasing tension between responsible and responsive government. The 'republican intergovernmentalism' of Bellamy and Weale (2015) explores what is required to observe this dual duty and proposes a stronger role for national parliaments in EU policymaking. In terms of the instrumental two-level game, this forecloses the use of the international level to achieve domestic reform leverage.

The positions of Germany and the UK in the recent reforms of economic governance will be used in the following to illustrate—and hopefully illuminate—the usefulness of the two-level game framework in both versions. It is incumbent upon any German government to ensure European integration, which is a tenet of its post-war constitution. The win-set in this respect is large for Germany, which is the set of all international agreements that stand a good chance of being ratified domestically (Putnam 1988: 437). This has not prevented German governments from exploiting their veto-player position in monetary integration and insisting on a policy framework which both in substance (to ensure above all price stability) and in form (rule-based) suits German interests. The imperative of this stance is to preserve its strong export position, and avoid possible fiscal exposure through instability.

UK governments have always had an ostentatiously utilitarian view of European integration, and, until recently, they played the two-level game competently in the original sense of Putnam (Hancké 2016). The UK's small win-set tended to give its diplomats the upper hand in negotiations, and both the Blair and the Cameron administrations underscored that with the threat of referenda. But the peculiar situation that the UK is the financial centre of a monetary union to which it does not belong also made its win-set large in specific reforms to solve the euro area crisis (Schelkle 2016). It agreed to a banking union that split the Single Market, indicating that it had a large win-set, thanks to a political system in which the government has clear majorities and the opposition

Table 6.1 Stylised two-level game representations of German and UK positions

	Germany	*United Kingdom*
Closer European integration	Big win-set due to normative obligation to support European integration	Small win-set due to Eurosceptic public opinion made politically binding with announced referendum
Euro area governance reforms	Small win-set whenever solutions lead to fiscal exposure	Big win-set due to unique position of being the euro area's financial centre

exercises only weak control. The executive is more constrained by internal party conflict that did not materialise on this occasion.

The two countries therefore had diametrically opposed positions in the two-level game of European integration in general, and reforms of euro area economic governance in particular (Table 6.1).

For Germany, this constellation raised the question of whether it would manage to give up the fiscal taboo when the euro area was confronted with an existential crisis that arguably asked for some fiscal integration. For the UK, the puzzle is why the Cameron government could not exploit its small win-set to its own advantage when it had done so successfully for over 40 years.

THE INS AND OUTS OF TWO-LEVEL GAMES

This section sketches three significant innovations that characterise the new economic governance of the EU: the Fiscal Compact, the ESM, and the banking union.[3] A remarkable feature of all three is how fiscal governance, in particular, is quietly shifting while many observers still accuse the EU of being stuck with the same old Stability and Growth Pact. The analysis focuses on whether we can understand these innovations as the outcome of a two-level game with participants who had different preferences and different stakes in achieving collective EU action. For each innovation, the analysis zooms in on Germany, because this indispensable insider was involved in initiating but also limiting integration, and on the UK as the critical case of an explicit outsider that still had a part in these integration efforts.

---

[3] For details on the latter see Lucia Quaglia's chapter.

THE FISCAL COMPACT

The Fiscal Compact was initiated by French President Sarkozy and German Chancellor Merkel in a letter to Herman van Rompuy in August 2011. The timing of this Compact as well as its motivation is rather obscure. The letter was sent one and a half years after the Council President had been asked to convene a task force that would come up with fundamental reforms to economic governance.[4] The Compact is the fiscal section of a contract between signatory states, an intergovernmental 'Treaty on Stability, Coordination and Governance in the Economic and Monetary Union'. All EU member states could sign up although it was initially meant to include countries in the euro area only. It came into force when at least twelve member states had signed which was the case by 1 January 2013. In the meantime, all EU members except the UK and Croatia have signed it. The Czech government decided in March 2014 to join.

The timing is odd because the Commission had already presented legislative proposals for the reform of fiscal surveillance almost a year earlier, in September 2010 (Beach 2013: 114). The five Directives and one Regulation, known as the 'Six Pack', contain a 'muscular' package of reforms that was in crucial respects plagiarised by the Fiscal Compact. The Six-Pack contains an extension of the Excessive Deficit Procedure to debt above 60% and, in case of violation, foresees an obligation to bring this debt down by a prescribed amount (a twentieth of the difference between the actual debt ratio and a 60% debt-to-GDP ratio). A qualified majority is now required to reject (rather than endorse) a Commission proposal for opening an Excessive Deficit (and Debt) Procedure. This 'reverse' QMV (qualified majority voting) was meant to make for quasi-automatic sanctions, as Christian-Democratic German finance ministers had demanded for some time. Member states were also obliged to introduce independent Fiscal Councils, which would assess the budgetary plans of the government.

Only two features distinguished the original Compact from provisions in the Six-Pack: the Compact requested that an automatic debt brake should be written into each signatory's constitution. And it envisaged giving

---

[4]It was published as the Four Presidents report (Van Rompuy et al. 2012) and quickly shelved by the European Council; its successor, the Five Presidents report (Juncker et al. 2015), fared no better.

the Court of Justice (CJEU) powers to sanction a non-compliant state, which would align sanctions in fiscal surveillance with the normal legal infringement procedures of the Court (Dehousse 2012: 1), thus replacing this role of the Council of Economic and Finance ministers (Ecofin). However, both stipulations were watered down considerably (Burret and Schnellenbach 2013: 9): constitutional implementation became an equivalent hard law implementation (Article 3) and the powers of the Court were confined to overseeing the balanced budget rule (Article 8). These two amendments spared willing signatories the trouble of finding supermajorities for constitutional changes and/or holding referenda because of the fundamental Treaty changes that would otherwise have been necessary.

The Treaty asked the Commission to provide a Communication and a report about the Compact's transposition in signatory states. This request was made in early 2014 but the report was not forthcoming until 22 February 2017, so deficiencies that the Commission had found (EPSR 2016: 8) earlier did not have to be corrected. The Communication is lukewarm and notes a lot of 'heterogeneity' in the transposition of the new rules; it also announced incorporation into EU law by early 2018 as the Compact itself foresaw (European Commission 2017: 4).

It is arguable that the Compact has been in abeyance ever since it was ratified. Independent evaluations about its implementation come to rather mixed conclusions (Burret and Schnellenbach 2013; EPRS 2016): member states use its flexibility to the maximum and often follow more the letter than the spirit of the Compact. The strictest implementation can be observed in Spain and Portugal while Germany and the Netherlands have opted for weaker rules, for instance as regards correction mechanisms (Burret and Schnellenbach 2013: 9–10). Last but not least, despite all the talk about tougher rules, the sanctions envisaged by the Compact have not been applied as of December 2017. The thresholds for admissible deficit and debt ratios have been exceeded by several member states, among them Spain, Portugal and the Netherlands (EPRS 2016: 9–10). The Compact shares this fate with the Six-Pack as far as sanctions are concerned: even the German finance minister Schäuble shied away from endorsing them when they jeopardised a cooperative administration belonging to his own party family in Spain (Eder 2016).

One might thus conclude that the Fiscal Compact was manifestly redundant and, for better or worse, has not achieved its goal of making the new economic governance more disciplinarian. It was also not very helpful in easing negotiations with the UK ahead of the Brexit referendum (Beach 2013: 118). In preparation for the summit in December 2011, the French and German governments reiterated their commitment to the proposal for a Compact and called for amendments of the TFEU. Prime Minister Cameron expressed willingness to go along with Treaty changes but combined this with a list of demands for concessions, especially regarding financial regulation.[5] German politicians, including Chancellor Merkel, rejected any such *quid pro quo*; a member of her CDU called it 'a massive attempt at blackmail' (quoted in Beach 2013: 118). When Cameron presented his wish list at the Council, at 2 a.m. in the morning, Council President van Rompuy cut short any discussion and closed the proceedings. In the end, only the Czech Government joined David Cameron in not signing the Fiscal Compact. President Sarkozy blamed the British Prime Minister for the fact that the Compact had to remain an intergovernmental treaty outside the EU framework (BBC 2011).

The mystery of Cameron's blunder can be dispelled with the help of the concept of a two-level game. At a time when the euro area crisis was still escalating, Cameron's negotiation tactics were seen as shamelessly exploiting the fact that the rest of the union was desperate to get a deal on the Fiscal Compact. Support for the Fiscal Compact by other member states was not for reasons of substance; they recognised the constraints faced by Germany. Angela Merkel was involved in a precarious two-level game of her own. Other member states urged the German Chancellor to agree to bring forward the implementation of the permanent ESM, scheduled for 2013, to calm down panicking markets in Italian and Spanish government bonds (Beach 2013: 126). Domestic opposition made it imperative for Merkel to have some assurances that member states would change their ways and exercise preventive fiscal discipline. This domestic constraint allowed her to dictate the terms of the Fiscal Compact, making her domestic weakness international strength.

A German Chancellor could not, however, let the euro area implode, especially after Italy had got Mario Monti as a prudent technocratic leader. With respect to this bigger game, Merkel was vulnerable to getting a raw deal. Other governments seem to have understood the

---

[5]The key word for these demands was 'flexibility', meaning that Cameron wanted the freedom to both slap higher (sic) capital requirements on UK-resident banks and to exempt banks from tighter bonus rules of the EU (see below on the banking union).

Chancellor's predicament, even though most had as little stake in the Compact as the British. Cameron's blunt strategy jeopardised the entire plot. He treated the Fiscal Compact as a bargaining chip when Merkel wanted it to be seen as the sea change that would make the required massive support for Italy and Spain acceptable. It was particularly sensitive that Cameron pretended to need special treatment for the UK financial sector while the euro area went through another episode of financial market panic. Cameron's demand was also far from the truth—he had not consulted the City on this, representatives of which were actually quite taken aback by his tactics (Schelkle and Lokdam 2015: 15). Cameron's bluff was called by van Rompuy's short shrift. The UK's leader had not recognised the bigger game, presumably because Cameron was notoriously disinterested in policy detail. He and his administration assessed the payoffs incorrectly: the other member states did not need UK agreement for the Fiscal Compact to fulfil its function. Or put the other way round: they would only have to respond to the UK's other small win-set if it was essential to have the UK on board.

From the UK's point of view, its failure in the two-level game meant the beginning of the end of British EU membership.[6] Cameron had to return empty-handed which was grist to the mill of Eurosceptics. In the EU, his ill-judged tactics had destroyed trust in his ability and willingness to navigate the difficult terrain of honouring international commitments and representing domestic constituencies. From the German point of view, the double two-level game it was involved in was a success. The tightened rules could be used to soften domestic opposition against more taboo breaks to come (see next two sections).

For the EU, we can see how a step towards closer integration had disintegration in its wake: the attempt at closer fiscal coordination created an institution outside the EU's treaty framework and exposed the alienation of one member state from its partners. Ironically, the Compact outside the Treaties was arguably more in line with the normative logic of the two-level game than if all had gone according to the Franco-German plan. The Fiscal Compact is not part of the legal constitution of the EU, so the Commission does not have to cooperate in the implementation

---

[6]Thompson (2017) argues that, in a longer time horizon, the beginning of the end for British membership came with the creation of the euro. This conclusion does not necessarily contradict my analysis although the two-level game framework has inherently more space for contingencies than her structural analysis.

of it; it promptly dragged its feet and did not publish its implementation report in a timely fashion. The competence of the CJEU is equally ambiguous with respect to an institution outside the Treaty and it is doubtful that fiscal disciplinarians will want to test the robustness of its role in the Compact. This has helped to let governments off the hook exactly when implementing the fiscal rules would be counterproductive economically. In this, the implementation of the Fiscal Compact arguably conforms the normative logic of two-level games, even though Bellamy and Weale (2015: 262, 271) seem to have a different empirical interpretation: they take the legal phrasing for political reality. The evidence suggests that the Fiscal Compact became a dead letter as soon as it had fulfilled its role in the instrumental and normative two-level game that the Franco-German initiative had set up. This interpretation can also explain why the French President went along with it.

THE EUROPEAN STABILITY MECHANISM

The ESM was indeed brought forward by a few months (September 2012), thanks to the introduction of the Fiscal Compact. Access to its funding was made conditional on signing the Fiscal Compact. This condition is obviously meant to be a preventive mechanism against moral hazard: countries must be deterred from behaving recklessly in fiscal terms, knowing that there is an emergency fund that can bail them out when investors turn away. The problem with this explanation is that the intrusive and harsh conditionality imposed on distressed countries before this stipulation was added should have been sufficient deterrent, if deterrents work at all.[7]

The two-level game framework provides a more convincing answer than the pervasive moral hazard explanation. In order to be able to bail out Greece in May 2010, governments had to circumvent the 'no bailout' clause that they had so publicly proclaimed to be the bulwark against fiscal excess. This was particularly difficult because Greece was

[7]One can legitimately doubt that deterrence in fiscal surveillance works, not because incentives for moral hazard are so powerful, but because a fiscally unsustainable situation may not be due to reckless behaviour of governments. When a private sector boom ends, no democratically elected government can let households, firms and banks simply go bust; it will have to come to their rescue, irrespective of who is to blame (Rodrik and Zeckhauser 1988).

the disciplinarians' showcase of fiscally unsustainable government policy. The first temporary emergency fund was based on voluntary bilateral guarantees of bond issues that would finance the Greek loan, so as to be compatible with Article 125(1) TFEU: 'The Union [...] [or a] Member State shall not be liable for or assume the commitments of central governments, regional, local or other public authorities, other bodies governed by public law, or public undertakings of another Member State, without prejudice to mutual financial guarantees for the joint execution of a specific project'. This bailout clause still had its uses, even though it had to be bent. It allowed guarantor countries to exploit the paradox of weakness in conditional lending.

This weakness (small win-sets) was not self-evident. The guarantors had enormous interest in avoiding another Lehman moment in general and in the rescue of domestic banks exposed to Greece in particular. At the end of 2009, when the Greek budget data began to unsettle markets and officials, banks in the euro area held claims to the tune of around €1100bn, that is 62% of all foreign bank claims on Greece, Ireland, Portugal and Spain. This figure related to claims consolidated on an ultimate risk basis; in other words, if those countries defaulted, losses would have to be borne by these euro area banks. French and German banks were particularly exposed, holding more than half of the combined exposure (€345bn and €325bn, respectively).[8] Thus, it was not so much Greece as financial panic that forced a bailout. The systemic crisis made everybody's win-set large. But the guarantors could claim that having to break a very public political commitment that exercises national voters made them domestically constrained. They could thus impose one-sided and harsh adjustment on Greece, in return for unprecedented bailouts that were simultaneously bailouts for the guarantors' banks.[9]

The voluntary nature of strictly bilateral guarantees meant, however, that small member states could refuse to participate. This was the choice

---

[8] There was also the real threat of a domino effect among vulnerable economies: for instance Spanish banks were the largest creditors of Portugal (€77bn). Data is from BIS (2010: 18–19), US $ amounts converted at a historical (interbank) exchange rate of 0.7 $/€.

[9] It stands to reason whether the guarantors could have asked banks to share more in the pain, given that domestic opinion was favourably disposed towards seeing bankers 'bashed'. While even the Obama administration urged the Council of heads of state to bail out Greece (Barber 2010), an orderly write-down of Greek debt, as the IMF recommended, could have bailed-in banks earlier (Mabbett and Schelkle 2015: 524–528).

of Slovakia. Its right-of-centre government pointed out that it could not ask domestic voters for fiscal restraint while helping to rescue a profligate richer member state like Greece (*Economist* 2010). The bigger guarantor countries thus felt acutely that their bigger win-sets made them bear the brunt of the responsibilities. They had to ensure that a permanent solution would make them less vulnerable. This was soon in the offing: the ESM is based on callable capital to the tune of €80bn, to which member states must commit when they become a member of the emergency fund. While the guarantees are still bilateral, members cannot simply refuse to pledge them, so if the guarantee of the bond issue becomes necessary (because the borrowing country cannot pay back), the capital is called from member states according to a key that is based on the share in the paid-in capital of the ECB.

The ESM provides a stark example for the simultaneity of disintegration and integration. Its conditional lending is politically extremely divisive (disintegrating) while the fund also represents a significant step towards integration and solidarity at the same time. This new fiscal capacity has been used in historically unprecedented amounts of actual sovereign lending. This becomes clear if we compare EU lending to IMF credit outstanding. At its peak, IMF lending amounted to €112bn, at the end of December 2012.[10] The Spanish bank restructuring programme alone, which proceeded without the involvement of the IMF, had an envelope of €100bn, of which €41bn was used. The Greek rescue was the biggest in the history of sovereign lending, amounting to €289.6bn (the disbursed credit of the first two programmes plus committed sum of the third programme). In return, the guarantor countries used their leverage to reign deeply into the policies of a distressed country. Fiscal governance thus exercised is effective and has led to a turnaround of budget balances at the most difficult of economic times. But it raises serious concerns about the legitimacy of such outside interventions in sovereign democracies.

One might expect the UK to be a complete outsider to this evolution of emergency funding, officially so when Cameron did not sign the Fiscal Compact. But HM Government did take part in the Irish bailout programme. Banks headquartered in the UK were the largest creditors of Ireland (€160bn) on an ultimate risk basis and held large claims on Spain

[10] Source: IMF data on total credit outstanding and on historical SDR rates, accessed October 15, 2016.

(€98bn) (BIS 2010: 18–19). According to a Treasury insider at the time, the department was very happy to pay a 'small insurance premium' for its banks by contributing €3.8bn to the Irish bailout programme of €85bn.[11] This was an admission that every bailout of euro area members is also a bailout of UK's financial system, a gesture of goodwill that came with a conveniently low price tag.

The two-level game has thus worked well for the UK in the case of emergency funding. There was never any discussion that the voluntary contribution to the Irish bailout programme could be formalised in the set-up of the ESM and made a regular feature if the UK had a large stake in a rescue. This is less absurd than such a request would surely have been portrayed by British Eurosceptics: the City of London is the euro area's financial centre and has fought hard to remain so. It thus has a vital self-interest in its preservation (and we will see below that the Chancellor at the time admitted this). But its hands were tied so tightly by domestic hostility to the euro experiment that it could not even enter the game. This is in line with playing a normative two-level game: the UK could not have entered an international commitment in good faith because it would have gone so much against the mainstream voter sentiment. This was also instrumentally what worked for the apparent outsider in the sense that its financial system got the insurance: the 'voluntary nature' of the ex-post insurance gave the UK the upper hand, as the guarantors had to bail out Ireland anyhow. Outsider status inside the EU was actually advantageous and made Chancellor Osborne an ardent defender of continued membership, in line with the utilitarian tradition of Britain's attitude towards the EU.

THE BANKING UNION

In the context of this chapter, the banking union is remarkable for the attempt to resist further fiscal integration when this clearly diminishes its benefits. This resistance defies the most immediate goal of the banking union, namely to break the negative feedback loop between weak bank balance sheets and weak fiscal positions, transmitted through banks' holdings of government bonds. The diabolic loop jeopardises the neat

---

[11] The Commission fund EFSM contributed €22.5bn, the IMF €22.5bn; the predecessor to the ESM, the EFSF €17.7bn; the Irish Treasury and Pension Fund €17.5bn; UK €3.8bn, Sweden €0.6bn, Denmark €0.4bn.

separation of a single monetary policy from national fiscal policies that so many elements of the euro area's economic governance try to ensure.

For the same reason, namely jeopardising the separation of monetary and fiscal policy, financial supervision was a known problem area of economic governance before the crisis. Member state authorities were responsible for the prudential supervision of banks, for resolution of insolvent banks and for deposit insurance schemes. They conducted these tasks in accordance with EU rules and regulations, but without any shared fiscal resources. Each of these responsibilities may require fiscal backing. In a systemic crisis, accumulated resolution and deposit insurance funds, typically financed by industry levies, may be too small to deal with the fallout and governments have to make up the balance, at least in the first instance. When supervisors order a bank to close, savers may have to be compensated for their losses—in fact, protection of small depositors is typically the main reason why governments across the party-political spectrum come so readily to the rescue of banks (Brunnermeier et al. 2009: 68).

But keeping supervision, resolution and deposit insurance as national responsibilities contributed directly to the fragmentation of banking during the crisis as well as to the negative feedback loop between banks and sovereigns (ECB 2015: 88–90). This fragmentation can be seen in the differentiation of interest rates on new loans to non-financial firms in 'peripheral countries'[12] compared to non-distressed EA members, as well as shrinking credit to the distressed economies since 2008 (ECB 2015: Charts S32 and S34). Banks posted much less cross-border collateral in liquidity operations with the ECB after the crisis, again a tendency driven by distressed countries (ECB 2015: 127). The home bias in banks' holdings of government bonds had fallen before the financial crisis, but, by 2015, it had returned to the levels of the early 2000s (ECB 2015: 89).

The June 2012 European Council decided to introduce a banking union, in the context of dangerously rising risk premia on Italian and Spanish bonds. In a backroom deal, the heads of the four biggest euro area member states also gave ECB President Draghi the green light for his 'Do whatever it takes' speech (Draghi 2012) before he proposed this to the ECB Governing Board, notably his internal opponent

---

[12] The ECB (2015: 88) includes in this category the five programme countries, Italy and Slovenia.

Bundesbank President Weidmann. Draghi's speech at an investment bankers' forum in London announced Outright Monetary Transactions (OMT): the promise to buy government bonds in secondary markets in unlimited amounts, provided the bonds were issued by a government with an ESM programme; the ECB would not claim senior status among creditors. This speech marked a watershed that turned a virulent into a latent crisis. It supposedly shows the ECB at the height of its power, having silenced Bundesbank opposition by going directly to the top, i.e. Chancellor Merkel.

This coincidence—of an agreement on the banking union with the announcement that the ECB could act, if necessary, as an indirect Lender-of-Last-Resort to sovereigns—was enough to calm down markets. These were undoubtedly two significant steps of integration and the setting up of the Single Supervisory Mechanism as the world's largest financial supervisor and regulator within two years is an extraordinary achievement. But the sudden stop of financial panic also allowed Germany to backtrack on promises to agree to a deposit insurance guarantee and some fiscal backstop at the height of the crisis. The 'Do whatever it takes' speech worked too well. Inadvertently and unintentionally, ECB President Draghi reduced the win-set of the German Government, leading it to block all immediate moves to a European Deposit Insurance Scheme (FAZ 2015). Reassuring steps towards more integration helped to sustain disintegration in fiscal terms.

Somewhat surprisingly, the British government did not stop the move towards banking union. In the most basic sense, it encouraged the banking union, hence Quaglia's verdict of 'constructive fence-sitting'. The UK wanted to see the troubled currency union stabilised and accepted 'the remorseless logic' towards closer integration, as finance minister Osborne put it (Giles and Parker 2011). Contrary to earlier German wishes, the ECB was put at the helm of the SSM and created a two-tier Single Market. While open to all EU members, nine non-euro countries stayed out of the SSM, including its financial centre, the UK. Supervision of its banking system by a supranational authority was unacceptable even though the UK had just abolished its own pre-crisis supervisor. More astonishingly still, the UK government asked for remarkably little in return for the two-tier Single Market in financial services that the banking union implied (Schelkle and Lokdam 2015: 3–4). The only concession it requested concerned the voting rules for decisions by the European Banking Authority (Quaglia, Chap. 5). The escalation of the euro area crisis made even a hard-nosed British government concede, as it feared for its own stability. There were apparently no domestic constraints, from organised banking interests, on this accommodating stance (Quaglia, Chap. 5).

But the permanent split also deprived the UK government of a lever vis-à-vis its own financial system. Banks are domestically unpopular and able to create huge costs for the government but are too important for the UK economy, as a major source of employment, income and tax revenue, to be abandoned. Sharon Bowles, the influential chair of the European Parliament's economic and financial committee until 2014, said at an LSE hearing that Cameron's demand for 'flexibility' from the EU meant protection of the taxpayers from the City, not of the City from Europe; evidence for this is that the UK government lobbied hard to be allowed to impose higher capital requirements than the EU Directive foresaw (Schelkle 2016: 160). Losing the protection of the EU creates a problem for the new government in regulating the City. Against this background, it is noticeable how the new Prime minister, Theresa May, signalled early on to the City that she will not fight its corner in the Brexit negotiations. Her pledges to care more about 'ordinary, working-class families' than the 'wealthy' is an act of public hands-tying, telling the financial service industry that the constraint from 'Brussels' had been replaced by the constraint that popular opinion represents to her government. Her government tried to sideline Parliament as both Houses have too many pro-integrationist members which would get in the way of a shift to compassionate nationalist Conservatism.[13]

Her re-positioning was a transparent attempt to replace the two-level game when it can no longer be played in reverse by using restrictive 'Brussels' to rein in domestic opposition. For the normative two-level game, this contains the important qualification that supranational agreements are not always in a normative tension with domestic democracy. In the presence of unduly powerful special interests at home, supranational commitments may strengthen democracy by tying the hands of the executive. No member state has a fully functioning representative democracy, immune from special interests, as the theory so far seems to assume.

---

[13]This strategy floundered when Theresa May lost her majority in the House of Parliament after the June 2017 elections.

CONCLUDING REMARKS

This chapter started out with a criticism of the existing integration literature, especially the neo-functionalist supranational strand. It cannot coherently explain processes of integration and disintegration. Realist intergovernmentalism does better and it is no wonder that it was inter-governmentalism—both new and Republican, as advanced by Bickerton et al. (2015a, b) and Bellamy and Weale (2015), respectively—that has grasped the centrifugal tendencies within a theory of European integration. This chapter takes cues from this recent literature but focuses on the notion of two-level games that revolve around the interaction of supra-/international level and the domestic level of interstate cooperation. It provides the analytics that makes us see the twists and turns of recent institution-building, in particular the strategies of the indispensable insider, Germany, and the deliberate outsider, the UK.

Another conceptual advantage of the two-level game is arguably that it does not predispose the analysis towards finding integration. New intergovernmentalists tend to be dismayed when integration does not occur, ignoring all we know about the likelihood of collective action failure. By contrast, two-level game analysis alerts us to the astonishing amount of cooperation and institution-building that has taken place over recent years, under the most difficult of circumstances (Moravcsik 2012). This is easily forgotten given the limitations and deficiencies of each reform of economic governance recently agreed upon.

The three case studies—Fiscal Compact, ESM and banking union—were chosen because they are significant innovations in economic governance. They illustrate a shift away from the emphasis on fiscal surveillance (for which the Fiscal Compact still stands) to fiscal capacity building (ESM) and monetary-fiscal interfaces (banking union). To summarise briefly what the two-level game analysis of each showed:

- The Fiscal Compact became a dead letter as soon as it had served its role of bringing forward the creation of a permanent fiscal capacity. David Cameron, who had not cared to understand the game that was going on, came back empty-handed from his first attempt at invoking the UK's small win-set to bargain over signing up to the Fiscal Compact. While the Fiscal Compact represents a 'de novo institution' (Bickerton et al. 2015a: 705) created by interstate cooperation, it was also a further step towards ending UK membership.

- The ESM had to be built in open breach of the no-bailout clause. It managed to become an intergovernmental emergency fund that, in terms of actual sovereign lending, surpasses the IMF. The *quid pro quo* was intrusive and harsh conditionality on lending to distressed countries, and this divides the euro area deeply. The UK's domestic opposition to European integration could only grow in the light of these interventions. This allowed the UK Treasury to exploit the paradox of weakness and even combine it with a gesture of goodwill at its discretion by contributing voluntarily to the Irish bailout, which benefitted UK banks disproportionately.
- The banking union was a major step towards further integration but as such a classic example of Monnet's curse that Europe will be forged in crisis. As soon as this crisis receded, Germany backtracked on promises of targeted joint liability and a common deposit insurance fund, regressing to its original position that the single monetary policy should be isolated from national fiscal policies. The UK was surprisingly adamant in letting a banking union come about, even though it split the Single Market, under the pressure of an escalating euro area crisis. Being no longer part of an integration project that is of such vital interest to the UK economy would have raised in any case the issue with which the new administration under Prime Minister May is confronted acutely: how to impose constraints on special interests at home when domestic democracy has proven too weak in the past.

The two-level game analysis of the UK brings into sharp focus how membership in the EU extends the policy space of national executives. Compared to full members of EMU, the UK after Brexit can no longer exploit the instrumental logic of two-level games to the same extent. Its outsider position will mean that its win-set is always larger than that of a diverse union of 27 other countries. The UK will lose more from the more constrained access to the Single Market than any other member state, with the exception of Ireland that therefore proves to be the most difficult veto-player in the Brexit negotiations. Hancké (2016) argues that the referendum destroyed the basis on which the two-level game worked so well for the UK while the country was in the EU. Others had to accommodate the 'recalcitrant member' to preserve the union. When the UK referendum called off this union, its recalcitrance became an empty threat.

At the same time, two-level games of interstate cooperation will have to be played still, especially if an economy houses one of the world's financial centres. Policymaking is then still subject to normative tensions inherent in such games. But Theresa May's initial strategy gave us a glimpse of the new dilemma: it will no longer be about fighting 'flexibly' the corner of Britain (read: the City and/or the taxpayers), but about pitching an international elite (read: banks) against the people (read: a mix of losers from open borders and right-wing internal opposition). Future British governments will find that the two-level games inside the EU were actually fun to play once one mastered the rules, while nobody knows yet how to play the anarchic games ahead.

References

Barber, T. (2010, October 11). Dinner on the Edge of the Abyss. *Financial Times*.

BBC. (2011, December 9). David Cameron Blocks EU-Wide Deal to Tackle Euro Crisis. *BBC*. http://www.bbc.co.uk/news/uk-16104275. Accessed October 22, 2016.

Beach, D. (2013). The Fiscal Compact, Euro-Reforms and the Challenge for the Euro-Outs. *Danish Foreign Policy Yearbook, 13*, 113–133.

Bellamy, R., & Weale, A. (2015). Political Legitimacy and European Monetary Union: Contracts, Constitutionalism and the Normative Logic of Two-Level Games. *Journal of European Public Policy, 22*(2), 257–274.

Bickerton, C. J., Hodson, D., & Puetter, U. (2015a). The New Intergovernmentalism: European Integration in the Post-Maastricht Era. *Journal of Common Market Studies, 53*(4), 703–722.

Bickerton, C. J., Hodson, D., & Puetter, U. (Eds.). (2015b). *The New Intergovernmentalism: States and Supranational Actors in the Post-Maastricht Era*. Oxford: Oxford University Press.

BIS. (2010, June). *Quarterly Review*. Basel: Bank for International Settlements.

Brunnermeier, M., Crockett, A., Goodhart, C., Persaud, A. D., & Shin, H. S. (2009). *The Fundamental Principles of Financial Regulation*. Geneva and London: International Center for Monetary and Banking Studies and Centre for Economic Policy Research.

Burret, H. T., & Schnellenbach, J. (2013, November). *Implementation of the Fiscal Compact in the Euro Area Member States* (Working Paper No. 08/2013) (Updated January 2014). German Council of Economic Experts (Sachverständigenrat).

De Grauwe, P. (2013). *Design Failures in the Eurozone: Can They Be Fixed?* (LEQS Paper No. 57/2013). London: LSE European Institute.

Dehousse, R. (2012, February). *The Fiscal Compact: Legal Uncertainty and Political Ambiguity* (Notr Europe Policy Brief No. 33). Available at: http://infoeuropa.eurocid.pt/database/000048001-000049000/000048296.pdf. Accessed October 16, 2016.

Draghi, M. (2012, July 26). Speech: Mario Draghi, President of the European Central Bank at the Global Investment Conference, London. Press Release. Available at: http://www.ecb.europa.eu/press/key/date/2012/html/sp120726.en.html. Accessed October 22, 2016.

ECB. (2015, April). *Financial Integration in Europe*. Annual Report. Frankfurt: European Central Bank.

Economist. (2010, August 13). Slovakia's Revolt Against Solidarity. Available at: http://www.economist.com/blogs/easternapproaches/2010/08/slovakia_and_greece. Accessed October 22, 2016.

Eder, F. (2016, July 27). *Wolfgang Schäuble Bails Out Spain, Portugal.* Politico. Available at: http://www.politico.eu/article/wolfgang-schauble-bails-out-spain-portugal-sanctions-juncker-german-finance-minister/. Accessed October 22, 2016.

EPRS. (2016, June). *Fiscal Compact Treaty: Scorecard for 2015*. European Parliament Research Service, PE 581.403. Brussels: Stanislas de Finance.

European Commission. (2017). *The Fiscal Compact: Taking Stock*. Communication from the Commission, C(2017) 1200 Final. Brussels: European Commission.

FAZ. (2015, December 9). Schäuble nennt Bedingungen für europäische Einlagenversicherung. *Frankfurter Allgemeine Zeitung, 286*, 18.

Giles, C., & Parker, G. (2011, July 20). Osborne Urges Eurozone to 'Get a Grip'. *Financial Times*. Available at: http://www.ft.com/cms/s/0/e357fe94-b2ec-11e0-86b8-00144feabdc0.html#axzz3ub8U1MJT.

Hancké, B. (2016). Brexit, Red Lines and the EU: The Two-level Game Revisited. EURPP Blog. http://bit.ly/2i7BJ8y. Accessed November 2, 2018.

Johnston, A., & Regan, A. (2016). European Monetary Integration and the Incompatibility of National Varieties of Capitalism. *Journal of Common Market Studies, 54*(2), 318–336.

Juncker, J.-C., Tusk, D., Dijsselbloem, J., Draghi, M., & Schulz, M. (2015). *Completing Europe's Economic and Monetary Union*. Brussels: European Commission.

Mabbett, D., & Schelkle, W. (2015). What Difference Does Euro Membership Make to Stabilization? The Political Economy of International Monetary Systems Revisited. *Review of International Political Economy, 22*(3), 508–534.

Mair, P. (2009). *Responsible Versus Responsive Government* (MPIfG Working Paper No. 09/8). Cologne: Max-Planck Institut für Gesellschaftsforschung.

May, T. (2016, October 5). Keynote Speech: Theresa May at Conservative Party Conference, Birmingham. Full Transcript. Available at: http://www.independent.co.uk/news/uk/politics/theresa-may-speech-tory-conference-2016-in-full-transcript-a7346171.html. Accessed October 22, 2016.

Moravcsik, A. (1998) *The Choice for Europe: Social Purpose and State Power from Messina to Maastricht.* London: UCL Press.

Moravcsik, A. (2012). Europe After the Crisis: How to Sustain a Common Currency. *Foreign Affairs, 91*(3), 54–64.

Parsons, C., & Matthijs, M. (2015). European Integration Past, Present and Future: Moving Forward Through Crisis? In M. Matthijs & M. Blyth (Eds.), *The Future of the Euro* (pp. 210–232). Oxford: Oxford University Press.

Putnam, R. D. (1988). Diplomacy and Domestic Politics: The Logic of Two-Level Games. *International Organization, 42*(3), 427–460.

Quaglia, L. (2019). European Union Financial Regulation, Banking Union, Capital Markets Union and the UK. In C. Hay & D. Bailey (Eds.), *Diverging Capitalisms* (pp. 99–123). Cham: Palgrave Macmillan (this volume).

Rodrik, D., & Zeckhauser, R. (1988). The Dilemma of Government Responsiveness. *Journal of Policy Analysis & Management, 7*(4), 601–620.

Rosamund, B. (2000). *Theories of European Integration.* Basingstoke: Palgrave Macmillan.

Schelkle, W. (2016). Financial Centre and Monetary Outsider: How Precarious Is the UK's Position in the EU? *Political Quarterly, 87*(2), 157–165.

Schelkle, W., & Lokdam, H. (2015, November 27). *Financial Regulation and the Protection of Eurozone Outs.* Report of the Hearing on Brexit. London: LSE. Available at: http://eprints.lse.ac.uk/66945/1/Hearing-1—Financial-regulation-and-the-protection-of-Eurozone-outs.pdf.

Schelling, T. C. (1960). *The Strategy of Conflict.* Cambridge, MA: Harvard University Press.

Stiglitz, J. (2016). *The Euro: How a Common Currency Threatens the Future of Europe.* New York and London: W. W. Norton.

Thompson, H. (2017). Inevitability and Contingency: The Political Economy of Brexit. *British Journal of Politics and International Relations, 19*(5), 434–449.

Van Rompuy, H., Barroso, J. M., Juncker, J.-C., & Draghi, M. (2012). *Towards a Genuine Economic and Monetary Union.* Brussels: European Union.

CHAPTER 7

The UK's Growth Model, Business Strategy and Brexit

Scott Lavery

INTRODUCTION

The UK's growth model is distinguished by two key characteristics: its position as a hub of international finance and its maintenance of a highly 'flexible' labour market regime. Since the signing of the Maastricht Treaty in 1992, EU integration has both underpinned and at key moments threatened to undermine elements of this growth model. The City of London benefited greatly from EU financial integration and from its access to deepening capital markets on the European continent. Immigration from EU member states contained labour costs and ameliorated bottlenecks in the UK's low skill sectors. UK trade in goods and services became deeply integrated into EU supply chains. Simultaneously, European integration has often been in tension with underlying elements of the UK's growth model. The development of EU employment policy represented a latent but persistent threat to the UK's flexible labour

S. Lavery (✉)
Sheffield Political Economy Research Institute,
University of Sheffield, Sheffield, UK
e-mail: scott.lavery@sheffield.ac.uk

© The Author(s) 2019
C. Hay and D. Bailey (eds.), *Diverging Capitalisms,*
Building a Sustainable Political Economy: SPERI Research & Policy,
https://doi.org/10.1007/978-3-030-03415-3_7

regime. Deepening integration amongst Eurozone states threatened the City of London's ability to shape its external environment (Thompson 2017). European integration has therefore both *underpinned* and threatened to *undermine* the UK's growth model at crucial moments. Navigating these complex and contradictory dynamics has been a persistent challenge for powerful interests within the British state and civil society.

This chapter begins from the premise that 'growth models' are not abstract systems which operate according to a self-sustaining 'economic' logic. Growth models are underpinned by the support of underlying coalitions of social forces (Jessop 1990). In the case of the UK, powerful business interest groups have historically played an important role in promoting and defending the UK's growth model. This is reflected most clearly in the long history of the financial sector's ability—through the 'City-Bank-Treasury' nexus—to shape macroeconomic policy in decisive ways (Ingham 1984). Organised 'umbrella' organisations such as the Confederation of British Industry (CBI) and the Institute of Directors (IOD), although arguably less powerful and effective than their European counterparts (Moran 2006), have also been able to shape UK economic policy in important respects (Farnsworth 1998). However, the role of business groups in mobilising to defend the UK's growth model in a context of European integration has been neglected in the recent literature.

This chapter fills this gap in the literature by focussing on two European policy spheres: EU employment policy and Capital Markets Union (CMU). Analysing business interest group mobilisation between 2010 and 2016, the chapter argues that British business has attempted to 'defend and extend' a liberalising bias within the Single Market. In the case of EU employment policy, business groups have lobbied hard to prevent supranational social policy activism from encroaching on the UK's lightly regulated labour market. City-based interests also proactively engaged with the Commission's flagship CMU initiative. Crucially, both of these objectives involved British business groups mobilising to deploy the power of British officials *inside* the EU institutions. *Influence over* as well as *access to* the Single Market has been a key consideration for business elites within Britain. Brexit fundamentally disrupts this strategic orientation, generating a series of dilemmas from the perspective of both British capital and the UK growth model more broadly.

The chapter proceeds as follows. Section one outlines the core features of the UK's growth model and argues that EU membership has both underpinned and at times threatened to undermine this distinctive model of capitalism. Section two reflects on the relation between business strategy and state power in a context of European integration. The following two sections then advance an empirical analysis of the European strategy of British business groups since 2010. Section three interrogates how business groups mobilised to limit the impact of EU employment policy on the UK's flexible labour market. Section four turns to the flagship initiative of CMU and shows how business groups and officials in the UK played a key part in shaping this agenda in its early stages. Section five then argues that Brexit poses a series of challenges to British business strategy in these two spheres. The final section concludes.

THE UK'S GROWTH MODEL
AND THE EUROPEAN SINGLE MARKET

As outlined by Talani in this volume, the City of London has long occupied a position of crucial importance within British capitalism (Talani 2019). The City's position as an 'entrepôt' for international financial transactions and commercial activity more broadly has decisively shaped the UK's integration into the world market (Ingham 1984). It has also had profound implications for British domestic development. In the 1980s, huge volumes of mobile capital flowed into the City as a result of high interest rates and deregulatory reforms (Jessop et al. 1988: 171). As manufacturing declined and the UK experienced persistent deficits on its 'visible' trade balance, the ability of the City to generate trade surpluses and attract external investment grew in salience for the British economy. Throughout the 1990s and 2000s, the City consolidated its position as a pivotal hub of global finance, with the financial sector's trade surplus rising from £8.7 billion to £25.1 billion in the 2000s (Shaw 2012: 231). On the eve of the 2008 financial crisis, the UK held the highest amount private debt of any G7 economy, accounted for primarily by the financial sector (Thompson 2013: 471).

The dominance of the City has had profound implications for the UK's growth model (Engelen et al. 2011). The rapid expansion of financial services contributed to growing Treasury tax revenues during the long upswing of the 1990s and 2000s. In 2011, tax receipts associated with the financial services sector amounted to £63 billion. Furthermore, the growth of the City has underpinned job creation within the financial services sector and within ancillary industries such as legal and business services, consultancy and marketing (Sassen 2011). The UK's highly liquid capital market has also underpinned credit growth domestically, contributing to rising household debt, house prices and consumption in a context of relatively stagnant income growth (Crouch 2009). On the other hand, critics point out that the dominance of the City has generated a series of difficulties for the UK's growth model. Hosting an international financial centre creates an upward pressure on the real exchange rate, undermining the export competitiveness of non-financial sectors. The dominance of the City has also been associated with facilitating 'brain drain' from non-financial sectors, entrenching geographical unevenness and increasing the susceptibility of the UK to financial crises and to prolonged economic downturns (Christensen et al. 2016). For these reasons, the City can be viewed as both a source of dynamism and dysfunctionality for the UK's growth model.

The second key feature of the UK's model of capitalism is its flexible labour market regime. Since the early 1980s, a series of highly restrictive trade union laws have been passed in order to enhance managerial control over the workforce. As a result, UK workers today encounter the fourth lowest level of employment protection of any advanced economy. Economic growth has overwhelmingly been generated by the services sector, which experiences both low levels of unionisation and a tendency to generate low productivity jobs, in particular when compared to the manufacturing sector. The result is that whilst the UK sustains a number of well-paid sectors and professions, large swathes of the UK labour market are subject to high levels of precariousness, low pay and in-work poverty. These trends have intensified since the 2008 crisis (Lavery 2018). New legislation designed to further intensify the UK's 'flexible' labour market regime was introduced in this period. Fees for employment tribunals were increased, preventing workers from seeking recompense for managerial malpractice (Heyes and Lewis 2015). These processes have consolidated the UK growth model's reliance on low pay work. Low productivity, stagnant living standards and volatile anti-systemic politics have been the result (Hopkin 2017).

The UK's internationalised financial sector and flexible labour market regime do not exist in a geographical vacuum. The UK's growth model position inside the European Single Market has conditioned its development in a number of important respects. The Single Market significantly reduced non-tariff barriers between member states through enhanced regulatory convergence and 'mutual recognition'. The Single Market has acted as an important outlet for UK exports, particularly from the UK's services sector. For example, in 2016, 30% of financial services exports were destined for the EU whilst the UK emerged as the EU's de facto 'investment banker' (James and Quaglia 2017). The Single Market also provides an important outlet for the export of manufactured goods from the UK to the EU, with 56% of the UK's pharmaceuticals exports, 51% of its automotive exports and 27% of its aerospace exports typically ending up on the European continent (CBI 2013). The geographical proximity of the EU to the UK and the deep integration of intra-European supply chains have underpinned these close trading relations. As a result, between 2000 and 2010, regions outside of London and the South East saw their dependence on EU demand for the export of goods and services increase substantially (Los et al. 2017: 789).

EU membership has also bolstered the UK's flexible labour market. As a result of 'free movement', high-skilled workers have poured into the UK and in particular to London from the EU (Ryan and Mulholland 2014: 3). At the same time, high levels of 'low skilled' EU migrants have entered the UK labour market in recent decades. The Blair Government's decision in 2004 to eschew transitional controls on inflows of labour from the central and eastern European 'accession' states was crucial here. The Treasury noted that the inflow of workers would act as a brake on wage growth and inflation in the UK (Thompson 2017: 238). As such, UK business models within high-wage sectors such as finance and business services and in low wage sectors such as agriculture, retail and hospitality have increasingly come to depend on labour inflows from EU member states.

BRITISH BUSINESS STRATEGY AND THE STATE

European integration has unleashed a series of contradictory dynamics within British capitalism. On the one hand, regulatory convergence between EU member states and European enlargement together opened-up new opportunities for British business expansion. On the other hand, the growing power of the European institutions—most notably the European Commission and European Parliament—placed constraints on the degree to which UK policymakers could 'tailor' economic policy to the requirements of the UK's liberalised growth model. Historically, this tension between integration and sovereignty has generated intractable political conflict within and between the Conservative and Labour Parties. At the same time, European integration has also generated important strategic dilemmas for powerful groups within British civil society. Business groups based within the UK have had to contend with the transfer of policymaking powers 'upwards' to the European level. However, no comprehensive analysis of British business group mobilisation in relation to European integration has been advanced. This chapter addresses this gap in the literature. Before turning to the empirical material, it is necessary to briefly reflect on a number of conceptual and methodological issues relating to the question of business strategy, domestic political economy and the state.

The notion of business 'strategy' implies that business is capable of organising itself as a collective actor. However, there are numerous barriers which can prevent the emergence of a common political will (Jessop 1990). Distinct 'fractions' of capital—embodied most obviously in financial and industrial circuits—are likely to hold divergent strategic priorities. Competition between firms is endemic, as businesses vie for market position. Businesses which are oriented towards the international or domestic markets are also likely to display distinct strategic priorities (Frieden 2006). Despite these divergent 'particular' interests, there is some common ground upon which a 'general' capitalist interest can be constructed. Most firms agree on the need for strong managerial control over the workforce, the need to avoid 'excessive' taxation and the imperative to cultivate a political environment which is amenable to enterprise. Capital is simultaneously divided and driven to articulate a common political will. Precisely because of these internal divisions, a business must actively *construct* a collective programme if it hopes to influence policy. Business must institutionalise its power. It can do this in a variety of ways. It can organise within or across sectors, forming 'umbrella' organisations which seek to represent the general interest. In the case of the UK, the CBI, the IOD, the Chambers of Commerce and the Federation of Small Businesses (FSB) are all bodies which seek to express the 'general' interest of their members and of the 'business community' more broadly. We can therefore identify inductively British 'business strategy' through close empirical examination of these organisations and their strategic orientations (Lavery 2017).

A second issue relates to the extent that we can talk of a 'British' business interest and strategy. Since the 1970s, capital has become increasingly integrated along transnational lines. The UK economy is particularly 'open' to international capital flows and hosts numerous corporations with a distinctly 'transnational' character. Under these conditions, a cynic might argue that there can be no such thing as 'British' business strategy, only global business strategy which incidentally takes place within the jurisdiction of the UK. However, capital does not freely float in an unbounded, transnational space. It must 'territorialise' itself within specific national contexts. In the case of the UK, a whole series of institutional peculiarities help to attract capital flows. The UK's common law system, its reputation as a creditworthy sovereign, the historic proximity between its core state institutions such as the Treasury and the Bank of England and the financial sector, and its relatively 'light touch' regulatory regime all act as inducements to external investment (Palan 2015). Over time, business models become integrated into the regulatory context of their 'host' state. This entanglement between private and public power can incentivise business to protect the legal infrastructure of their 'host' state from external encroachment. As we shall see below, this helps to explain why the City has regularly mobilised to defend UK sovereignty over financial regulation inside the EU.

These two tendencies—for business to organise its power into 'peak' organisations and for business power to become entangled with the regulatory infrastructure of its 'host' state—have important analytical implications. Powerful business interests characteristically attempt to penetrate the state apparatus and to directly shape government policy. This blurs the lines between 'private' and 'public' power. In neo-Gramscian terms, the co-articulation of the state and capital gives rise to distinctive 'state-society complexes' which are capable of projecting power 'outwards' (shaping the external environment) and 'downwards' (managing tensions internal to a particular domestic political economy) (Cox 1981). The core conceptual claim of this chapter is that this fusion of private and public power has historically been at the heart of the European strategy of British-based businesses. However, Brexit disrupts this 'state-society complex', unleashing a series of dilemmas for British business and the UK's growth model more broadly. The following sections advance an empirical analysis which seeks to substantiate this claim. Two EU policy areas are analysed in particular: EU employment policy and the CMU agenda. Each of these policy spheres has potentially far-reaching consequences for the UK's growth model. In both cases, the chapter argues that British business has aimed to 'defend and extend' the UK's growth model inside the EU by deploying the power of the British state inside the European institutions.

The CBI, Business Strategy and EU Employment Policy

Since the relaunch of European integration under the Delors Commission, there have been numerous attempts to embed a 'social' dimension at the EU level (Bailey 2008; Forde and Slater 2016: 594). The tentative development of 'European' employment policy has long been viewed by British business and the Conservative Party as a threat to the UK's flexible labour market regime. In the early 1990s, the CBI and the IOD pressurised the Major Government to secure an 'opt-out' from the Social Chapter (Lourie 1997). When New Labour reversed this position in 1998, the CBI claimed that this would increase compliance costs for British firms and would undermine UK competitiveness. One Whitehall official stated that the 'overwhelming view' of industry at the time was 'that acceptance of the social chapter would seriously damage competitiveness and employment because it would allow the United Kingdom to be out-voted on measures imposing unnecessary burdens and costs on businesses' (cited in Lourie 1997: 19). EU employment policy was subsequently transposed into UK law. As a result, a persistent challenge for British business has been how it might mobilise to 'defend' the UK's flexible labour market from the growth of EU employment policy.

The following material focuses on the CBI's approach to EU employment policy. The CBI is the UK's largest 'peak' business organisation, representing 190,000 companies which together employ one-third of the private sector workforce (CBI 2015b: 2). The CBI therefore provides us with a useful lens through which to interrogate the relation between British business strategy and EU S&EP in the period prior to the EU referendum. For the research, all publicly available policy documents released by the CBI between 2010 and 2016 were reviewed, with a specific emphasis on the CBI's approach to EU employment policy.

Throughout the documents, the CBI identifies two specific ways in which EU employment policy negatively impacts on its members' interests. First, the CBI claims that the Commission often proposes 'one size fits all' policies which are not well-suited to the specific needs of British firms (CBI 2015a: 3; 2016b: 4). The Agency Workers Directive (AWD) is identified as one initiative which threatens the UK's flexible labour market regime in this way. In one key CBI report, the organisation points out that agency workers in the UK already receive 92% of equivalent employees' wages (CBI 2013: 73). Whilst the AWD might have helped to liberalise labour markets on the European continent, the CBI claims that it was unnecessary in the UK context and simply heaped £1.9 billion of compliance on British firms. Second, the CBI identifies 'mission creep' as another area of concern (CBI 2015a: 2). The Working Time Directive (WTD) is regularly highlighted as an area of EU employment policy where 'mission creep' poses a threat. The UK had previously secured an 'opt-out' from the WTD's maximum 48-hour working week requirement. However, in the late 2000s, forces within the European Parliament, European trade unions and the Commission actively pushed for this 'opt-out' to be repealed. The CBI, along with numerous other British business interest groups, persistently expressed concern over these manoeuvres and agitated for the UK's 'opt-out' to be made permanent (CBI 2013: 171).

The CBI's ability to 'defend' the UK's flexible labour market was bolstered by the UK's position as a powerful member state inside the EU. Strategically, the CBI emphasises time and again the importance of the *formal* and *informal* power of UK officials inside the EU in securing the British business interest. In terms of 'formal' power, the CBI regularly emphasises the ability of UK officials to utilise their power within the Council of Ministers and the European Parliament. In a 2016 consultation with the Treasury Committee, for example, the CBI stated that the UK had, 'a powerful voice at the table, enabling us to have influence over the rules that business has to comply with and to achieve the reform of the European Union that the UK wants to see' (CBI 2016b). The consultation continues, 'by being round the table in EU institutions, the UK can help to shape the EU legislative agenda and ensure the Commission regulates only where necessary' (CBI 2016b). UK membership of the EU was therefore not simply preferable because it provided business with 'access' to the Single Market; the capacity of the UK government to *shape* EU legislation was of equal salience to the CBI's European strategy. In addition, the CBI places a special emphasis on the UK's capacity to build cross-country support for a liberalisation agenda with other member states. For example, in one intervention, it points out that, 'the UK is not alone in wanting [liberal] reform…by working with our European partners… we have the opportunity, right now, to achieve reform for a more outward looking, open and competitive European Union' (CBI 2015b). In these ways, the CBI sought to deploy the formal power of the UK inside the EU in order to protect its members' interests. For example, when David Cameron sought to 'renegotiate' the UK's relationship with the EU prior to the referendum, the CBI pushed hard for him to secure a 'moratorium' on the development of future EU employment policy (CBI 2016a: 10). In common with other business groups, it also agitated for the UK's WTD 'opt-out' to be made permanent.

The documents also reveal that the CBI was attentive to the ways in which the *informal* influence of UK officials inside the EU could be deployed to 'defend' the UK's liberalised labour market and growth model. One report notes that, 'the UK also has notable informal influence in the EU legislative process and has, for example, leveraged its ability to build alliances and use British expertise to help shape the agenda' (CBI 2016b). The CBI explicitly recommends that these informal channels influence should be strengthened. For example, in its submission to the Treasury Committee, the CBI (2016b: 14) states that, 'British MEPs must step up engagement in the law-making process and represent the interests of British business. To boost UK informal influence in the EU, the UK must do more to ensure it has personnel in key positions to help frame the debate. The UK…is underrepresented in staffing across the European Parliament and European Commission generally. Despite making up 12.5% of the EU population, in 2013 UK nationals represented only 4.6% of EU Commission staff, 5.8% of staff in the EU parliament and 4.3% in the Council of the EU' (CBI 2016b: 14). 'Access' to the Single Market was therefore not the only concern of the CBI in the period prior to the referendum. The ability to deploy the formal and informal power of British officials inside the EU was also a key element in the CBI's attempts to 'defend' the UK's flexible labour market regime.

THE CITY AND CAPITAL MARKETS UNION

There is a long history of attempts by the Commission to deepen European capital markets, dating back to the Treaty of Rome's commitment to support the free movement of capital across European borders. The Segre Report (1966), the Single European Act White Paper (1985) and the Financial Services Action Plan (1999) all attempted to deepen and integrate European capital markets. However, numerous barriers have stood in the way of this objective. Divergent domestic banking models, legal systems and political constraints have all militated against the formation of an integrated European capital market. The CMU programme, proposed initially by the Junker Commission in 2014, followed by a Green Paper (2015), Action Plan (2015) and Mid-term Review (2017), therefore embodied the latest in a long line of attempts to establish a single European capital market. British-based business interests, as we shall see, played a pivotal role in the emergence of this agenda in its early phases.

CMU is underpinned by two core objectives: to *deepen* and to *integrate* European capital markets. The central premise of CMU is that investment and growth in Europe are currently undermined by a number of supply-side factors. CMU advocates claim that the EU suffers from a lack of financial diversity. For example, bank loans account for 79% of EU corporate debt whilst in the US the figure is 26%. Since the Eurozone crisis, banks have become more risk-averse and face new capital adequacy requirements. According to CMU advocates, this acts as a drag on investment and economic growth. A second impediment is the slow pace of European financial integration. Differing insolvency rules, supervisory practices and tax regimes between member states ensure that European capital markets remain fragmented. Furthermore, this fragmentation has increased in the wake of the Eurozone sovereign debt crisis. For example, in 2008 euro area institutional investors held 27% of their assets in other euro-area states but by 2014 this figure had fallen to 21%. As the European Central Bank (ECB) remarked in 2012, the Eurozone crisis 'led to a marked deterioration in European financial integration', particularly in bond markets (ECB 2012). CMU attempts to circumvent these barriers by both deepening and integrating European capital markets. These include activities such as private equity, corporate bonds, securitisation, hedge funds and venture capital.

As the host of Europe's pre-eminent hub of global finance, the UK was set to be one of the main beneficiaries of CMU. 85% of the EU's hedge funds and 42% of its private equity are concentrated within the City. As Lucia Quaglia has argued, powerful actors within the UK therefore became 'pace setters' on CMU, enthusiastically engaging with and shaping the agenda in its early stages (Quaglia 2016; Quaglia et al. 2016).

Powerful financial interests based in the City of London enthusiastically embraced the CMU agenda. The City of London Corporation and CityUK—two pre-eminent lobbying groups at the heart of the square mile—published numerous documents which endorsed the core principles of Juncker's capital markets programme. In 2014, through their co-sponsored 'International Regulatory Strategy Group' (IRSG), they published a document entitled *Principles for a Capital Markets Union in Europe* (IRSG 2014). This was followed by detailed responses to the Commission's Green Paper (IRSG 2015a) and Action Plan (IRSG 2015b). Throughout these interventions, the IRSG emphasised the ways in which CMU could positively contribute to European growth, employment, infrastructure investment and lending to small and medium-sized enterprises (SMEs). In addition, a constellation of think tanks, consultancy firms and networks within the City proactively embraced the CMU agenda. For example, one group—New Financial—was set-up to directly feed into the CMU process, promoting the perspectives and interests of capital market participants in general. New Financial was clear that CMU opened-up opportunities for UK based financial services firms. One report noted that, 'capital markets in the UK are twice as developed relative to GDP as in the rest of Europe, and between 40 and 80% of all capital markets activity in the EU is conducted in the UK' (Wright 2016: 3). This link between CMU and the potential for UK financial services growth was widely acknowledged across the City in the early stages of the Commission's initiative. Indeed, as Quaglia points out, 25% of submissions to the Commission's consultation on CMU were from City-based firms. In addition, the pre-Brexit Commissioner for CMU—UK national Jonathan Hill—held numerous meetings with interest groups from the UK's financial sector.

Officials within the British state also took a positive view of CMU and proactively engaged in promoting the agenda in its early stages. Harriet Baldwin, economic secretary to the Treasury, stated in 2015 that the UK government was a 'staunch supporter' of CMU (HM Treasury 2015). In particular, Baldwin welcomed CMU as a positive programme which sought to 'make' rather than 'shape' financial market activity as, she claimed, had been the case with much of the Commission's post-crisis interventions. The UK government's response to the Commission's Green Paper also stated that the government was 'fully committed' to the CMU agenda, emphasising the need to prioritise the development of securitisation, pan-European private placement markets and reform to the Prospectus Directive amongst other areas. Similarly, the Bank of England in an extensive analysis of CMU argued that deepened European capital markets could contribute positively both to growth and financial stability (Bank of England 2015). Through facilitating portfolio diversification, the Bank argued that CMU could both protect European borrowers against exposure to credit downturns in one country and could facilitate more rapid recovery of investment and growth in times of crisis.

In the early stages of CMU, there was therefore a marked complementarity between the positioning of the City and the core institutions of the British state. This was not entirely coincidental. Numerous forums brought together private and state actors within the UK to respond to the Commission's CMU proposals. A 2015 House of Lords consultation was emblematic in this regard (House of Lords 2015). It brought together key stakeholders from the Treasury, the City, the Commission and the UK's regulatory authorities. The report from the consultation counselled that CMU would represent a 'fillip to the UK economy and the City of London in particular...[and as such] the UK must ensure that it is at the forefront of the debate as the CMU agenda takes shape in the coming months' (House of Lords 2015: 32). The report was clear that a joint effort between British business and the UK government would be key to maximising the benefits from CMU. In this regard, the report stated, 'the UK must ensure that it is at the forefront of the debate as the CMU agenda takes shape in the coming months. It will not suffice simply to react to others' proposals: the City and the Government should be active in responding to the Commission's initiative' (House of Lords 2015: 32).

UK engagement in the early stages of the CMU programme demonstrates the ways in which British business and state power came to be co-articulated under conditions of European financial integration. The Treasury was eager to promote the UK's pre-eminent export sector and to bolster state revenues. More generally, the Cameron Government saw CMU as an opportunity to demonstrate the economic benefits of European integration amidst a context of entrenched Euroscepticism. The City, for its part, sought to promote CMU both through engaging directly at the supranational level with the Commission and through shaping the orientation of the UK government. In this way, the financial lobby sought to 'extend' one core element of the UK's growth model—its deep and liquid capital markets—outwards into the Single Market. From the perspective of the EU institutions, CMU had been crafted in part as a way to appease the UK (Ringe 2015). Since 2010, numerous initiatives, such as Banking Union, had been advanced to bolster the Eurozone's financial architecture. This had raised concerns amongst the City and the UK government that a new 'core' organised around Economic and Monetary Union (EMU) was taking shape to the detriment of the UK. CMU was explicitly designed to appease these concerns. It was framed as a 'Single Market' programme with the UK at its heart. Indeed, in its early stages, CMU advocates sought to push the agenda forward through incremental, market-based initiatives in line with UK preferences rather than through deep institutional reform which would have involved the further centralisation of supervisory powers at the EU level. In these ways, the UK's 'state-society complex' profoundly shaped the development of CMU in its early stages. Private and public actors could 'extend' the UK's growth model outwards in a form that was compatible with domestic political imperatives.

British Business, the UK's Growth Model and the Political Economy of Brexit

The vote to leave the EU in June 2016 has far-reaching implications for both the UK's growth model and British business strategy. The economic impact of Brexit is often thought of in terms of the degree of 'access' which UK firms will enjoy after exiting the Single Market. One possible outcome is that the UK remains closely aligned with the structures of the EU and thereby maintains close trading links with its European neighbours. This, however, would likely involve continued payments into the EU budget, the continued jurisdiction of the European Court of Justice (ECJ) and the continuation of free movement for EU citizens. At the other end of the spectrum, a 'hard' Brexit involves precipitating a sharp break from the EU. This would involve decoupling the UK from the structures of the Single Market and the Customs Union. In this scenario, increased trade with non-EU countries such as the US, China and India would be necessary to compensate for negative trade and investment effects associated with leaving the Single Market. Critics suggest that this would be a gargantuan task. As widely pointed out in the economic geography and international political economy literature, 'globalisation' has in fact involved a deepening of economic linkages within *regional blocs* of the world economy, such as the NAFTA, ASEAN and the EU (Gamble and Payne 1996).

In the UK case, 'globalisation' has been paralleled by a deep process of *Europeanisation*, with supply chains, investment flows and economic linkages significantly deepening between European member states (Hay 2002). De-linking from the regulatory structures of the EU in a 'hard' Brexit is therefore unlikely to be a costless exercise.

What implications does Brexit have for British business strategy? Before the EU referendum, powerful business interests, including the CBI, the CityUK, the City of London Corporation, the British Bankers' Association and the Institute of Directors supported a 'Remain' position. Since the 'leave' vote, leading voices from within the British business community have made it clear that of the 'soft' and 'hard' Brexit scenarios, its preference is for the former. The CBI, for instance, has stated that its top priority is to maintain 'a barrier-free relationship with our largest, closest and most important trading partner' (CBI 2016c: 4). In contrast to the 'globalist' vision of Brexit advanced by some on the right of the Conservative Party, the CBI state that, 'the UK's new trading relationship with the EU must appreciate the current importance of the EU market to every sector, the level of integration between the UK and EU economies, and its future significance as a market. These factors set the EU apart from other markets for business. For every major sector of the UK economy, the EU is currently more important than any other international market' (CBI 2016c: 12). Similarly, powerful voices from the City have emphasised the need to secure comprehensive access for services in the aftermath of Brexit. As the IRSG puts it in one report, 'it is in the mutual interest of the EU27, the UK, businesses and the financial services sector for the existing, heavily integrated, cross border flows in finance to continue in order to sustain jobs and growth across the whole of Europe' (IRSG 2017).

Securing close proximity between the UK and the EU's regulatory structures in order to maintain a high level of 'access' to the Single Market has therefore been a key priority for British business since the June 2016 referendum. As argued previously, 'access' to the Single Market has not been the only concern for British-based firms historically. The ability to *influence* the shape of Single Market rules through the supranational activism of UK officials has also been a central component of the European strategy of British businesses. Brexit fundamentally disrupts this approach. British officials will no longer be able to shape EU rules in the ways they have done in the past. Regulatory alignment might preserve a high degree of access to the Single Market in both goods and services but the UK will become a *rule-taker* rather than a *rule-maker* in relation to EU legislation. This creates a number of dilemmas for British business. Returning to the policy areas outlined above— EU employment policy and CMU—we can briefly outline some of the challenges this is likely to pose to British firms and the UK's growth model more broadly.

Between the June 2016 referendum and the Article 50 'trigger' in March 2017, statements from the CBI suggested that its central objective was to secure a high degree of 'regulatory harmonisation' with the EU after Brexit (CBI 2016c: 18). This would ensure barriers to trade would be kept to a minimum. However, the existing models which guarantee this relationship—for example, Norway's membership of the European Economic Area (EEA)—require not only product market harmonisation but also compliance with EU employment policy. In this situation, the UK would have to comply with EU employment and social policy directives whilst being unable to 'defend' the UK's flexible labour market regime in the ways it has done in the past. Concretely, a range of EU employment directives—such as the WTD and the AWD—which in the eyes of the business community are 'ill-suited' to the UK's flexible labour market could be strengthened. This prospect was anticipated by the CBI. It's report *A Whole Economy View of Brexit* states that, 'business and government must work together to agree how to secure long-term regulatory cooperation between the EU and UK markets after the UK leaves … [however] it is not in the UK's interests to be a rule taker. In areas such as social and employment regulation in particular, it would not be acceptable for the UK to implement laws over which is has had no say' (CBI 2016c: 18). This basic dilemma is likely to continue to shape British business strategy as the politics of Brexit unfolds. Indeed, as the CBI puts it in its post-referendum strategy document *Shaping Our Future*, 'UK policymakers must continue to engage on the EU legislative agenda. A long-term strategy for influencing new EU rules and standards that may still apply to UK businesses after exit will have to be established' (CBI 2016d: 6). Deploying the power of the British state in order to shape EU legislation therefore remains part of British business strategy. The reality is, though, that without formal voting rights and the informal channels of influence which the UK enjoyed as an EU member state, the UK's ability to shape the policymaking process in Brussels has been irredeemably diminished. Proximity to the Single Market may be secured, but (co)authorship of its rules has been forfeited.

Brexit and the associated loss of UK influence within the EU institutions also has far-reaching implications for the CMU agenda. As outlined above, British business and government mobilised effectively to shape the CMU programme in its early stages. Two competing 'visions' of CMU have been advanced. The first, advanced by member states who seek to move the EU towards a more federalist structure, argue that capital market integration requires the further transfer competences and powers to the European Supervisory Authorities. The European Commission and the ECB have both countenanced the prospect of the need to create a 'single European capital markets supervisor' (see, for example, The European Commission 2015). This direction of travel was anathema to the UK government, the UK's regulatory authorities and the City, who advanced a different approach to CMU in its early stages. British officials and business interests staunchly opposed ceding further regulatory sovereignty to the EU level, preferring instead to advocate a piece-meal approach which respected the autonomy of national supervisory authorities (House of Lords 2015: 44; CBI 2015c: 3). Prior to Brexit, UK opposition to the 'federalist' vision of CMU was effective, shaping the agenda in line with the preferences of the UK's state-society complex.

With the Brexit vote, the UK's ability to shape CMU in line this way has been fatally undermined. The UK's exit removes one of the principal impediments to further supervisory convergence. For example, UK policymakers consistently resisted the further empowerment of the European Supervisory and Markets Authority (ESMA), the agency charged with ensuring that member states adequately apply capital market legislation. ESMA's lack of supervisory 'muscle' was frequently cited as a barrier to a fully-functioning CMU. Brexit creates an opportunity for those forces who would like to empower ESMA in order to drive through capital market integration. For example, John Berrigan, Deputy Director General of the CMU portfolio, recently stated that, 'Brexit makes regulatory and supervisory convergence more important to avoid fragmentation and to promote more efficient capital markets. This will accelerate market integration by avoiding regulatory arbitrage and a race to the bottom'. Proceedings from the EuroFi 2016 conference—a high-level forum of financial institutions and European regulators—echoed this sentiment. Their report states that 'the idea of a CMU with 40 national supervisors will not work. ESMA needs to be strengthened. In such a context…CMU must be more ambitious in response to Brexit'. European institutions' tacit commitment to creating a 'single European capital markets supervisor' has therefore become increasingly explicit since Britain voted to leave the EU in June 2016. The implication is that the design of CMU is less likely to reflect British preferences as the agenda develops into the future.

CONCLUSION

The UK's growth model is characterised by its large, internationalised financial sector and its flexible labour market regime. Since the 1990s, this growth model has been profoundly shaped by the UK's position inside the Single Market. European integration both underpinned and threatened to undermine the UK's growth model at critical moments. This chapter has examined how British business strategy has evolved in relation to the contradictory dynamics unleashed by European integration within the UK. It has argued that this British business attempted to 'defend and extend' the UK's growth model through deploying the power of UK officials inside the EU institutions. UK membership of the EU was therefore key to British business both because it provided *access* to the Single Market and because it allowed for UK officials to have *influence* over the EU's rules. In the fields of EU employment policy and CMU, British business successfully mobilised the power of UK officials inside the EU institutions to advance its interests. Brexit undermines this strategic orientation. By reducing the UK's power inside the formal structures of the EU, Brexit ensures that the UK is likely to become a 'rule-taker' rather than a 'rule-maker' at the EU level. This generates a series of challenges both for British business strategy and for the UK's growth model more broadly.

This analysis has a number of implications for the themes of this *Diverging Capitalisms* volume. First, divergent 'growth models' are not reified economic structures. They are always underpinned and supported by underlying coalitions of social forces. Powerful business interest groups are one key coalition which can mobilise to defend growth models over time. Although business groups certainly organise at the 'transnational' European scale (van Apeldoorn 2003), as the above case studies of the CBI and the City of London demonstrate, business power also tends to become entangled with domestic politics and regulatory structures. A renewed focus on the relation between the strategies of domestic business interest groups and the development of divergent growth models therefore remains a key area for future comparative enquiry (Baccaro and Pontusson 2016). Second, this chapter has referred to the British 'business' interest as if it is a unified whole. Whilst it is true that business shares a number of generally defined interests, it is of course also the case that different firms in different sectors have numerous divergent and often contradictory objectives. Brexit therefore impacts differentially on firms depending on a number of factors, including, for example, whether their business models are oriented towards the domestic, European or international market. Future research should unpack the divergent strategic orientation of distinct sectors and fractions of capital in the context of Brexit. Third, the 'embeddedness' of business power within distinct domestic contexts has important implications for how we might analyse the European integration process. In contrast to accounts which perceive the transfer of power to supranational scale as a 'functional' response to deepening economic interdependence (Sweet and Sandholtz 1997), European integration is better viewed as the 'emergent' outcome of competing projects organised primarily at the domestic scale (Bulmer and Joseph 2016). As argued above, the development of CMU in its early stages was strongly conditioned by the orientation of the UK's 'state-society complex' inside the EU. Focussing on the co-articulation of public and private interests within member states and the ways in which these can 'project' power outwards provides us with an invaluable lens which can overcome teleological readings of EU integration. Fourth, the emerging political economy of Brexit reminds us that 'globalisation'—increased levels of economic integration at the transnational scale—is not an inevitable process. It is always underpinned by politics. Brexit embodies a moment where democratic politics 'trumped' the preferences of powerful business interests in the UK. As the UK embarks on the process of leaving the EU, a key area for future research will be to analyse the ways in which business mobilises to secure its interests within this altered context.

REFERENCES

Baccaro, L., & Pontusson, J. (2016). Rethinking Comparative Political Economy: The Growth Model Perspective. *Politics & Society, 44*(2), 175–207.

Bailey, D. J. (2008). Explaining the Underdevelopment of 'Social Europe': A Critical Realization. *Journal of European Social Policy, 18*(3), 232–245.

Bank of England. (2015). *A European Capital Markets Union: Implications for Growth and Stability.* London: Bank of England.

Bulmer, S., & Joseph, J. (2016). European Integration in Crisis? Of Supranational Integration, Hegemonic Projects and Domestic Politics. *European Journal of International Relations, 22*(4), 725–748.

CBI. (2013). *Our Global Future: The Business Vision for a Reformed EU.* London.

CBI. (2015a). *Arguments for and Against the UK's European Union Membership.* London.

CBI. (2015b). *Choosing Our Future: Why the European Union Is good for Business, but How It Should Be Better.* London.

CBI. (2015c). *The Business Vision for a Capital Markets Union in Europe.* London.

CBI. (2016a). *A Business Assessment of EU Reforms.* London.

CBI. (2016b, January 11). *CBI Response to Treasury Committee Inquiry: The Economic and Financial Costs and Benefits of the UK's Membership of the EU.* CBI Website. Available at: http://www.cbi.org.uk/business-issues/uk-and-the-european-union/eu-business-facts/cbi-response-to-treasury-committee-inquiry-pdf/.

CBI. (2016c). *Making a Success of Brexit: A Whole-Economy View of the UK-EU Negotiations.*

CBI. (2016d). *Shaping Our Future: Key Business Principles for the UK-EU Negotiation.* London.

Christensen, J., Shaxson, N., & Wigan, D. (2016). The Finance Curse: Britain and the World Economy. *The British Journal of Politics and International Relations, 18*(1), 255–269.

Cox, R. (1981). Social Forces, States and World Orders: Beyond International Relations Theory. *Millenium, 10*(2), 125–155.

Crouch, C. (2009). Privatised Keynesianism: An Unacknowledged Policy Regime. *British Journal of Politics and International Relations, 11*(3), 382–399.

ECB. (2012). *ECB's Report on Financial Integration in Europe.* Retrieved January 12, 2018 from: https://www.ecb.europa.eu/pub/pdf/other/financialintegrationineurope201404en.pdf.

Engelen, E., Erturk, I., Froud, J., Johal, S., Leaver, A., Moran, M., & Nilsson, A. (2011). *After the Great Complacence: Financial Crisis and the Politics of Reform.* Oxford: Oxford University Press.

Farnsworth, K. (1998). Minding the Business Interest: The CBI and Social Policy, 1980–1996. *Policy Studies, 19*(1), 19–38.

Forde, C., & Slater, G. (2016). Labour Market Regulation and the 'Competition State: An Analysis of the Implementation of the Agency Working Regulations in the UK. *Work, Employment & Society, 30*(4), 590–606.

Frieden, J. A. (2006). *Global Capitalism: Its Fall and Rise in the Twentieth Century.* New York: W. W. Norton.

Gamble, A., & Payne, A. (1996). *Regionalism and World Order.* Basingstoke: Macmillan.

Hay, C. (2002). Globalisation, "EU-isation" and the Space for Social Democratic Alternatives: Pessimism of the Intellect: A Reply to Coates. *The British Journal of Politics and International Relations, 4*(3), 452–464.

Heyes, J., & Lewis, P. (2015). Employment Protection Legislation and the Growth Crisis. In J. Green, C. Hay, & P. Taylor-Gooby (Eds.), *The British Growth Crisis: The Search for a New Model.* Basingstoke: Palgrave.

HM Treasury. (2015). *Harriett Baldwin on the European Commission's Action Plan for a Capital Markets Union.* London: HM Treasury.

Hopkin, J. (2017). When Polanyi Met Farage: Market Fundamentalism, Economic Nationalism, and Britain's Exit from the European Union. *The British Journal of Politics and International Relations*. https://doi.org/10.1177/1369148117710894.

House of Lords. (2015, March 9). Capital Markets Union: A Welcome Start. *EU Economic and Financial Affairs Sub-Committee*. Available at: https://www.parliament.uk/business/committees/committees-a-z/lords-select/eu-economic-and-financial-affairs-and-international-trade-sub-committee-a/news/capital-markets-union-welcome-start/.

Ingham, G. K. (1984). *Capitalism Divided?: The City and Industry in British Social Development*. New York: Schocken Books.

IRSG. (2014). Briefing on the Principles That Should Underpin the Development of a Capital Markets Union in Europe. Retrieved January 12, 2018, from: https://www.irsg.co.uk/resources-and-commentary/principles-for-a-capital-markets-union-in-europe/.

IRSG. (2015a). *IRSG Response to Commission Green Paper on Long-Term Financing of the EU Economy*. Retrieved January 12, 2018, from: https://www.irsg.co.uk/resources-and-commentary/irsg-response-to-commission-green-paper-on-building-a-capital-markets-union/.

IRSG. (2015b). *IRSG Response to Capital Markets Union Action Plan*. Retrieved January 12, 2018, from: https://www.irsg.co.uk/assets/IRSGResponse-to-CMU-Action-Plan.pdf.

IRSG. (2017). *A New Basis for Access for EU/UK Financial Services Post Brexit*. January 12, 2018. Available at: https://www.irsg.co.uk/resources-and-commentary/a-new-basis-for-access-to-eu-uk-financial-services-post-brexit/.

James, S., & Quaglia, L. (2017). *Brexit and the Limits of Financial Power in the UK* (Working Paper). University of Oxford.

Jessop, B. (1990). *State Theory: Putting the Capitalist State in Its Place*. Cambridge: Polity Press.

Jessop, B., Bonnett, K., Bromley, S., & Ling, T. (1988). *Thatcherism: A Tale of Two Nations*. Cambridge: Polity Press.

Lavery, S. (2017) "Defend and Extend": British Business Strategy, EU Employment Policy and the Emerging Politics of Brexit. *British Journal of Politics and International Relations, 19*(4). https://doi.org/10.1177/1369148117722713.

Lavery, S. (2018). The Legitimation of Post-crisis Capitalism in the United Kingdom: Real Wage Decline, Finance-led Growth and the State. *New Political Economy, 23*(1). https://doi.org/10.1080/13563467.2017.1321627.

Los, B., McCann, P., Springford, J., & Thissen, M. (2017). The Mismatch Between Local Voting and the Local Economic Consequences of Brexit. *Regional Studies, 51*(5), 786–799.

Lourie, J. (1997). *The Social Chapter*. London.

Mcrae, S. (n.d.). *Hidden Voices the CBI, Corporate Lobbying and Sustainability*.

Moran, M. (2006). The Company of Strangers: Defending the Power of Business in Britain, 1975–2005. *New Political Economy, 11*(4), 453–477.

Palan, R. (2015). Futurity, Pro-cyclicality and Financial Crises. *New Political Economy, 20*(3), 367–385.

Quaglia, L. (2016). *European Union Financial Regulation, Banking Union, Capital Markets Union and the UK* (SPERI Paper No. 38). Sheffield: University of Sheffield.

Quaglia, L., Howarth, D., & Liebe, M. (2016). The Political Economy of European Capital Markets Union. *JCMS: Journal of Common Market Studies, 54*(S1), 185–203.

Ringe, W.-G. (2015). Capital Markets Union for Europe: A Commitment to the Single Market of 28. *Law and Financial Markets Review, 9*(1), 5–7.

Ryan, L., & Mulholland, J. (2014). Trading Places: French Highly Skilled Migrants Negotiating Mobility and Emplacement in London. *Journal of Ethnic and Migration Studies, 40*(4), 584–600.

Sassen, S. (2011). *Cities in a World Economy.* London: Sage.

Shaw, E. (2012). New Labour's Faustian Pact? *British Politics, 7*(3), 224–249.

Sweet, A. S., & Sandholtz, W. (1997). European Integration and Supranational Governance. *Journal of European Public Policy, 4*(3), 297–317.

The European Commission. (2015). *The Five Presidents' Report: Completing Europe's Economic and Monetary Union.* European Commission. March 9, 2017. Available at: https://ec.europa.eu/commission/publications/five-presidents-report-completing-europes-economic-and-monetary-union_en.

Thompson, H. (2013). UK Debt in Comparative Perspective: The Pernicious Legacy of Financial Sector Debt. *British Journal of Politics and International Relations, 15*(3), 476–492.

Thompson, H. (2017). Inevitability and Contingency: The Political Economy of Brexit. *The British Journal of Politics and International Relations.* https://doi.org/10.1177/1369148117710431.

van Apeldoorn, B. (2003). *Transnational Capitalism and the Struggle over European Integration.* London: Routledge.

Wright, W. (2016). *The Potential Impact of Brexit on European Capital Markets.* London: New Finance.

CHAPTER 8

The Bed You Made: Social Democracy and Industrial Policy in the EU

Angela Wigger and Laura Horn

INTRODUCTION

Many observers seem puzzled by the demise of social democracy in the context of the EU. While some frame the developments in the context of the electoral woes of the centre-left at Member State level (Pauly 2018), others see a paradox: while social democratic policies and parties are highly in favour of the European project, the European project damages their electoral chances the most (Holmes and Lightfoot 2014: 228). This apparent paradox can be resolved quite easily, however, when adopting a critical political economy perspective and investigating the dissonance between social democratic commitments and the actual policies pursued at EU level. From a critical perspective, the current struggles of social democracy in national electoral arenas seem to be mainly an aftershock of the failure of Third Way politics—a politics that has

A. Wigger (✉)
Radboud University, Nijmegen, The Netherlands
e-mail: a.wigger@fm.ru.nl

L. Horn
Roskilde University, Roskilde, Denmark
e-mail: lhorn@ruc.dk

© The Author(s) 2019
C. Hay and D. Bailey (eds.), *Diverging Capitalisms*,
Building a Sustainable Political Economy: SPERI Research & Policy,
https://doi.org/10.1007/978-3-030-03415-3_8

171

been compromised at the outset with an essentially neoliberal agenda at EU level and that has ruled out 'traditional' social democratic policies anchored in welfare state interventions indefinitely (see, e.g., Bailey et al. 2014). While the 'European Social Model' and its vaguely progressive outlook once had offered the legitimising discourse to Third Way politics (Bailey 2016), after years of an ongoing constitutionalisation of austerity that has been negotiated, managed and implemented also by social democrats in response to the 2007/2008 financial and economic crisis, the European Social Model has become completely amorphous. What has long been the 'substitute collective horizon of future' (Miró Artigas 2017: 6) rather seems to have been turned into a mere rationalisation for austerity and neoliberal supply-side policies.

Now that the socially disastrous consequences of austerity have been fiercely criticised not only by social protest movements but also the IMF, and even EU institutions themselves, is there still a future for a social democratic reincarnation of the European Union (EU)? Jeroen Dijsselbloem (2017a), Dutch Minister of Finance and former President of the Eurogroup, also referred to as the 'red engineer' from the Dutch social democrats, the Partij van de Arbeid (PvdA), announced that austerity was no longer at the heart of the debate in the Eurogroup, and that 'there will be a change in the policy mix […] moving away from austerity and putting more emphasis on deep reforms'. In its manifesto 'Towards a New Europe' (2014), the Party of the European Socialists (PES) suggested such deep reforms in the form of an 'ambitious European industrial policy'. Similarly, on the website of the Progressive Alliance of Socialists and Democrats (see S&D 2018), the political group in the European Parliament of the PES, we can read: 'We have a vision for Europe: to put industry back at its heart. Together we can renew European industry, create jobs, shift to a more sustainable model of production and strengthen European competitiveness'. The European Commission's Communication, entitled 'For a European Industrial Renaissance' in 2014 already heralded a new common industrial policy, announcing that the manufacturing share of the EU's GDP would increase from currently 15 to 20% by 2020, provided that competitiveness measures would be adopted (European Commission 2014). Commission President Jean-Claude Juncker, reaffirmed the commitment towards an EU industrial policy in his 2017 State of the Union speech (European Commission 2017a). Are we indeed witnessing the return of industrial policies inspired by a social democratic leitmotif?

A cursory inspection of the recent EU crisis management packages may give the impression of a 'good old' social democratic industrial policy—one that in the spirit of competitiveness supports knowledge-intensive sectors and that tackles the persistently high unemployment in the EU since 2009. Reforms in the context of the new common industrial policy are however highly deceptive. As we argue in this chapter, competitiveness is primarily understood as 'price and cost' competitiveness, allowing EU industries to compete on global markets on the basis of lower prices (European Commission 2016a). The suggested reform strategy is internal devaluation by first, depreciating real wages and inducing further labour market reforms; second, intensifying inter-company competition to lower prices; and third, lowering the overall level of corporate taxation. Thereby, the neoliberal structural adjustment that we have seen hitherto will be further recalibrated, putting the primary burden of adjustment on labour rather than capital: while wage repression, labour market reforms and intense price competition directly and indirectly deflate labour, the reduction of corporate taxes expedites the redistribution of wealth from labour to capital. Social democrats like Dijsselbloem (2017b) have warned that despite the reform zealousness, the EU should also hold on to its unique European social model and modernise it so that it can survive in the future. However, Dijsselbloem's statements are quite indicative of the overall social democratic stance that portrays the EU as competitive, post-austerity and prosocial. This chapter engages critically with the EU's new common industrial policy initiative and its broader framing within social democratic visions of Europe, and argues that with the particular direction that the new common EU industrial policy is taking, social democracy in the EU, once more, is failing to steer the EU towards a more radical social agenda and to capitalise politically on the 'deep reforms' that have recently been announced. As a result, assumptions about a rekindling of 'social democratic Europe' through an industrial policy flanked by the European Pillar of Social Rights (EPSR) initiative remain fundamentally flawed.

The argument unfolds as follows: in the next section, the shift towards an EU industrial policy discourse is located within the wider EU approach to crisis management since 2008. Section two outlines the new common industrial policy, including the defence industry policy, and discusses the prevailing political project of competitiveness through internal devaluation. Section three shows how internal devaluation exacerbates existing structural asymmetries and economic disintegration further, which renders a socially more equitable European economic fabric—just like earlier forms of neoliberal crisis management—a fundamental failure, and it puts these findings in the context of recent and ongoing developments of social democratic political projects in the EU, particularly the EPSR. In concluding, the chapter highlights the tensions between the social democratic vision for a 'Social Europe', and the means in the name of competitiveness and the new common industrial policy.

THROUGH THE COMPETITION GLASS: EU CRISIS MANAGEMENT REVISITED

When the European Commission took more than 500 emergency state aid decisions from 2008 to 2015 to give its generous permission to bail out of 117 European banks (European Commission 2016b), other industries in distress, such as the car, steel, construction or shipbuilding industries, also demanded emergency state aid to cope with the worsening crisis. However, the Commission was no longer so permissive and declared state aid to be a distortion to competition in the common market. At the time, a common industrial policy seemed far away. The Commission construed the crisis as a crisis within the financial sector only, and optimistically expected the crisis to be over by 31 December 2010, the expiry date of permitted state aid schemes for the financial sector (Wigger and Buch-Hansen 2014). When excessive government spending to bail out the financial sector, in conjunction with the overall lower GDPs and declining tax revenues, exhausted national budgets (see Heinrich 2015 on crisis management dynamics), the crisis was no longer interpreted as a crisis of the financial sector but as a sovereign debt crisis. Particularly Southern Eurozone members suffered from growing current account imbalances and rapidly accumulating public debt, and faced acute difficulties to sell bonds (and thus, public debt) on financial markets. Subsequently, crisis-hit Eurozone members were accused to have lived beyond their means, which served as a political legitimation for the imposition of painful austerity programmes. The Eurozone-specific and more general EU-28 regulatory and treaty-based measures that were adopted imposed a strict EU monitoring of national budgets, limiting the capacity to run budget deficits and adopt costly social and economic policies. Tightening member states' fiscal discipline and enhancing their ability to service their debt served the purpose of regaining the trust of financial markets and its rating agencies. As austerity packages merely targeted ongoing budget deficits, while protecting the accumulated stock of existing debt, deficit and debt ratios stayed high, while economic contraction and depression aggravated. Even IMF economists eventually concluded that austerity did more harm than good (see for example Blanchard and Leigh 2013, or Clift in this volume). EU bureaucrats and politicians, however, continued to push for strict budget rules. In parallel, the improvement of competitiveness of EU economies has been put high on the EU agenda.

Competitiveness performance indexes and scoreboards have formed the apex of the neoliberal organisation of capitalism in Europe for decades. As Miró Artigas' (2017: 13) trenchant analysis shows, the 'neo-liberal need to improve competitiveness became a depoliticised and apolitical normative imperative that came to guide the construction of the EU, to the extent that it was assumed by those parties claiming to confront neoliberalism'. Already the Lisbon Agenda of 2000 and its successor strategy Europe 2020 were imbued with notions of competitiveness. When the crisis hit, 'competitiveness' moved up further on the EU agenda. In 2011, the Commission (2011: 21–22) announced that '[w]hile fiscal imbalances are at the forefront of the current policy debate, they are by no means the only area where policy action is needed. Recent developments have highlighted the urgent need for some euro-area Member States to restore their external balances and to improve their competitiveness'. A year later, the *Four Presidents' Report* (2012) prepared by the European Commission's President, in cooperation with the Presidents of the Euro Summit, Eurogroup, and the ECB, suggested that EU member governments should conclude annual contractual arrangements with the Commission, targeting areas where competitiveness was weak. In January 2013, German Chancellor Merkel proclaimed at the World Economic Forum in Davos, Switzerland, that 'Competitiveness Pacts', along similar lines to the Fiscal Compact, should create the prerequisite to get access to financial aid from EU budgets under what euphemistically had been termed the 'solidarity mechanism'. Only a month later, the Commission launched a proposal for a 'Convergence and Competitiveness Instrument', which suggested a procedure according to which the Commission would make recommendations to individual member governments on how to regain competitiveness (European Commission 2013). Almost simultaneously, the European Council committed itself to negotiate 'Partnerships for Growth, Employment and Competitiveness', entailing that individual member governments and the Commission would conclude bilateral reform contracts, which would be subject to approval by Council, notably in the configuration of the Competitiveness Council (European Council 2013: 17–20). In contrast to the reform requirements spelled out in the Memoranda of Understanding (MoU) between member states and the Troika or the IMF/EU, the envisaged competitiveness treaties would encompass all Eurozone members. Furthermore, in contrast to the Country-Specific Recommendations (CSRs) issued *ex ante* by the Commission under the European Semester procedure of 2011, the competitiveness treaties would be legally binding, which would make them enforceable through *ex post* litigation before the EU Courts.

In the absence of political support, the Council negotiations stalled in June 2014; yet the idea of member state-specific competitiveness reforms has persisted ever since. The *Five Presidents' Report*, which included also the President of the European Parliament, Martin Schulz, a social democrat, proposed establishing 'National Competitiveness Authorities' (see Five President's Report 2015). The Commission subsequently renamed the envisaged 'Competitiveness Authorities' into 'Competitiveness Boards', and in September 2016, the Council—upon the recommendation of the Commission—subsequently issued a recommendation calling upon Eurozone members to establish 'National Productivity Boards' as part of the wider new common industrial policy. These productivity boards, which are currently being established in all member states, will be entrusted with the supervision of policies and performances in the field of competitiveness. As will be shown below, they will form one of the key touchstones of the new common EU industrial policy. Moreover, the centrality of competitiveness, which will be governed by National Productivity Boards, forms part of the several instances where tensions between key social democratic themes and the concrete manifestation of progressive positions at EU become manifest.

Towards a Social Democratic Vision
of Industrial Policy?

The Commission Communication 'For a European Industrial Renaissance' (2014) prophesies a vast re-industrialisation of Europe, provided that competitiveness measures will be adopted. In addition to increasing the manufacturing share of the EU GDP from 15 to 20% by 2020, keeping pace with China, India or Brazil takes centre-stage. According to the Commission, the EU's relative weight in world trade and share of world capital flows vis-à-vis emerging markets has declined steadily. The Chinese economy, for example, no longer exclusively caters for labour-intensive low value-added production but is increasingly moving into high-quality, high value-added segments, notably in the computer and electronics sector. The Commission notices that China has become the world's largest exporter at country-level, while attracting a share of FDI equal to the EU (European Commission 2015: 14, 98). To keep up the competition with emerging markets is foregrounding in the EU's long-term development and industrial policy plans, as the Commission reaffirmed in September 2017 (European Commission 2017a).

The new common industrial policy is multifaceted and a range of the so-called industrial policy packages have already been adopted, such as the European Fund for Strategic Investments (EFSI) established in June 2015, also referred to as the Juncker Funds, named after Commission President Jean-Claude Juncker, which seeks to co-finance and leverage risky 'infrastructure and innovation projects' around Europe that would not otherwise be funded. The EFSI forms a key node in the mobilisation of private financing of investments and stands for a 16 billion euro guarantee anchored in the EU budget. In addition, the European Investment Bank (EIB) has committed up to 5 billion euro of its own capital to unlock private investment. The so-called Juncker Plan has however been implemented only slowly. As the 2017 EuroMemorandum argues (2017: 11), 'there are substantial hints that the positive investment effects have not been additional, but that instead the EFSI has largely financed investment projects that would have been undertaken anyway'. Yet, the EFSI is but one among several measures. In parallel, the Programme for the Competitiveness of Enterprises and Small and Medium-sized Enterprises (COSME) seeks to improve SMEs' access to credit on the basis of guarantees and counter-guarantees, as well as through using the securitisation of debt-finance portfolios as leverage. In the same vein, also the funding through Horizon 2020 is being subsumed under the new common industrial policy. More recently, the European Commission (2017b) even announced specific action plans for almost every imaginable industrial sector, ranging from chemical, automotive, raw materials, metals, minerals and forest-based industries to food, healthcare, biotechnology, aeronautical, maritime industries, textiles, fashion, tourism and creative industries.

The Commission also pushed for a European Defence Fund as part of the 'defence industrial policy', which supports investment in research and development in the defence industry, and includes a significant funding to encourage and facilitate private investments in collaborative research and capacity development between member states—all in the name of 'boosting the competitiveness of the European defence industry' (European Commission 2017c, 2018). In this context, the Permanent Structured Cooperation on Security and Defence (PESCO), established in December 2017, allows the Member States to develop joint projects and acquisitions with funding from the Defence Fund. While the initial framework with regard to deployment of military forces was something of a compromise, in particular between the pragmatic integration agenda of the Merkel Government, and the Macron Government's ambitious vision for military development of the EU, there is an important linkage between the PESCO and the European Defence Fund. An in-depth position paper by the Progressive Alliance of Socialists and Democrats, the S&D, summarised the nexus between industrial policy and defence industry rather neatly, arguing that '[t]he defence industry is a key sector for Europe's ongoing development as world leader in manufacturing and innovation. Also, a competitive European defence industry is vital for the credibility of the Common Security and Defence Policy (CSDP)' (S&D 2017: 66). Social democrats in the formation of the S&D thereby put the militarisation of the EU in the same bracket as innovation in renewable energies or manufacturing of sustainable products. The invocation of a social democratic motif becomes more than clear in the same position paper, where it is argued 'that security interests, industrial competitiveness and human rights considerations can go hand in hand' (S&D 2017: 22). This is not an isolated view but reproduced, for example, in the Progressive Post, a European level think tank that seeks to establish an intellectual crossroad between social democracy and the European project, and that has both the S&D and the PES as partners. In a critique on the projects chosen for defence funding in 2018, it was lamented that 'softer' projects, such as a medical command centre, have been prioritised over the development of High-Altitude Long Endurance (HALE) drones (Besch 2018). Even 'progressive' observers might see that strengthening of the military-industrial nexus at EU level can hardly be reconciled with the peace narrative permeating social democratic visions of European integration.

While the aforementioned investment programmes, albeit problematic in themselves, may give the impression of an active industrial policy to counter the decline in Europe's industrial base, they have been quite marginal thus far. Moreover, they camouflage the competitiveness agenda, *inter alia*, internal devaluation, which also forms part of the new common industrial policy.

Industrial Renaissance Through Internal Devaluation

As former Commissioner Almunia, a social democrat himself, affirmed, the new industrial policy differs markedly from that employed during the crisis of the 1970s; '[…] with governments picking winners and all that' (Almunia 2014). Rather than a commitment to state intervention to steer companies and industries towards a socially and ecologically innovative future, the Commission holds the view that the EU's future prosperity depends on its ability to attract investments, most notably Foreign Direct Investment (FDI) to compensate for the low domestic investments. Such investments, so the idea goes, would then boost a re-industrialisation across Europe, enhance economic growth and heighten net exports, with a 'trickle down' effect on employment. Indeed, since the 1970s, investments in the production sphere in relation to GDP have been declining, which is due to several factors, such as saturated markets, lingering over-capacity, slowly growing aggregate demand and a vast tertiarisation that came with outsourcing production to cheap labour areas. Measured in terms of gross fixed capital formation, investments decreased from 22.1% of GDP in 2000 to 19.3% in 2014, which is compared to 45% in China or 30% in India (European Commission 2015: 8). From 2000 to 2014, de-industrialisation accelerated in the EU: the share of manufacturing of the total EU GDP fell by 3.5 percentage points in nominal value-added terms (from 18.8 to 15.3%), and employment in manufacturing 16%, which translates in a reduction of 6 million jobs (ibid.: 5–7, 14).

In addition to the various investment programmes, the Commission suggests boosting the competitiveness of European economies as the prevailing way to create more investment opportunities in the real economy and to re-industrialise Europe. Competitiveness is almost exclusively understood in terms of internal devaluation, which can 'mimic the expenditure-switching effects of "external" exchange rate devaluation' (European Commission 2011: 22). In particular wage moderation is expected to make 'labour' less costly for business, and to translate into overall lower prices for goods and services. In addition, intense price competition, alongside a vast deregulation of product markets and further privatisations, is expected to lead to lower prices and hence overall lowered production costs. Last but not least, reduced corporate tax burdens, reduced taxes on exports and a 'revenue-neutral' shift from taxes on labour to consumption are expected to restore an attractive investment climate in Europe (ibid.). Or, as German Chancellor Merkel (2013) declared, the yardstick of competitiveness 'should be whether our products can compete in global markets'.

The competitiveness agenda and the internal devaluation strategy have been actively promoted and supported by organised (transnational) capital. The so-called Captains of Industry, assembled in the European Round Table of Industrialists (ERT), were invited to a meeting in Berlin in March 2013, bringing together the German Chancellor Merkel, French President Hollande and Commission President Barroso, where it was jointly agreed that industrial competitiveness should be at the centre of EU policy-making (ERT 2013). The ERT made its position unequivocally clear: to be competitive, the EU needed more business-friendly regulations, such as tax reductions, less labour protection and more labour market flexibilisation, lower wages and severance payments, further privatisations as well as the facilitation of mergers and acquisitions, or what the ERT calls 'market-driven consolidation' (ibid.). In June 2014, the ERT (2014: 1) issued an Agenda for Action 2014–2019 for the newly appointed Commission, titled 'EU Industrial Renaissance', echoing the Commission's documentation and demanding that 'industrial competitiveness should be mainstreamed throughout all policy areas and at all policy levels'. To achieve price competitiveness, the costs of labour, energy, finance and administrative requirements had to be reduced, while non-price competitiveness had to be fortified by an improved regulatory environment for enterprises (ERT 2012, 2014; BDI 2014). The joint articulation of national and transnational business seems to have borne fruit: internal devaluation achieved through lowering the costs of labour, reducing prices and taxes has currently become the most prevailing agenda point in EU crisis management.

Internal Devaluation Through the Labour Market

Emulating the emerging markets' comparative advantage of cheap labour constitutes a cornerstone of the EU internal devaluation strategy. The national productivity boards that are currently being established form the governance apparatus for the internal devaluation strategy: a central task will consist of monitoring that member states 'raise productivity while containing unit labour costs', as well as suggesting policies when 'cost competitiveness lags behind the euro area average' (Council of the European Union 2016). These national productivity boards will issue annual reports, which the European Commission can use as a basis for its CSRs in the European Semester and the Macroeconomic Imbalance Procedure (European Commission 2016a; Council of the European Union 2016). Unit labour costs have been a longstanding measure to assess and compare the evolution of competitiveness in the EU. While the components can vary, unit labour costs generally comprise the ratio between productivity and total labour compensation (direct and indirect labour costs). A reduction of unit labour costs is believed to have positive signalling effects to investors. Unit labour costs can be reduced either by increasing productivity or reducing elements of the total labour costs structure. However, since de-industrialisation in the 1970s, productivity in the EU has slowed considerably, and productivity gains in the tertiary sector are limited. Consequently, labour market adjustments, notably through wage suppression or labour market flexibilisation, are strongly emphasised, particularly as wages for temporary and flexible labour tend to be lower, and as social security benefits or experience-rated pay can be avoided. Chancellor Merkel (2013), has been quite outspoken in this respect when proclaiming that it was vital to keep driving down labour costs to create a regulatory environment in Europe that is attractive to investors.

The EU competitiveness agenda is implicitly premised on inflexible labour, rising and hence too high labour costs, unproductive labour and too powerful trade unions, as the root cause for the ongoing crisis. Although the Commission maintained that it will not intervene directly in wage levels and collective bargaining rules, it advocated that social partners should use the annual reports from national productivity boards as a guidance during wage-setting negotiations. The umbrella organisation of national trade unions, the European Trade Union Confederation, ETUC (2015), vehemently condemned neoliberal structural adjustments through the labour market and responded that 'we are only a hair's breath away from setting maximum wage standard for collective bargaining that are legally binding, or from questioning the validity of strike action [...]'. In marked contrast, social democratic parties seem entangled by the enthralling competitiveness rhetoric; at least, they have hitherto not discredited and de-legitimised the prevailing narrow vision of competitiveness. This is surprising as the use of unit labour costs as a core indicator for competitiveness has received its share of criticism. It appears that even ECB researchers have raised their doubts and admit that '[m] acroeconomic considerations have traditionally been the core element of competitiveness assessment. Macro indicators, such as unit labour costs (ULCs) or current account deficits, are both easy to communicate and related to the macroeconomic instruments that generally policy-makers can avail themselves of. However, in light of the renewed focus on growth, there is a need for a broader and more precise assessment of competitiveness' (ECB 2013).

The Competition-Competitiveness Nexus in Internal Devaluation

The Commission readily admits that internal devaluation through reducing unit labour costs is not the only strategy required, as only the cost of labour is targeted, thereby neglecting variable production costs such as energy and raw materials (European Commission 2015: 57). Thus, it also advocates a strict enforcement of competition rules as one of the main levers to reduce the cost of capital, energy, raw materials and other production inputs. Particularly the prices in the non-traded intermediate sectors, like electricity and energy, are in the spotlight. In addition, a range of 'pro-competition' reforms have been announced, notably reforms that remove perceived (regulatory) market barriers in product markets. According to the Commission, high levels of restrictiveness in national product and service markets inhibit cross-border expansion and investments, such as in utilities sectors such as energy, and network industries (European Commission 2016b: 34). Moreover, flanking regulatory packages, such as the 'Regulatory Fitness and Performance Programme' (REFIT) and 'Competitiveness Proofing' have already been employed to remove existing legislation and to screen future legislation regarding their impact on competitiveness.

The competitiveness agenda is thus premised on the idea that Eurozone economies can compete themselves out of the crisis based on an overall lowering of price levels. According to former Competition Commissioner Almunia (2012a, b), competition policy is 'the cheapest and most effective structural reform', 'at no extra cost for the taxpayer'. Competition, he argued, enhances 'competitiveness and innovation, creates jobs and drives economic expansion'. The Commission's faith in capitalist competition as the backbone for economic growth builds on the axiom that positive feedback loops in the form of higher competitiveness and better performance of entire economies can be expected if a plethora of discrete companies strive to become more efficient, increase their productivity and stay ahead of rivals through lower prices. The benefits of capitalist competition are presented as inherently positive-sum, lifting society to ever-higher standards of economic wealth, or, in the words of the Commission (2016b), 'consumers, taxpayers, workers and businesses – everyone is better off overall when competition exists in our markets'. Competition policy is also portrayed as a redistributive policy: through competition, prices are expected to converge towards marginal production costs, thereby reducing the portion of realised surplus value for capitalists and benefiting consumers.

Once more we can see that social democrats are strong supporters of a strict EU competition policy. The S&D group (2008, 2010) associates EU competition control with positively connoted terms such as 'freedom and equality', 'sustainability', 'economic and social solidarity', 'social and territorial cohesion', 'quality of life and an efficient and dynamic economy'. Competition policy is moreover considered 'a vital instrument for economic and social integration', 'guaranteeing consumer welfare and encouraging the optimum allocation of resources and in granting economic agents the appropriate incentives to pursue productive efficiency, quality and innovation but also low prices and employment' (ibid.).

Putting 'the Social' Back into Competitiveness?

What, then, are we to make of the EU industrial policy project in light of broader discussions about the European Social Model? Internal devaluation as a cornerstone of the EU's industrial policy needs to be discussed in the broader context of a concomitant renaissance of 'social Europe' through the EPSR. The core contradiction in the current conjuncture of social democratic Europeanism rests in propagating industrial policy reminiscent of Keynesian tradition, paired with a non-binding pillar framework invoking social rights, while at the same time buying into a competitiveness discourse that fundamentally undermines any chance for even remotely reconciling the economic and social objectives put forward. The 'paradox' of social democratic Europeanism as referred to in the introduction (see Holmes and Lightfoot 2014: 228) hence requires a critical reading.

The recent initiative for the EPSR should be seen against the institutional architecture that facilitates competitiveness as 'master policy paradigm' (Miró Artigas 2017). The rigid disciplinary rules and institutions of the Economic and Monetary Union (EMU) have already prefigured internal devaluation over the past decades: by warding off inflation and precluding national governments from unilaterally making exports cheaper via exchange rate adjustments, while the budgetary straitjackets and the absence of a common fiscal shock absorber ruled out the possibility of Keynesian-style industrial policies through deficit spending. Under the yoke of the Maastricht orthodoxy, adjustments to the labour market constituted the prime cure to improve trade balances. Moreover, far-reaching internal devaluation measures have already been employed in the context of MoU and the new economic governance packages, such as the European Semester of 2010 or the Euro Plus Pact of 2011. Under the euphemistic label of a new common industrial policy, not only the most crisis-hit member states but the entire EU has to step up reform efforts. EU economies not only have to undercut each other's cost and price competitiveness, or corporate tax rates in a competitive, beggar-thy-neighbour fashion but also those of the main trading partners or rivals.

In fact, experiments with internal devaluation through the labour market have hitherto fostered structural asymmetries in Europe. The example of Greece is pertinent here, where between 2008 and 2012 unit labour costs were reduced by 20% on the basis of rigorous interventions in the wage bargaining process, labour market flexibilisation and a reduction of minimum wages by 22% and an additional 10% for the young (ETUI 2014). So far, internal devaluation has increased neither employment levels nor exports. Labour costs have foremost been reduced in the public sector, which therefore left the export position unaffected. Moreover, Greek exports are concentrated in capital-intensive low and medium technology sectors, and not labour intensive sectors. Lower wages did also not translate into lower prices. In fact, Greek export prices increased by 20% between 2009 and 2013—the highest increase in the Eurozone (ibid.: 17). Reducing unit labour costs, in other words, merely served to improve returns on capital, and these returns have not been invested in long-term productivity, or in projects that improve the structural position of existing industries. As Sablowski (2012) explains, lowering wages in Greece cannot solve the problem that Greek industries cannot keep up the competition with Germany's in high-tech manufacturing, automobile production or the machine-tools industry, simply because such industries (or equivalents that would allow for high-value-added production for export) do not exist. Furthermore, a competitive reduction of unit labour costs cannot solve structural economic asymmetries between European economies. EU economies cannot all expand their industries and pursue an export-led growth pattern with a large trade surplus, particularly as a reduction of unit labour costs in one member state will weaken unit labour costs in others. Wage repression, in combination with austerity, undermines not only domestic but also intra-EU consumption, while triggering also deflation. All these factors combined render the proclaimed export-led growth strategy a farce, particularly against the backdrop of weak global demand. As extra-EU exports account for a relatively small share of the EU's GDP (ranging between 12 and 15%, see Eurostat 2017), internal devaluation will have a moderate effect on the EU's net-export position, if any at all (Stockhammer and Onaran 2012: 195–196). Internal devaluation will mainly increase the number of 'working poor' and precarious workers, hitting the youth, women and migrants, particularly non-EU migrants, and low-skilled workers the hardest (EuroMemorandum 2013: 39; ETUI 2014: 10). The effects of EU crisis management have already led to considerable social unrest and political contestation, contestation that directly targeted the EU. Notably Southern Europe has seen concerted actions, such as a series of transnational campaigns, manifestos and petitions, as well as joint strike days and weeks of action against EU austerity policies (see Wigger and Horn 2014). Established social democratic parties, however, maintained their uncritical pro-EU stance, and were unable to chart an alternative future for European integration. As a result, social democratic parties have not managed to win the support of a vast constituency, while neo-populist Eurosceptic, radical right and even neo-fascist parties successfully harness feelings of discontent and insecurity.

Against this background, the EPSR seems to put forward a strong emphasis on salvaging the European Social Model discourse, bolting it onto the industrial policy package. The Commission's position on this is rather clear in prioritising one over the other, arguing that, while 'economic and social progress are intertwined', social rights are, at the end of the day, means to the end of competitiveness: 'The establishment of a European Pillar of Social Rights should be part of wider efforts to build a more inclusive and sustainable growth model by improving Europe's competitiveness and making it a better place to invest, create jobs and foster social cohesion' (European Commission 2017b). The EPSR is mainly meant for the Euro area, as 'a stronger focus on employment and social performance is particularly important to increase resilience and deepen the Economic and Monetary Union'. Perhaps not unintentionally, the Commission has here conveniently left out that part of the story where EU crisis management and austerity have contributed to, if not caused, the social crisis that the EPSR is now seeking to address.

In terms of content, the principles at the heart of the EPSR cover three broad chapters; equal opportunities and access to the labour market, fair working conditions and social protection and inclusion. Its institutional form essentially consists of a recommendation (under Article 292 TFEU), which does not have any binding force, as well as a statement of commitment in form of a proclamation of the European Commission, the European Parliament and the Council. The latter is an interesting but mainly symbolic instrument, previously and most notably used for the EU Charter of Fundamental Rights. The EPSR is subject to intensive debate, politically as well as academically. It has been critiqued as 'neither very organised nor very clear' (Pochet 2017). Two illustrations here resonate with the arguments made earlier. On the one hand, the launch of the EPSR, and the choice of parental leave as one of the pilot initiatives, indeed indicates a concern with social rights that corresponds to social democratic themes. The vocal protests from, for example BusinessEurope (2017) against revisiting the parental leave directive (e.g. guaranteeing a paternity leave of at least ten days, carer's leave and transfer of leave between parents), indicate that the initiative is not wholly without traction. Overall, in light of the EPSR process BusinessEurope was adamant that the social dimension should be a means to the end of competitiveness: 'A genuine and appropriate social dimension of the EU/EMU can help underpin convergence. This should be a convergence towards the outcomes, i.e. restoring competitiveness, growth, employment and productivity [...] we believe that [...] priority areas for benchmarking [should be] reducing labour costs to facilitate job creation and labour market integration' (BusinessEurope 2016). Notably, it is not only the content of the proposed changes, which according to BusinessEurope would undermine competitiveness but also the fact that the Commission is suggesting harmonising measures that have previously been within the purview of welfare state provision. In his discussion of the EPSR draft in 2016, Seikel (2017) raises another pertinent point in the juxtaposition of competitiveness versus social rights. The EPSR is mainly focusing on individual rights, consistent with an overall focus of policy making on the individualisation of rights and responsibilities. Allowing for an integration into the EPSR, he argues, would 'otherwise highlight the illegitimacy of interventions in national wage policies and collective bargaining systems – be it by the Troika or the macroeconomic imbalance procedure'. The subjugation of collective rights such as wage bargaining to the overall aim of bringing wages in line with productivity is clearly outside of the range of the EPSR. And how could it be, as long as 'the European Pillar of Social Rights is part of the efforts to launch a new process of convergence within the EMU [...]. The future success of the euro area depends, in no small measure, on the effectiveness of national labour markets and welfare systems and on the capacity of the economy to swiftly absorb and adjust to shocks and to effectively tackle their social implications' (European Commission 2017b).

As long as this convergence is still fundamentally based on internal devaluation, as argued above, the invocation of the elusive European Social Model remains a futile and ultimately counterproductive venture for social democracy. It appears that these contradictions are becoming more explicit in the actual social democratic political project. Whereas the vote on the social pillar in the European Parliament in 2017 was hailed as 'one piece of evidence that this progressive cooperation is possible' even by the leader of the GUE/NGL group (EUObserver 2017), a recent discussion in form of an open letter on the EPSR by members of the S&D group illustrates clearly that there is an increasing awareness that the 'EPSR illustrates well the political trap we need to get out of as social democrats' (Beres 2017). Arguing that '[i]f Social Europe today is in such a poor state, it is largely the responsibility of the EPP family', the letter then makes the case for strengthening the EPSR further, beyond 'a proclamation of rights pre-existing since years in more important texts' (ibid.). In a similar vein, Pochet (2017), albeit cautiously, suggests that despite its vagueness and weaknesses, the Social Pillar has potential 'if (powerful) actors seize it' (Pochet 2017), with the potential for 'creating long-term change through a Polanyian approach aimed at rebalancing the social and the economic'. The argument that the social dimension would mainly require a stronger political coalition in order to be expanded might seem intuitively clear from an EU perspective. However, as our critical political economy perspective has shown, it is at the fundamental level of socio-economic governance that the bed for the social model has already been made, so to speak. In a recent contribution to the discussion of social Europe versus neoliberal development, Parker and Pye (2017) provide a nuanced discussion of the 'unfulfilled promise of social rights' in the EU, arguing that, to the extent that the EU has developed a discourse on the social, it has been recast in a manner compatible with the competitiveness agenda. 'Social Europe' as a reference point for debates is often much more broadly conceived than a focus on the limited social policies of the EU, and, as mentioned above, seen as a protective shield against market pressures emanating from the global economy (aka 'globalisation', see Dannreuther 2014; Nölke 2017). Once the social model is however irrevocably associated as a flanking measure for the endgame of competitiveness, with 'a great array of social and labour policy areas have been subsumed within macroeconomic coordination (Parker and Pye 2017: 7), even a limited claim to social protection becomes quite untenable. This leaves advocates of the competitiveness-cum-social project with rather empty hands. As Ryner (2014: 62) argues in his analysis of European social democracy, it is 'so deeply imbricated with the system that is in crisis that it is in no position to offer an alternative to it'.

CONCLUDING REFLECTIONS

The prevailing interpretation of the crisis at EU level has shifted over time from a crisis within the financial system to a crisis of sovereign debt, and more recently, to a crisis of competitiveness of European economies. As German Chancellor Merkel (2013) stated: '[…] from a European standpoint we must aim to be so competitive that we not only stay prosperous but become even more prosperous'. The question is, however, who will become more prosperous on the basis of the EU competitiveness agenda. Competitiveness is now conflated with lower wages, lower prices and lower corporate taxes, thereby construing the crisis in terms of inflexible labour markets, and high labour and production costs. What has been disguised as the new common industrial policy primarily serves to maximise the freedom of capital to exploit labour, which implies that less surplus from the production sphere will have to be redistributed to wage earners.

Ever since the adoption of neoliberal policies in the late 1970s, average wage shares of GDP have been on a downward trend, and so have corporate taxes. In a context where member states will have to undercut each other's internal devaluation policies in a 'beggar-thy-neighbour' fashion, labour will be even further devalued. We see thus more of the same neoliberal remedies. As competition disunites more than it unites, the competitiveness agenda, alias industrial policy, also jeopardises the establishment of a solid basis for future social cohesion and pan-European worker solidarity.

What is more, the competitiveness strategy is counterproductive and will only worsen the vast structural imbalances and uneven economic development in Europe, and if aggregate demand is tempered further, the propensity to invest in real production will stay weak. Due to the structural problem of overaccumulation, even more surplus capital will be freed for circulation in the financial sphere with the prospect that the next manifestation of this crisis will again be in the financial sector; however, this time far more dramatic that what we have seen since 2007/2008. This gloomy yet highly likely scenario raises rather uncertain prospects for the future of a social democratic vision of the EU. It also tasks critical observers with considering possible alternatives. In this context, Parker and Pye (2017) for instance introduce an interesting suggestion, calling for the Commission to strengthen the relevance of social rights with an *ex ante* constitutional check on EU policies, drawing on the Council of Europe's European Committee for Social Rights. Rasnača and Jagodziński (2017) draw on a suggestion in Juncker's 2017 State of the Union speech, namely the introduction of a European Labour Authority to facilitate monitoring the impact of cross-border company mobility on workers' rights, assistance in developing transnational collective bargaining system, implementation of the Directive on Workers Involvement in the Societas Europaea (SE) and European Cooperative (SCE) and the implementation of the European Works Councils Directive (2009/38/EC). In recent years, various alternative proposals for a productive transformation within the European Union have been discussed (e.g. Transform 2014). Suggestions that might replace the obsession with export-orientation fuelled by competitiveness could point towards an increased focus on domestic demand, just energy transition or infrastructural development. If the EU, and in particular progressive social forces within social democracy were to take social integration seriously, industrial policy would have to become a means towards a different endgame than competitiveness.

References

Almunia, J. (2012a). *The Role of Competition Policy in Times of Crisis.* Speech 12/917. Brussels.

Almunia, J. (2012b). *Policy Competition Policy for Innovation and Growth: Keeping Markets Open and Efficient.* Speech 12/172. Copenhagen.

Almunia, J. (2014). *Competition Policy Enforcement as a Driver for Growth.* Speech 14/178. Brussels.

Bailey, D. (2016, March 1). The End of the European Left? Social Democracy, Hope, Disillusion, and Europe. *Near Futures Online.*

Bailey, D., De Waele, J. M., Escalona, F., & Viera, M. (Eds.). (2014). *European Social Democracy During the Global Economic Crisis: Renovation or Resignation?* Manchester: Manchester University Press.

BDI. (2014). A Call from BDI and Confindustria to the German and Italian Government Ahead of the Spring European Council. *Joint Declaration with Confindustria.* Available at: http://www.bdi.eu/bdi_english/download_content/BDI_Confindustria_Joint_Declaration_EN.pdf. Accessed April 22, 2017.

Beres, P. (2017). *Open Letter.* Available at: https://www.pervencheberes.fr/?p=11556.

Besch, S. (2018, February 9). PESCO Unlikely to Deliver Much in the Short Term. *The Progressive Post.* Available at: https://progressivepost.eu/pesco-unlikely-deliver-much-short-term.

Blanchard, O., & Leigh, D. (2013). *Growth Forecast Errors and Fiscal Multipliers* (IMF Working Paper, WP/13/1), pp. 1–43.

BusinessEurope. (2016, August 24). *European Pillar of Social Rights—BusinessEurope Contribution to the Debate*. Available at: https://www.businesseurope.eu/publications/european-pillar-social-rights-businesseurope-contribution-debate.

BusinessEurope. (2017). *European Pillar of Social Rights—Right Aims, Wrong Approach*. Available at: https://www.businesseurope.eu/publications/european-pillar-social-rights-right-aims-wrong-approach.

Council of the European Union. (2016). Recommendation for a Council Recommendation on the Establishment of National Productivity Boards, ECOFIN 590, UEM 248, Brussels.

Dannreuther, C. (2014). The European Social Model After the Crisis: The End of a Functionalist Fantasy? *Journal of Contemporary European Studies, 22*(3), 329–341.

Dijsselbloem, J. (2017a). Remarks Following the Eurogroup Meeting of 20 February 2017. Press Release 77/17. Brussels.

Dijsselbloem, J. (2017b). Speech by the President of the Eurogroup, Jeroen Dijsselbloem, at the Future of Europe Event, 24 January 2017. Brussels.

ECB. (2013, June). *Competitiveness Research Network First Year Results, European Central Bank*. Available at: http://www.ecb.europa.eu/pub/pdf/other/competitivenessresearchnetworkfirstyearresults201306en.pdf.

ERT. (2012). *ERT's Priorities for an Integrated Industrial Policy*. Brussels: ERT.

ERT. (2013, March 18). *ERT Meets with Merkel, Hollande and Barroso on Europe's Competitiveness*. Press Release. Brussels: ERT.

ERT. (2014). *EU Industrial Renaissance: ERT Agenda for Action*. Brussels: ERT.

ETUC. (2015). *ETUC Position on National Competitiveness Boards*. Available at: https://www.etuc.org/documents/etuc-position-national-competitiveness-boards#_ftnref1. Accessed April 22, 2017.

ETUI. (2014). *Benchmarking Working Europe 2014*. Brussels: ETUI.

EUObserver. (2017, January 20). *New EU Parliament Coalitions Get in Shape*. Available at: https://euobserver.com/institutional/136612.

EuroMemorandum. (2013). *The Deepening Crisis in the European Union: The Need for a Fundamental Change*. Available at: http://www.euromemo.eu/euromemorandum/euromemorandum_2013/. Accessed April 20, 2017.

EuroMemorandum. (2017). *The European Union: The Threat of Disintegration*. Available at: http://www2.euromemorandum.eu/uploads/euromemorandum_2017.pdf.

European Commission. (2011). *The Effects of Temporary State Aid Rules Adopted in the Context of the Financial and Economic Crisis* (Commission Staff Working Paper). Brussels.

European Commission. (2013). *Towards a Deep and Genuine Economic and Monetary Union: The Introduction of a Convergence and Competitiveness Instrument*. COM(2013) 165 Final, Brussels.

European Commission. (2014). *For a European Industrial Renaissance.* Communication, Brussels.

European Commission. (2015). *EU Structural Change 2015.* Luxembourg: Publications Office of the European Union.

European Commission. (2016a). *Industrial Policy.* Available at: https://ec.europa.eu/growth/industry/policy/index_en.htm. Accessed April 20, 2017.

European Commission. (2016b). *EU Competition Policy in Action.* Available at: http://ec.europa.eu/competition/publications/kd0216250enn.pdf. Accessed April 20, 2017.

European Commission. (2017a). *State of the Union 2017—Industrial Policy Strategy: Investing in a Smart, Innovative and Sustainable Industry.* Available at: http://europa.eu/rapid/press-release_IP-17-3185_en.htm.

European Commission. (2017b). *Establishing a European Pillar of Social Rights.* COM(2017) 250 Final, Brussels.

European Commission. (2017c). *The European Defence Fund: Questions and Answers.* Available at: http://europa.eu/rapid/press-release_MEMO-17-1476_bg.htm.

European Commission. (2018). *European Defence Industrial Policy.* Available at: http://ec.europa.eu/growth/sectors/defence/industrial-policy_en.

European Council. (2013). *Conclusions.* EUCO 217/13. Brussels.

Eurostat. (2017). *International Trade.* Available at: http://ec.europa.eu/eurostat/. Accessed April 21, 2017.

Five President's Report. (2015). *Completing Europe's Economic and Monetary Union.* Available at: https://ec.europa.eu/commission/sites/beta-political/files/5-presidents-report_en.pdf. Accessed October 25, 2018.

Four Presidents' Report. (2012). *Towards a Genuine Economic and Monetary Union.* Available at: http://www.consilium.europa.eu/uedocs/cms_Data/docs/pressdata/en/ec/134069.pdf. Accessed April 22, 2017.

Heinrich, M. (2015). EU Governance in Crisis: A Cultural Political Economy Perspective on European Crisis Management 2007–2014. *Comparative European Politics, 13*(6), 682–706.

Holmes, M., & Lightfoot, S. (2014). Limits of Consensus? The Party of European Socialists and the Financial Crisis. In D. Bailey, et al. (Eds.), *European Social Democracy During the Global Economic Crisis.* Manchester: Manchester University Press.

Merkel, A. (2013, January 24). *Speech at the World Economic Forum Annual Meeting.* Available at: http://www.bundeskanzlerin.de/ContentArchiv/EN/Archiv17/Reden/2013/2013-01-24-merkel-davos.html. Accessed April 20, 2017.

Miró Artigas, J. (2017). European Integration, Social Democratic Europeanism and the Competitiveness Discourse: A Neo-Poulantzian Approach to Discursive Policy Analysis. *Palgrave Communications, 3,* 17060.

Nölke, A. (2017). Financialisation as the Core Problem for a "Social Europe". *Revista de Economia Mundial, 46*(2), 27–48.

Parker, O., & Pye, R. (2017). Mobilising Social Rights in EU Economic Governance: A Pragmatic Challenge to Neoliberal Europe. *Comparative European Politics, 16*(5), 805–824.

Pauly, M. (2018, January 26). *European Social Democracy Extinct?* Social Europe Blog. Available at: https://www.socialeurope.eu/pauly.

PES. (2014, March 31). *Towards a New Europe: The Manifesto of the Party of European Socialists.* Brussels.

Pochet, P. (2017, November 16). *The European Pillar of Social Rights in Historical Perspective.* ETUI blog. Available at: https://www.etui.org/News/The-European-Pillar-of-Social-Rights-in-historical-perspective.

Rasnača & Jagodziński. (2017, October 12). *Giving Juncker's Proposed European Labour Authority Real Clout.* ETUI blog. Available at: https://www.etui.org/News/Giving-Juncker-s-Proposed-European-Labour-Authority-Real-Clout.

Ryner, M. (2014). Why Has the Financial Crisis Not Generated a Social Democratic Alternative in Europe? In D. Bailey, et al. (Eds.), *European Social Democracy During the Global Economic Crisis: Renovation or Resignation?* Manchester: Manchester University Press.

Sablowski, T. (2012, May 16). The Global Economic Crisis: Impoverishing Europe. *Global Research.*

Seikel, D. (2017). The European Pillar of Social Rights. An Analysis. *Policy Brief WSI/Institute of Economic and Social Research, 17*(11), 1–19.

S&D Group. (2008). *Competition Policy, European and State Aid.* Brussels: Group of the Progressive Alliance of Socialists and Democrats in the European Parliament.

S&D Group. (2010). *European Competition Policy. For Social Cohesion, Quality of Life and an Efficient and Dynamic Economy.* Brussels: Group of the Progressive Alliance of Socialists and Democrats in the European Parliament.

S&D. (2017, September 26). *Security and Defence: Foreign Affairs, Human Rights, Security and Defence.* Position Paper. Available at: http://www.socialistsanddemocrats.eu/sites/default/files/position_paper/Security%20%26%20defence_en_171108.pdf.

S&D. (2018). *Industry, Research and Energy.* Available at: http://www.socialistsanddemocrats.eu/policies/industry-research-energy-0.

Stockhammer, E., & Onaran, O. (2012). Rethinking Wage Policy in the Face of the Euro Crisis: Implications of the Wage-Led Demand Regime. *International Review of Applied Economics, 26*(2), 191–203.

Wigger, A., & Buch-Hansen, H. (2014). Explaining (Missing) Regulatory Paradigm Shifts: EU Competition Regulation in Times of Economic Crisis. *New Political Economy, 19*(1), 113–137.

Wigger, A., & Horn, L. (2014). Uneven Development and Political Resistance Against EU Austerity Politics. In L. Pradella & T. Marois (Eds.), *Polarizing Development: Alternatives to Neoliberalism and the Crisis.* London: Pluto.

CHAPTER 9

Unusual Bedfellows? The IMF, Tackling Inequality and Social Democratic Policy Renewal

Ben Clift

Introduction: Inequality, Nationalism and Social Democratic Policy Space

Social democracy has always been about living with capitalism. This entails coping with capitalism's inherent instabilities and their social consequences. The desire to tackle inequality is a defining characteristic feature of social democratic political projects, arguably distinguishing social democracy from other liberal and centre-right political programmes. Historically, social democracy has been and arguably needs to remain, at the heart of the politics of struggles to achieve a more equitable distribution of wealth and power, and efforts to create the political authority structures which could create it.

B. Clift (✉)
Department of Politics and International Studies,
University of Warwick, Coventry, UK
e-mail: B.M.Clift@warwick.ac.uk

© The Author(s) 2019
C. Hay and D. Bailey (eds.), *Diverging Capitalisms,*
Building a Sustainable Political Economy: SPERI Research & Policy,
https://doi.org/10.1007/978-3-030-03415-3_9

The focus here is on inequality and the politics of seeking its redress for twenty-first century social democracy. It argues that the deep-rooted methodological nationalism at the heart of the traditional social democratic project is a major source of its weakness as a reforming political force in contemporary advanced economies. This national perspective characterised the political economy of social democracy as a political movement throughout the twentieth century, but the failure to 'move beyond the national' in convincing fashion is an important source of the problems facing social democratic ideological renewal in the twenty-first century (see Gamble 2009; Ferrera 2005, 2009). There is a pressing need for a post-national social democracy, or at least to post-nationalise social democracy (Gamble 2009). Yet cosmopolitan democratic thought—one vision for a scaling up of traditional social democracy notions—indicates the paucity of thinking on this topic (see, e.g., Smith and Brassett 2008; Brassett and Bulley 2007; Brassett 2010; Archibugi 2004; Archibugi and Held 1995).

The demise of social democracy has been pronounced repeatedly, with varying degrees of conviction in recent decades (Dahrendorf 1990; Giddens 1994; Gray 1996, 1998; Bailey et al. 2014). Power has shifted from labour to capital, and from the public sector to forms of private authority, both national and transnational. A globalising world economy characterised by heightened international capital mobility, advancing deregulation and privatisation, fragmenting class identities and a changing international division of labour are all seen to contribute to a more adverse environment for social democratic economic policy, progressive taxation, redistribution of wealth and regulation of firms and capitalism.

In response to this colder ideological and institutional climate, there have been successive waves of social democratic introspection, and attempted ideological redefinition and *aggiornamiento*. This attests to the *potential* capacity for ideological innovation, and renovation, within social democracy. However, the analysis of social democracy tends to become wedded to particular means through which, across the twentieth and twenty-first centuries, in different national contexts, the political aspirations of social democracy have been channelled—notably Keynesian political economy. Keynesianism has been identified closely with social democracy (see Przeworski 1985; Pierson 2001). Its role as a legitimating discourse was crucial to social democrats' perceived 'fitness to govern', justifying state intervention in the economy in a socially just direction in terms of economic efficiency. Keynesianism laid down a blueprint of how the economic regulatory potentialities of the nation-state could be tailored to secure the social democratic goal of full employment.

There is an elision within some studies of social democracy, assuming that because the political claims of social democracy were advanced through a particular set of policies or institutions (e.g. the welfare state and Keynesian economic policies), therefore social democracy is ultimately *reducible to* those elements. It 'follows' that the continuing viability of these institutions or policy approaches is a necessary condition of the enduring viability of social democracy. Yet this excessively static, indeed ahistorical conception misconstrues the relation between social democracy's programmatic goals and the institutional and ideational means deployed in pursuit of social democratic ends. So, the decreasing viability of national level Keynesian demand management in an adverse international economic environment, as was demonstrated by the Mitterrand experiment in the early 1980s, is read across to entail the decreasing viability of social democracy. Fundamentally, such an interpretation misunderstands the nature of social democracy and prematurely discounts its capacity for renewal (see Clift 2003a).

There are problems of diagnosis and prognosis with how the Keynesian policy paradigm is understood within means-based approaches which deem social democracy to be past its sell-by date (Gray 1996, 1998). The characterisation of Keynesianism (like social democracy more broadly) is often static, generalising too widely (across time and space) from a particular historically contingent articulation of Keynesianism and social democracy. This was always about Keynesianism in one country, pursued in a manner shrouded from international economic forces. Such an understanding downplayed the possibility and import of international coordination, and the application of Keynesian insights at a wider, regional or even global level. The focus in the social democracy literature on social democratic means, almost to the exclusion of ends, explains the confidence in assigning social democracy to the rubbish bin of history. National Keynesianism of the 'Keynesianism in one country' variety constituted but one 'strategic amalgam' (Pierson 1995: 34) through which to pursue the politics of social democracy. That all elements of this approach no longer retain the same relevance should not surprise us. Nor should it lead us to write off social democracy as a spent force. Rather, the changed international economic and domestic political context requires us to look how social democratic goals are pursued today, and seek to trace the outline of a new 'strategic amalgam'—or amalgams.

Paul Hirst offered an ends-oriented definition of social democracy which identifies its core elements, 'minimising the cost of capitalism for individuals, either through growth and employment enhancing policies, and/or, through welfare state provision for the contingencies of unemployment, ill-health and old age'. Secondly, it 'attempts to tackle and reduce major and unjustifiable inequalities in power and wealth', and thirdly it seeks to 'accomplish these objectives within the limits set by parliamentary democracy on the one hand, and private property and the market economy on the other' (1999: 87). In a similar vein, Karl Polanyi highlighted the dangers of social tensions arising from freer markets in his analysis of the Gold standard in the nineteenth century ([1944] 2001). Polanyi identified a dialectic between 'economic liberalism' and 'social protection'. The violent imposition of 'market organisation on society' ([1944] 2001: 258) risked ultimately 'annihilating the human and natural substance of society' ([1944] 2001: 3). If market relations are not embedded in society 'human beings would perish from ... social exposure', and suffer 'acute social dislocation' due to the 'congenital weaknesses' of market society, and 'the pernicious effects of a market-controlled economy' ([1944] 2001: 76). This desire for the social protection of vulnerable groups in society as a necessary accompaniment to the expansion of the market economy is a key *raison d'être* for social democracy. Operating with this more ends-oriented approach to social democracy, this chapter asks if the increasing concern to tackle inequality with the Bretton Woods institutions, especially the IMF, provides new opportunities for social democratic renewal in the post-crash context.

The focus on political actors other than social democratic parties, and on levels of action other than the nation-state is important because in the struggle for the creation of the political authority structures which could redistribute wealth, nation-states will arguably not be the primary actors. The new focus on inequality amongst international organisations—not just the IMF but also the OECD, could offer a conducive international environment to transcend social democracy's historic methodological nationalism. Might we see the emergence of a global public sphere where egalitarian policy coordination and promotion can be discussed and advanced? The goal of this chapter is to consider another alternative avenue for change presented by the current conjuncture. It asks to what extent does a confluence of interest in tackling inequality between Bretton Woods institutions, notably the IMF, and European social democracy change the contours of the policy space. How far does this increase the likelihood of progress on reducing capitalisms' inequalities? This context, and the kind of thinking about inequality and economic policy prevalent in the post-crash IMF (Clift 2018) has the potential to facilitate a more 'post-national' social democracy. This is something social democracy sorely needs (Gamble 2009), but social democratic parties find it very difficult, given their ideational and institutional legacies, to achieve.

THE ENDS OF SOCIAL DEMOCRACY: TACKLING INEQUALITY AND THE BRETTON WOODS ORDER

Tackling, mitigating and reducing the growing inequalities associated with capitalism through policy, regulation and institutional reforms are a particular concern to social democrats animated by their defining concern for equality. Whilst the Bretton Woods order in the early post-war years kept inequality in advanced economies within limits, since the collapse of Bretton Woods and the liberalisation and deregulation of capital flows since the 1970s, inequality as measured by Gini coefficients has been rising steadily (Glyn 2001, 2006). Within twenty-first century capitalism, inequality is rising dramatically in most advanced economies in the world, including in the USA and UK, and across the traditional Western European heartlands of social democracy (Stiglitz 2012, 2015; Piketty 2014, 2015). What Hacker and Pierson have called *Winner Take All Politics* has been a major contributing factor, with vast concentrations of wealth at the very top of the income distribution explicable in terms of massive concentrations of market power leading to public policy changes reducing the progressivity of tax and increasing tax and regulatory loopholes enabling the income distribution to become increasingly skewed in favour of the very wealthiest 0.01% in society (Hacker and Pierson 2010). Moreover, if inequality is on the rise *within* affluent societies, the scale of inequality between the Global North and South is at troublingly high levels. Indeed, one critique of European social democracy is that by focusing only on national level wealth inequality within a small number of affluent West European democracies, the chasm of North/South inequalities of wealth and power between global rich and global poor gets neglected.

The standard view for many years has been that, where inequality is concerned, the IMF are part of the problem, not part of the solution. The Fund's structural adjustment programmes of the 1980s and 1990s and other policies exacerbated inequalities in developing countries. They enforced fiscal discipline, eroded social provision and the public sector through privatisations, and required the cutting of public expenditures in ways which exposed poor and vulnerable social groups and undermined the building of social safety nets (see, e.g., Peet 2009). The IMF's reputation for exacerbating inequalities and reducing policy space through the programmes which accompany its lending is, of course, not without foundation. Indeed, in the post-crash period, countries not deemed to enjoy sufficient 'fiscal space' to pursue progressive policies continue to experience the IMF as a powerfully constraining force. Greece and the other European programme countries offer prime examples of this (Varoufakis 2017; IEO 2016). The parts of the IMF involved on forging the Troika programmes in 2010–2011, especially the one with Greece, required retrenchment and extraordinarily deep cuts in social provision which exacerbated inequality (Vasilopoulou et al. 2014).

However, it is important to disaggregate the Fund and identify different parts of the organisation which have offered different economic policy prioritisations since the global financial crash. If we consider the intellectual production of the influential Research Department, as showcased in flagship publication such as *World Economic Outlook* which constitutes the voice of the Fund staff, we can see that this is not your grandmothers' IMF (Grabel 2011; Lagarde 2014). The current Chief Economist and the last one espouse some progressive views about economic policy which prioritise tackling inequality in the interests of securing economic stability and growth. These views are shared by a range of senior figures in the Fund. The Fund's reputation for conformity with fiscally conservative one-size-fits-all neo-liberalism is at odds with its significant shift since 2008 towards more varied, and often more growth-oriented, policy discourse emphasising, amongst other things, tackling inequality (Clift 2018).

The IMF has, on a contingent basis, developed a different prescriptive policy discourse (for countries that *do* enjoy 'fiscal space') which contrasts quite starkly with its traditional reputation for austerity. The Fund today champions the tackling of inequality as critical to securing the economic stability at the heart of its mandate. To do so, the IMF proposes raising progressive income taxation levels, in a way which seems still largely off limits in many national policy discourses. There are also entreaties to kick-start growth through boosting aggregate demand and to pursue counter-cyclical infrastructure-upgrading public investment programmes. These IMF policy positions have been advocated consistently for many years now, and by successive managing directors of the Fund. Such a recalibration of economic policy orthodoxy provides key potential resources for centre-left politicians looking to bolster the economic credibility of their progressive economic programmes. One of the puzzles this chapter explores is why these evolutions have been all but ignored by social democrats.

AUSTERITY AND ALL THAT

In the UK, especially after the Coalition Government was elected in May 2010, the IMF consistently underlined that the government had additional policy space to pursue macroeconomic policies more supportive of the recovery. The scale and pace of cuts in the austerity programme were not, the IMF argued, warranted either by UK economic conjuncture or by debt dynamics and prevailing sentiment in international financial markets. Successive IMF Article IV Missions to the UK, the chief economist, and others highlighted how the UK Government had more room to move, that they could attenuate the pace of fiscal consolidation. The case was consistently made that the UK Government could and should engage in more public investment and infrastructure spending in support of growth. Osborne and the Treasury claimed they had no option but to stick to announced plans cuts. Anything else would not only undermine credibility but also lead to a 'Greek-style' crisis (see Clift 2018: Ch. 6).

The approaches to debt and deficit discourse amongst what Krugman termed the 'austerians' induced a sticking to Osborne's 'plan A' mentality. This was linked to the Treasury's choice of anchors of credibility (its pre-announced fiscal plans). The IMF, which chose more cyclically adjusted anchors of credibility, felt that significant policy change was needed, and could be undertaken with no adverse effect on Britain's international economic or fiscal credibility (Chopra 2014). The prosecution of austerity policies meant that the burden of adjustment fell on poorer social groups and certain geographical sections of British society. Adding to this burden were stagnating wages and ongoing deepening of financialisation and the entrenching of an asset-based welfare regimes whose effects were widening inequality gaps.

These austerity-oriented responses to the global financial crash materially shaped and limited UK economic policy possibilities, but all this was, of course, a product of political perception, and a particular narration and definition of 'crisis' (a crisis of debt). That is why the IMF's very different narrative and interpretation of the UK's policy space post-crash is interesting and important. The Fund's intellectual authority could have been mobilised by national politicians—either in government or in opposition—to sustain an alternative narrative. Such a rebooting of the economic policy debate was sorely needed in Europe in this period, which was living through a decade of crisis and austerity. There *was* an interesting and stimulating 'politics of economic ideas' type debate about what UK macroeconomic policy can and should do, and what it should prioritise. However, in this period this was going on within the IMF, and amongst leading economic policy commentators (Wolf, Wren-Lewis, Portes, Skidelsky, and others). It was not within UK party politics because of the strictures of deficit discourse.

The intriguing question is why social democrats such as Ed Balls and Ed Miliband did not choose to mobilise the intellectual resources presented by IMF lines of interpretation. Instead, they accepted a deficit discourse which erroneously said both that nothing else could be done, and inaccurately accepted that New Labour profligacy pre-2008 was the source of the crisis. Credibility concerns seemed to prevent New Labour from articulating a different macroeconomic policy vision. It was left to the IMF, Simon Wren-Lewis, Jonathon Portes at NIESR and the like to do so in their stead.

The IMF were calling in 2014 for counter-cyclical public infrastructure investment. Meanwhile, Larry Summers was underlining the prospects of secular stagnation and the need for bold macroeconomic policy activism to counter it. Yet it seemed that all those policy avenues were closed off to UK social democratic policy elites. They could not risk such policy positions for reasons of fiscal credibility, or so they seemed to think. To some degree, this same Labour deficit discourse of the Miliband/Balls era was perpetuated under Corbyn—who tried to incorporate Wren-Lewis into Labour's economic policy team—only for him to depart, disaffected, soon afterwards. McDonald's inexplicable and economically illiterate selection of a 'fiscal credibility lock' as a major economic policy commitment in 2016 was one root cause of the Oxford academic's disquiet.

The IMF and social democrats in this period were operating with palpably different conceptions of how much economic credibility the UK enjoyed, and what anchors it was tied to, and what space for growth- or redistribution-oriented policies it left. The IMF were in a way hark- ing back to a watered down version of what used to be called Keynesian stabilisation policy, built on a critique of Say's Law and the broader insight that if the market economy is not functioning well, 'ways should be found through public agencies of correcting its outcomes' (Gamble 1990: 138). The IMF's was a more international variant of Keynesianism than the post-war model—focused on the merits of internationally coordinated approaches to economic management. The Fund consist- ently highlighted the folly of all advanced economies pursuing fiscal consolidation at once. This underlined their point that policies geared towards demand require international coordination to be effective. The IMF went out of its way from 2010 onwards to deride the stridently anti-Keynesian thinking of the 'expansionary fiscal contraction' theorists who had influenced George Osborne's first budget in June 2010 (IMF 2010). UK social democrats did not seize the opportunity to align with or draw succour from the reputable rehabilitation of Keynesian think- ing. Neither was this in evidence in France, despite the attachment to Keynesian thought being deep within the contemporary PS.

Social Democracy and Methodological Nationalism: The French Example

One of the recurrent themes of this chapter is how methodological nationalism is hard-wired into social democratic thought and practice. The 'problem', from the point of view of thinking about the ideologi- cal renewal of social democracy, is that social democrats took inspiration from a particularly national-level Keynesianism which reinforced their deeply embedded methodological nationalism. The kind of Keynesianism to which social democracy developed a strong attachment served to fur- ther entrench rather than challenge the focus on the national economy and the nation-state as the scale of reforming activism. This did not pro- vide the mental furniture necessary for social democracy to evolve its programmatic vision and find new 'strategic amalgams' through which to pursue its political aspirations in an increasingly globalising and inter- nationalising economic order of the late twentieth and early twenty-first century. The supranational Keynesianism of the Clearing Union which was central to Keynes' own initial draft proposals at Bretton Woods was stillborn. Only a staunchly national version of Keynesian emerged in post-war Europe, and within the *modus operandi* of the Bretton Woods economic institutions, adjustment burdens fell on debtors, not creditors. The variant of Keynesian which was pursued was, accordingly, somewhat hollowed out (Best 2005). Thus, the ability to deliver on egalitarianism via Keynesian political economy was limited to a very small number of countries, and limited in how fully the strategy could be prosecuted in those few countries.

This deep-seated methodological nationalism, despite all the rhetorical appeal to socialist internationalism, is one of the main reasons why French Socialists have failed to carve out a new and distinctive identity or programme since the Jospin era of the late 1990s and early 2000s. The Hollande *quinquennat* did not deliver a coherent vision, or even any new thinking about a new vision for French Socialism (Clift and McDaniel 2017). The current and long-standing state of ideological stagnation within French Socialism reflects a broader condition of ideological flux and soul-searching within the European Left (Clift 2011). The reasons for this ideational inertia are manifold, too numerous to fully cover here, but in the French case, we highlight two powerful ideological legacies, the French Republican tradition, and the political economy of Keynesianism. This doctrinal baggage has arranged the PS' mental furniture in such a way as to make thorough-going revision within French Socialism difficult. Both these frames of reference weigh heavily on the ideological production of the party, establishing programmatic parameters which successive leaders and party conference texts have not transcended. Considering recent French Socialist discourse and practice, the lack of innovation in political and economic strategy is striking. Equally familiar is the unrealistic nature of many positions and proposals espoused by the French Socialists, especially when in opposition.

In France, methodological nationalism is so deeply entrenched partly because of French Socialism's reliance for programmatic inspiration on a particular reading of the French Republican tradition. What Jack Hayward calls the contested 'normative legacy' (2007) of the revolutionary decade of 1789–1799 has shaped French political ideologies and state–society relations ever since. Within French Socialism throughout the twentieth and now into the twenty-first century, Jean Jaurès' interpretation of the Republican tradition—notably his concept of 'la République Sociale'—has been powerfully influential. This saw 1789 as but the first step towards a true republic, laying the political foundations, leaving French socialists the task of translating political equality (before the law) into a more thorough-going social equality (of condition). The role of the state, as the embodiment of the Republic, in this egalitarian mission was unquestioned, extending liberty, fraternity and equality from the political domain to the social and production spheres. Thus the egalitarian element in French Socialism has always been couched in Republican terms, with a resultant statist approach not just to equality of opportunity but also to greater equality of material conditions. Within French Socialism, this particular brand of Republicanism still influences attitudes towards the institutions of the French State.

The new international economic context and the bruising lessons of periods in government in the last 35 years have made the socialists painfully aware of the limits of the possible. From every corner, political projects were founded on the assumption that international competitiveness was a necessary precursor to socialist advance. This brought the tension between economic efficiency and social justice into sharp relief, yet the egalitarian commitments of the PS have had little revision or re-evaluation. Pursuing Socialist policies in an open economy in the late twentieth/early twenty-first century in a context of the advancing processes of globalisation has been shown to be an extremely difficult task.

French Socialist analysis of France's economic problems, and in particular proposed solutions to long-standing high unemployment, has always had a distinctly Keynesian flavour. The focus is on boosting the purchasing power of the poorer members of society by attempting by various means, notably progressive taxation and wages policy, to redistribute wealth to them. This 'crisis of under-consumption' analysis is less pronounced today than in the national Keynesian heyday of the Mitterrand experiment between 1981 and 1983 (Hall 1986), but a broadly Keynesian vision still underpins French Socialist economic strategy and its critique of financialisation and neoliberal capitalism (PS 2010b: 4–5, 23–24; Clift 2003a).

The PS has always appealed first and foremost to national-level Keynesianism, at times supplemented with a desire to reshape the European political economy (along with French lines) and infuse it with a Keynesian spirit. As the Mitterrand experiment demonstrated, national-level Keynesianism in an open economy is problematic. Nevertheless, the French Socialist international and European reform agenda has consistently sought the reinvigoration of international Keynesianism, and the establishment of a 'New Bretton Woods', as in their October 2010 convention text on a new International and European order (PS 2010a: 12–15). As a strategy for the renewal of the future of social democracy, the appeal for a New Bretton Woods lacks credibility because the international political economic conditions have evolved to make such a scenario much less possible.

For all its commitment to internationalism and lengthy periods of reflection on international issues, the PS has never convincingly mounted a search for a way of living with capitalism that goes beyond the national level. It either calls for bold but unrealistic reforms to the UN or Bretton Woods institutions (in the French image), or it restates Tobin-tax-style proposals. The French Socialists have long clung to the notion that their Keynesian aspirations could be realised at the EU level (Clift 2003b; PS 2010a). Given German attachment to ordo-liberal principles, and its power within the Euro and processes of European construction, this was unrealistic. It was a very long shot even before the current fiscal crisis and sovereign debt concerns of the Eurozone. In its wake, where Schauble and Merkel have been the champions of European-wide austerity for nearly a decade (Clift 2018: Ch. 5), it looks entirely fanciful.

The constant reference to the French Republican tradition explains another curious facet of French Socialist thinking. Despite a strong ideological commitment to internationalism, written into the party's statutes and recent party texts, contemporary PS elites—like so many before them—offer a singularly France-centric account of the problems facing international society and possible solutions to them. PS internationalism always entails a Republican 'civilising mission' trying to make the rest of Europe, or the world, more like France. A recurrent theme within French Socialist discourse and texts is the unrealistic re-describing and re-imagining of the international and European order along very French lines. This is scarcely a viable, practicable or credible position from which to pursue an internationalist or internationalising agenda. Yet there is at best limited recognition of the collective action problems such a *French* vision faces in attempting to transform the European or wider international political economy. Thus, for example, the French Socialist vision for 'Social Europe' remains very closely modelled on the PS' own idealised self-image of French welfare institutions and labour market practices. French Socialists also seek to re-constitute European economic governance along the lines of an 'economic government'—consistent with the Republican statist tradition wherein state intervention in economic activity is the 'guiding force', providing capitalism with the necessary direction (Jospin 1995, 1999, 2001). Both have gone unrealised since the 1980s because of the unenthusiastic responses of European partners.

These aspects of PS identity and thinking betray a methodological nationalism which is hard-wired into French Socialist, and more broadly into European social democratic, thought and action. This is amply illustrated in PS texts on the International and European order, and on 'real equality', adopted following its October and December 2010 conventions (PS 2010a, b). This national perspective characterised the political economy of social democracy as a political movement throughout the twentieth century, but the failure to 'move beyond the national' in convincing fashion is an important source of the problems facing social democratic ideological renewal in the twenty-first century (see Gamble 2009; Ferrera 2005, 2009). These are but the French expressions of a wider problematic aspect of social democracy—how social democracy's deep attachment to Keynesian political economic ideas (of the 'Keynesianism in one country' variety) reinforces methodological nationalism.

The Post-crash IMF and the Contingent Expansion of Policy Space

The somewhat surprising question the remainder of this chapter addresses is how far the IMF might offer intellectual resources which could help social democracy escape this methodologically nationalist impasse in seeking to develop a political economic strategy and vision for tackling inequality in the twenty-first century. Recent research has challenged totalising understandings of the IMF and its intellectual position, analysing how persuasive struggles play out amongst competing 'subcultures' of economic thinking within the Fund, shaped by internal power relations (Chwieroth 2010; Ban 2015a, b; Clift 2018). This work finds Fund thinking to be less homogenous, more iterative, contingent and pragmatic than some earlier studies have implied (Blyth 2003; Grabel 2003; Wade 2001; Peet 2009).

The interpretation of the IMF offered here challenges, advances and updates extant understandings of IMF economists' shared beliefs, charting a revival of more Keynesian and market-sceptical 'subcultures' in the Fund, and their increased influence since 2008 (see Clift 2018).

It reveals the wide range of economic insights—including unconventional elements—reconcilable to mainstream economic thought, and how this affords key IMF actors hitherto neglected scope to select and prioritise within this menu of respectable economic thinking. The Fund's leading lights thought their Keynesian interpretation of the crisis and appropriate responses—notably prioritising international coordination of demand-oriented macroeconomic policies—was right, and the more orthodox approaches of Germany and the ECB were misguided. The reinvigoration of the Fund's Keynesian heritage in the context of the global financial crisis was in part motivated by its self-allocated role as a font of economic policy knowledge and by the Fund's desire to be 'on the right side of history' in the international economic policy debate. These dimensions of Fund policy commentary have gone under-reported and appreciated by scholars keen to critique the austerity-centric approach of the IMF (see, e.g., Stiglitz 2002; Webb 2000; Wade 2001). The Fund of the New Classical 'silent revolution' during the 1980s prioritised low inflation and austerity as necessary preconditions for growth (Boughton 2001: 25–28; Babb and Buira 2005). By contrast, the post-crash IMF took a more activist approach identifying supporting aggregate demand through counter-cyclical policy, infrastructure investment and tackling inequality as key macroeconomic components of securing growth in advanced economies. In this way, it strayed further onto social democratic economic policy terrain than one might have anticipated.

The IMF was designed as part of the Bretton Woods plan to create domestic policy space to pursue objectives, even if at odds with international financial market integration (Ruggie 1982, 1983). The initial Bretton Woods settlement curtailed short-term capital flows to enhance policy autonomy, as Keynes put it 'the whole management of the domestic economy depends on being free to have the appropriate rate of interest without reference to the rate prevailing elsewhere in the world. Capital control is a corollary to this' (1980: 148–149). Scholarship on the IMF of the Washington Consensus era critiqued the Fund for betraying these principles, curtailing policy autonomy and inducing countries to adjust to international economic conditions in ways which harmed the domestic economy (Davidson 2007: 93–103). As Thirkell-White summarised this view in the early 2000s 'many currently feel the IMF has reversed these priorities … attempts to push countries to adapt their social and political environments to suit market imperatives' (Thirkell-White 2005: 7; Best 2003; Soederberg 2004). Unlike the confining and restricting of policy space which Robert Wade and others associate with an earlier phase of the Bretton Woods institutions' interactions with developing economies (Wade 2003a, b), the post-crash construction and deployment of fiscal space involve the IMF seeking to *expand* the policy space for a select group of advanced economies.

THE IMF, FISCAL SPACE AND TACKLING INEQUALITY

Within the politics of austerity, the Fund has used its concept of fiscal space, which it had been developing since the mid-2000s, to couch and frame its policy narrative (Heller 2005; Ostry et al. 2010). Its imprecision notwithstanding, fiscal space was crucially important in enabling the Fund to differentiate its policy message according to national conditions, trajectories and debt structures and maturities. The Fund's social construction of 'sound' economic policy was refracted through this prism. The fiscal space framing offered a licence for Fund staff and missions to adjust how, and how far, debt and deficit reduction should be prioritised over other objectives, such as boosting aggregate demand, securing growth and tackling inequality. Allied to this, following the global financial crash, there was an innovative reinterpretation of the IMF's mandate, wherein the concern with growth and stability has been extended. Specifically, the Fund directly linked inequality and iniquitous outcomes from macroeconomic policy to instability and to lower growth. Research found that higher inequality reduces the size and duration of growth spells (Berg and Ostry 2011). Senior Fund figures from the last two Managing Directors down identified inequality as 'a macro-critical social indicator' (IMF 2011).The Fund under Strauss-Kahn and then Lagarde shifted significantly to make tackling inequality a priority in terms of its commentary, policy advice, research and contributions to the international economic policy debate.

Mainstream economics argues that the market determines the distributional outcomes of economic activity, and does not focus on the iniquitous effects of economic policy. Economists' default eschewal of political or ethical commentary on questions of inequality only began to be countered some years after the global financial crash when Piketty (2014, 2015) and Stiglitz (2012, 2015) directly addressed this issue. In perhaps the most pointed use of fiscal space to counsel a policy change, Deputy Director of the Research Department Jonathan Ostry and colleagues brought together a range of IMF research and other work to highlight the adverse effects of austerity on inequality, and through that on growth (Ostry et al. 2016: 38–39). The merits of neoliberalism, they noted, had been oversold. The effects of both fiscal consolidation and capital account liberalisation had contributed to rising inequality and were jeopardising a durable expansion. Highlighting an 'adverse feedback loop', and underscoring the non-linearities to which the post-crash Fund is increasingly attuned, the Fund's critique of neoliberalism noted that higher inequality caused by 'the neoliberal policy agenda', both capital account liberalisation and austerity, can hurt the very growth the policies are designed to support. Linking the advice back to the Fund core mandate, Ostry, Berg and Tsangarides note 'strong evidence that inequality can significantly lower both the level and the durability of growth' (Ostry et al. 2014).

The IMF's new focus on tackling inequality through macroeconomic policy as a way to secure economic growth and economic stability not only chimes with social democratic policy agendas but also offers an implicit critique of how fiscal consolidation has been pursued, mostly by Conservative and Christian Democrat governments, in certain advanced economies since the crash. This is why the Fund's post-crash reinterpretation of its mandate to redefine certain economic policy issues as 'macro-critical', notably inequality, was of such high political salience (IMF 2011). The focus on inequality dovetails with work on fiscal multipliers to reinforce the case for targeting spending on lower earners, to get the greatest bang for buck in supporting economic activity in the face of a severe downturn. More broadly, it indicates a role for macroeconomic policy in managing aggregate demand to sustain a high level of employment in the economy, and is further testament to the renewed influence of Keynesian thinking (IMF 2013: 4).

As the Fund's own research has recognised, fiscal consolidation leads to increased inequality (Ball et al. 2013; Furceri and Loungani 2013: 25–27; Woo et al. 2013). Thus the benefits of fiscal consolidation for the public finances need to be weighed against the costs in terms of iniquitous economic and social outcomes, and potential damage to long-term growth. Moreover, leading Fund figures underlined, addressing equity and equality considerations was important in gaining social and political acceptance for fiscal adjustment measures which will take many years (Lipton 2013). Although couched in the technocratic terms of the 'optimal composition' of fiscal consolidation, this was the IMF engaged in the politics of economic ideas. Key players at the Fund sought to shift approaches to austerity, endeavouring to convince governments with fiscal space to alter the pace of adjustment to limit adverse effects on inequality, demand and growth. These were all part of the Fund's contribution to the economic policy debate of the post-crash era for advanced economies.

In this way, the IMF's critique of 'the neoliberal agenda' was an important intervention in the politics of austerity debates, much discussed in the *Financial Times* and selected broadsheets. Ostry et al. questioned the wisdom of prioritising both fiscal consolidation and paying down public debt in all cases. Ostry et al. argue that for countries with 'ample fiscal space' (such as the UK and Germany) focusing on growth, rather than paying down public debt, would make more economic sense; 'the need for consolidation in *some* countries does not mean *all* countries - at least in this case, caution about "one-size-fits-all" seems completely warranted' (Ostry et al. 2016: 38–39). Countries with a strong track record of sound fiscal responsibility—enjoying fiscal space— have 'latitude' not to cut productive spending or raise taxes when debt is high (Ostry et al. 2010, 2016; Ghosh et al. 2013). Those countries enjoying this 'latitude' should use it because the benefits of paying down the debt, even for countries with very high debt levels, are 'remarkably small'. Indeed, the costs of paying down the debt 'could be large, much larger than the benefit' since cutting productive expenditure does excessive harm to growth.

Thus slowly reducing high debt through growth makes more economic sense than 'deliberately running budgetary surpluses to reduce the debt', and the IMF's considered view is that 'governments with ample fiscal space will do better by living with the debt' (Ostry et al. 2016: 40). This view was directly counter to the standard 'crisis of debt' line emanating from the German Government, and the UK Government between 2010 and 2015. The costs of austerity (lower output and higher unemployment) had been 'underplayed' and the benefits of countries with fiscal space focusing on growth to get high debt ratios to decline 'organically' had, Ostry et al. point out, been 'underappreciated'.

On inequality, as with market instability, the Fund is camped out on unconventional territory. Most mainstream economists would leave distributional questions to the market, comforted by the presumption that 'a rising tide floats all boats'. The Fund, however, has deployed significant resources in recent years working to address equity and inequality through the design of economic policy. This accentuated focus on inequality had a very specific relevance to the politics of austerity and the post-crash fiscal policy debate in advanced economies. A standard mantra of Lagarde as IMF Managing Director, like Strauss-Kahn before her, emphasised how fiscal policy needed to focus 'not only on efficiency, but also on equity, particularly on fairness in sharing the burden of adjustment, and on protecting the weak and vulnerable' (Lagarde 2012). The Fund is wont to recommend tax rises and increasing the progressivity of income tax regimes in ways which seem beyond the pale, even for mainstream left parties, in many national political discourses.

The post-crash Fund has made a series of such carefully calibrated interventions in the international economic policy debate to try and shift shared understandings of 'sound' economic policy. The direction of travel, during the protracted post-crisis recession in Europe, was towards a 'less now, more later' approach to fiscal consolidation for those countries enjoying the requisite fiscal space. The Fund raised concerns about adverse feedback loops (such as that between higher inequality and lower growth), and highlighted other nonlinear threats such as secular stagnation, deflation and hysteresis to strengthen their case (see Clift 2018). Another aspect of Fund advocacy of activist fiscal policy which side-stepped some fiscally conservative objections was the call for public infrastructure investment which would pay for itself through its positive growth effects, thus bringing debt down (IMF 2014).

The post-crash evolutions in IMF understandings of markets and stability, and its approach to inequality took IMF commentary towards the terrain of social democracy. These were the kinds of themes and tropes of social democratic critique of financial capitalism expounded over many decades. The catalyst for both shifts was the global financial crash, and each is testament to a broader post-crash revisiting of IMF policy premises. The Fund has become more sceptical about the operation of financial markets and their relationship to economic stability. Official post-mortems on the Fund's failure to anticipate the 2008 crisis identified a hitherto prevailing faith in unfettered market forces as an important causal factor (see Moschella 2011). For example, the Fund's Independent Evaluation Office report on pre-crisis surveillance noted the dominant view amongst IMF staff 'that market discipline and self-regulation would be sufficient to stave off serious problems in financial institutions' and also unearthed issues of confirmation bias (IEO 2011: 17) and a common belief in the 'presumed ability of financial innovations to remove risks off banks' balance sheets' such that 'large financial institutions were in a strong position, and thereby, financial markets in advanced countries were fundamentally sound' (IEO 2011: 7); 'most staff saw financial markets as inherently stable' (IEO 2011: 10). Fund commentary and research had never wholly brought into the infamous efficient market hypothesis (Fama 1970), but Fund staff were too willing to trust market outcomes. After 2008, the Fund became increasingly sceptical about financial markets and their properties, and IMF staff no longer presumed financial markets to be self-stabilising. Fund understandings of the nature and potential scale of market instabilities and systemic risks posed by fragile financial systems have evolved markedly.

The post-crash conjuncture appeared to be an ideal set of circumstances in which to use IMF positions and arguments to strengthen the economic credibility of the case for tackling inequality within capitalism. The Fund's internationalised Keynesian case for demand-oriented international economic coordination called for a different approach to austerity than that pursued by Conservatives and Christian Democrats in the UK, Germany and elsewhere after 2010. What is curious is that, both in the UK and France, social democrats did not pick up on or engage with the Fund overtures in 'their' direction. This is all the more surprising because the IMF carries with it the possibility to convey economic respectability and credibility upon the policy ideas it embraces. Historically, social democracy, especially when in government, has struggled to maintain economic credibility with financial markets and others.

Conclusion

The methodological nationalism which characterised the political economy of social democracy as a political movement in the twentieth century is a crucial source of the problems facing social democratic renewal today. There is a pressing need for a post-national social democracy, able to articulate an international vision for policy activism beyond the nation-state in ways more attuned to the complex economic interdependence which characterises our world. Social democracy needs to participate in the mapping out of a public sphere beyond the nation-state.

This could be built around externalities and the securing of global public goods. Yet cosmopolitan democratic thought—which entails a scaling up of traditional social democratic notions—indicates the paucity of thinking to date on this topic.

This chapter has taken a different route, but has sought to offer small steps towards a social democratic vision beyond the nation-state. It does this by asking how a confluence of interest in tackling inequality between Bretton Woods institutions and European social democracy changes the contours of progressive economic policy. The Fund of the new classical 'silent revolution' during the 1980s prioritised low inflation and austerity as necessary preconditions for growth (Boughton 2001; Babb and Buira 2005). By contrast, the post-crash Fund adopts a more activist, internationally Keynesian approach, which prioritises international economic coordination and identifies supporting aggregate demand through counter-cyclical policy, infrastructure investment and tackling inequality as key macroeconomic components of securing growth in advanced economies. The Keynesian-sympathetic subculture within the Fund has been in the ascendancy since the crash—with influential interventions from key figures like Blanchard, Ostry and others making the case for using macroeconomic policy to tackle inequality and boost aggregate demand (Clift 2018). This was an opportunity to bask in the reflected economic credibility of the Fund's surprisingly egalitarian policy positions.

Thus far bolstering social democratic economic policy credibility through alignment with the IMF on tackling inequality has been an opportunity not taken by British and French social democrats, as well as those elsewhere in Europe. One reason, perhaps, is that a reinvigoration of this variant of Keynesian thought, even in ways attuned to the need for international coordination, may not be sufficiently firm grounds on which to found a viable 'post-national' political economy of social democracy. Faced with today's harsh global and European climate for social democracy, the French and wider European left arguably need to develop new and viable theories of intervention in the economy. Its governing philosophy needs to face up to the contemporary capitalist conditions, and set out novel rationales for and logics of intervention. This is the kind of thinking which has the potential to 'post-nationalise' social democracy, but the French Socialists, Labour and other social democrats find it very difficult—because of their ideological and institutional legacies—to achieve that shift.

REFERENCES

Archibugi, D. (2004). Cosmopolitan Democracy and Its Critics: A Review. *European Journal of International Relations, 10*(3), 437–473.

Archibugi, D., & Held, D. (1995). *Cosmopolitan Democracy.* Cambridge: Polity.

Babb, S., & Buira, A. (2005). Mission Creep, Mission Push and Discretion: The Case of IMF Conditionality. In A. Buira (Ed.), *The IMF and the World Bank at Sixty.* London: Anthem Press.

Bailey, D. J., De Waele, J.-M., Fabien, E., & Mathieu, V. (Eds.). (2014). *European Social Democracy During the Global Economic Crisis: Renovation or Resignation?* Manchester: Manchester University Press.

Ball, L., Furceri, D., Leigh, D., & Loungani, P. (2013). *The Distributional Effects of Fiscal Consolidation* (IMF Working Paper WP/13/151). Washington, DC: International Monetary Fund.

Ban, C. (2015a). Austerity Versus Stimulus? Understanding Fiscal Policy Change at the International Monetary Fund Since the Great Recession. *Governance, 28*(2), 167–183.

Ban, C. (2015b). From Designers to Doctrinaires: Staff Research and Fiscal Policy Change at the IMF. In G. Morgan, S. Quack, & P. Hirsch (Eds.), *Elites on Trial.* Bingley: Emerald Group Publishing Limited.

Berg, A., & Ostry, J. D. (2011). *Inequality and Unsustainable Growth: Two Sides of the Same Coin?* (IMF Staff Discussion Note SDN/11/08). Washington, DC: International Monetary Fund.

Best, J. (2003). From the Top-Down: The New Financial Architecture and the Re-embedding of Global Finance. *New Political Economy, 8*(3), 363–384.

Best, J. (2005). *The Limits of Transparency: Ambiguity and the History of International Finance.* Ithaca: Cornell University Press.

Blyth, M. (2003). The Political Power of Financial Ideas. In J. Kirshner (Ed.), *Monetary Orders: Ambiguous Economics, Ubiquitous Politics.* Ithaca, NY: Cornell University Press.

Boughton, J. M. (2001). *Silent Revolution: The International Monetary Fund 1979–1989.* Washington, DC: International Monetary Fund.

Brassett, J. (2010). *Cosmopolitanism and Global Financial Reform: A Pragmatic Approach to the Tobin Tax.* Abington: Routledge.

Brassett, J., & Bulley, D. (2007). Ethics in World Politics: Cosmopolitanism and Beyond? *International Politics, 44*(1), 1–18.

Chopra, A. (2014). *The IMF Was Right to Criticize UK Fiscal Policy.* Peterson Institute for International Economics Realtime Economics Issues Watch blog. Available at: https://piie.com/blogs/realtime-economic-issues-watch/imf-was-right-criticize-ukfiscal-policy.

Chwieroth, J. M. (2010). *Capital Ideas: The IMF and the Rise of Financial Liberalization.* Princeton: Princeton University Press.

Clift, B. (2003a). *French Socialism in a Global Era*. London: Continuum.

Clift, B. (2003b). The Changing Political Economy of France: *Dirigisme* Under Duress. In M. Ryner & A. Cafruny (Eds.), *A Ruined Fortress? Neo-liberal Hegemony and Transformation Europe*. New York: Rowman & Littlefield.

Clift, B. (2011). The Frozen Pendulum: The Ideological, Organisational and Electoral Travails of French Socialism. *Renewal: A Journal of Labour Politics, 19*(1), 16.

Clift, B. (2018). *The IMF and the Politics of Austerity in the Wake of the Global Financial Crisis*. Oxford: Oxford University Press.

Clift, B., & McDaniel, S. (2017). Is this Crisis of French Socialism Different? Hollande, the Rise of Macron, and the Reconfiguration of the Left in the 2017 Presidential and Parliamentary Elections. *Modern & Contemporary France, 25*(4), 403–415.

Dahrendorf, R. (1990). *Reflections on the Revolution in Europe*. Piscataway: Transaction Publishers.

Davidson, P. (2007). *Interpreting Keynes for the 21st Century: Volume 4: The Collected Writings of Paul Davidson*. Basingstoke: Palgrave Macmillan.

Ferrera, M. (2005). *The Boundaries of Welfare*. Oxford: Oxford University Press.

Ferrera, M. (2009). Solidarity Beyond the Nation State? Reflections on the European Experience. In O. Cramme & P. Diamond (Eds.), *Social Justice in the Global Age*. Cambridge: Polity.

Furceri, D., & Loungani, P. (2013). Who Let the Gini Out? *Finance & Development, 50*(4), 25–27.

Gamble, A. (1990). *Britain in Decline*. Basingstoke: Macmillan.

Gamble, A. (2009). Moving Beyond the National: The Challenges for Social Democracy in a Global World. In O. Cramme & P. Diamond (Eds.), *Social Justice in the Global Age*. Cambridge: Polity.

Ghosh, A., Kim, J., Ostry, J., Qureshi, M., & Mendoza, E. (2013). Fiscal Fatigue, Fiscal Space and Debt Sustainability in Advanced Economies. *Economic Journal, 123*(566), 4–30.

Giddens, A. (1994). *Beyond Left and Right: The Future of Radical Politics*. Stanford: Stanford University Press.

Glyn, A. (Ed.). (2001). *Social Democracy in Neoliberal Times: The Left and Economic Policy Since 1980*. Oxford: Oxford University Press.

Glyn, A. (2006). *Capitalism Unleashed: Finance, Globalization, and Welfare*. Oxford: Oxford University Press.

Grabel, I. (2003). Ideology, Power and the Rise of Independent Monetary Institutions in Emerging Economies. In J. Kirshner (Ed.), *Monetary Orders: Ambiguous Economics, Ubiquitous Politics*. Ithaca, NY: Cornell University Press.

Grabel, I. (2011). Not Your Grandfather's IMF: Global Crisis, 'Productive Incoherence' and Developmental Policy Space. *Cambridge Journal of Economics, 35*(5), 805–830.

Gray, J. (1996). *After Social Democracy* (p. 47). London: Demos.

Gray, J. (1998). *False Dawn*. London: Granta.

Hacker, J. S., & Pierson, P. (2010). *Winner-Take-All Politics: How Washington Made the Rich Richer—And Turned Its Back on the Middle Class*. New York: Simon and Schuster.

Hall, P. (1986). *Governing the Economy*. Cambridge: Polity.

Hayward, J. (2007). *Fragmented France: Two Centuries of Disputed Identity*. Oxford: Oxford University Press.

Heller, M. P. S. (2005). *Understanding Fiscal Space* (IMF Policy Discussion Paper PDP/05/4). Washington, DC: International Monetary Fund.

Hirst, P. (1999). Has Globalisation Killed Social Democracy? *The Political Quarterly, 70*(s1), 84–96.

IEO. (2011). *IMF Performance in the Run-Up to the Financial and Economic Crisis: IMF Surveillance in 2004–07*. Washington, DC: International Monetary Fund. Available at: http://www.ieo-imf.org/ieo/files/issuespapers/Crisis_Final_Issues_Paper_Web.pdf.

IEO. (2016). *The IMF and the Crises in Greece, Ireland and Portugal*. Washington, DC: International Monetary Fund.

IMF. (2010, October). *World Economic Outlook*. Washington, DC: International Monetary Fund.

IMF. (2011). *2011 Triennial Surveillance Review—Overview Paper* (approved by SPR). Washington, DC: International Monetary Fund.

IMF. (2013). *Key Aspects of Macroprudential Policy*. Washington DC: International Monetary Fund.

IMF. (2014, October). *World Economic Outlook*. Washington, DC: International Monetary Fund.

Jospin, L. (1995). *Propositions pour la France 1995–2000*. Paris: PS Presse.

Jospin, L. (1999). *Modern Socialism*. London: Fabian Society.

Jospin, L. (2001). *My Vision of Europe and Globalization*. Cambridge: Polity.

Keynes, J. M. (1980). *The Collected Writings of J.M. Keynes: Vol. 25 Activities 1940–44: Shaping the Postwar World: The Clearing Union* (D. Moggridge, Ed.). Cambridge: Cambridge University Press.

Lagarde, C. (2012, June 8). *Completing the Task: Financial Sector Reform for Stability and Growth*. Speech hosted by the Süddeutsche Zeitung, New York. https://www.imf.org/en/News/Articles/2015/09/28/04/53/sp060812a.

Lagarde, C. (2014, May 27). *Economic Inclusion and Financial Integrity— An Address to the Conference on Inclusive Capitalism*. London. Available at: https://www.imf.org/external/np/speeches/2014/052714.htm.

Lipton, D. (2013). *David Lipton's Opening Remarks at Fiscal Forum: The Evolving Role of Fiscal Policy*. International Monetary Fund. Available at: http://www.imf.org/external/np/seminars/eng/2013/fiscal/. Accessed May 2, 2017.

Moschella, M. (2011). Lagged Learning and the Response to Equilibrium Shock: The Global Financial Crisis and Imf Surveillance. *Journal of Public Policy, 31*(2), 121–141.

Ostry, M. J. D., Berg, M. A., & Tsangarides, M. C. G. (2014). *Redistribution, Inequality, and Growth* (IMF Staff Discussion Note SDN/14/02). Washington, DC: International Monetary Fund.

Ostry, J. D., Ghosh, A. R., Kim, J. I., & Qureshi, M. S. (2010). *Fiscal Space* (IMF Staff Position Note SPN/10/11). Washington, DC: International Monetary Fund.

Ostry, J. D., Loungani, P., & Furceri, D. (2016). Neoliberalism: Oversold. *Finance & Development, 53*(2), 38–41.

Parti Socialiste. (2010a). *Texte de la Convention nationale Pour unenouvelle donne internationale et européenne adopté à l'unanimité le 9 octobre 2010.* Paris, PS Presse. http://www.parti-socialiste.fr/static/8739/convention-internationale-texte-definitif-avec-tous-les-amendements.pdf?issuusl=ignore.

Parti Socialiste. (2010b). *Convention égalité réelle Texte présenté lors de la convention nationale Samedi 11 décembre 2010.* Paris, PS Presse. http://www.parti-socialiste.fr/static/9373/samedi-suivez-la-convention-egalite-reelle-en-direct-73415.pdf?issuusl=ignore.

Peet, R. (2009). *Unholy Trinity: The IMF, World Bank and WTO.* London: Zed Books.

Pierson, C. (1995). *Socialism After Communism.* Cambridge: Polity.

Pierson, C. (2001). *Hard Choices: Social Democracy in the 21st Century.* Cambridge: Polity.

Piketty, T. (2014). *Capital in the 21st Century.* Cambridge, MA: Harvard University Press.

Piketty, T. (2015). Putting Distribution Back at the Center of Economics: Reflections on Capital in the Twenty-First Century. *Journal of Economic Perspectives, 29*(1), 67–88.

Polanyi, K. ([1944] 2001). *The Great Transformation: The Political and Economic Origins of Our Time.* (2nd Beacon Paperback). Boston, MA: Beacon Press.

Przeworski, A. (1985). *Capitalism and Social Democracy.* Cambridge: Cambridge University Press.

Ruggie, J. (1982). International Regimes, Transactions and Change: Embedded Liberalism in the Post-war Economic Order. *International Organization, 36*(2), 379–415.

Ruggie, J. (1983). International Regimes, Transactions and Change: Embedded Liberalism in the Postwar Economic Order. In S. Krasner (Ed.), *International Regimes.* Ithaca, NY: Cornell University Press.

Soederberg, S. (2004). *The Politics of the New International Financial Architecture: Reimposing Neoliberal Domination in the Global South*. London: Zed Books.

Smith, W., & Brassett, J. (2008). Deliberation and Global Governance: Liberal, Cosmopolitan, and Critical Perspectives. *Ethics & International Affairs, 22*(1), 69–92.

Stiglitz, J. E. (2002). *Globalization and Its Discontents*. New York: W. W. Norton.

Stiglitz, J. E. (2012). *The Price of Inequality: How Today's Divided Society Endangers Our Future*. New York: W. W. Norton.

Stiglitz, J. E. (2015). The Origins of Inequality, and Policies to Contain It. *National Tax Journal, 68*(2), 425.

Thirkell-White, B. (2005). *The IMF and the Politics of Financial Globalization*. Basingstoke: Palgrave Macmillan.

Varoufakis, Y. (2017). *Adults in the Room: My Battle with Europe's Deep Establishment*. London: Bodley Head.

Vasilopoulou, S., Halikiopoulou, D., & Exadaktylos, T. (2014). Greece in Crisis: Austerity, Populism and the Politics of Blame. *JCMS: Journal of Common Market Studies, 52*(2), 388–402.

Wade, R. H. (2001). Capital and Revenge: the IMF and Ethiopia. *Challenge, 44*(5), 67–75.

Wade, R. H. (2003a). The Invisible Hand of the American Empire. *Ethics & International Affairs, 17*(2), 77–88.

Wade, R. H. (2003b). What Strategies are Viable for Developing Countries Today? The World Trade Organization and the Shrinking of 'Development Space'. *Review of International Political Economy, 10*(4), 621–644.

Webb, R. (2000). The Influence of International Financial Institutions on ISI. In E. Cardenas, J. Ocampo, & R. Thorp (Eds.), *An Economic History of Twentieth-Century Latin America: Volume I: The Export Age*. New York: Springer.

Woo, J., Bova, M. E., Kinda, M. T., & Zhang, M. Y. S. (2013). *Distributional Consequences of Fiscal Consolidation and the Role of Fiscal Policy: What Do the Data Say?* (IMF Working Paper 13/195). Washington, DC: Institute for International Economics.

INDEX

A

Anglo-liberal capitalism, 1, 6, 18
Austerity, 4, 7, 8, 13, 37, 172–174,
    185, 186, 200–202, 206,
    208–214

B

Banking Union (BU), 12, 99, 109,
    111, 162
Bank of England, 11, 31, 44–46, 48,
    78, 79, 81, 82, 84, 108, 109,
    155, 160
Barnier, Michel, 86
Barroso, 180
Basel, 106, 107, 121
Bretton Woods, 198, 199, 204, 206,
    208, 214
Brexit, 1, 4, 5, 9–11, 13, 18, 25, 36–
    40, 44, 47, 60–65, 67, 74, 75,
    77, 91, 92, 99, 100, 115–118,
    134, 142, 144, 149–151, 155,
    160, 162–167
Brown, G., 21, 33, 107

C

Cameron, D., 11, 12, 73, 75–77, 84,
    85, 87–91, 93, 130, 131, 134,
    135, 138, 142, 143, 158, 161
Capital Markets Union (CMU), 12,
    91, 92, 100, 102, 104, 112–115,
    117, 150, 151, 155, 158–161,
    164–167
China, 32, 62, 77, 83–85, 162, 177,
    179
The City, 3, 9–12, 19, 26, 43–54,
    57–61, 63–67, 73–93, 103,
    106, 107, 113–115, 117, 135,
    139, 142, 145, 150, 151, 155,
    159–163, 165, 166
City-Bank-Treasury nexus, 11
City of London, 3, 9–11, 19, 26,
    43–48, 50–54, 57, 59–61, 63–66,
    73, 83, 103, 106, 113, 114, 117,
    139, 149, 151, 160, 161, 163,
    166
City of London Corporation, 60, 160
Coalition Government, 36, 77

© The Editor(s) (if applicable) and The Author(s), under exclusive license   221
to Springer Nature Switzerland AG, part of Springer Nature 2019
C. Hay and D. Bailey (eds.), *Diverging Capitalisms*,
Building a Sustainable Political Economy: SPERI Research & Policy,
https://doi.org/10.1007/978-3-030-03415-3

Commission, 82, 90–92, 102, 107–110, 112–114, 126, 127, 132, 133, 135, 139, 150, 153, 156–158, 160, 161, 165, 172–183, 186, 189

Common Market, 26

Competition state, 2, 29

Competitive advantage, 10, 11, 53, 59, 66, 115

Competitiveness, 1–3, 8–10, 13, 14, 23, 33, 64, 65, 105, 152, 156, 172, 173, 175–184, 186–189, 205

Confederation of British Industry (CBI), 13, 50, 150, 153, 154, 156–158, 163–166

Conservative Party, 5, 6, 11, 21, 81, 115, 156, 163

Convergence, 1, 3, 4, 18, 39, 153, 165, 187

Coordinated Market Economy (CME), 2

Corbyn, J., 40, 63, 202

Council of Ministers, 111, 157

Customs Union, 5, 38, 162

D

Debt, 4, 7, 11, 32, 99, 109, 110, 132, 133, 137, 151, 152, 159, 174, 178, 189, 201, 202, 206, 209, 211, 212

Dollar, 11

Draghi, 140, 141

E

Economic and Monetary Union (EMU), 29, 66, 100–102, 104, 115, 117, 118, 144, 162, 184, 187

Economic growth, 4, 8, 10, 21, 29, 35, 39, 62, 79, 159, 179, 183, 210

EU Commission, 38, 115, 158

EU industrial policy, 13, 172, 173, 176

Euro, 11, 53, 91, 129, 131, 175, 184, 186, 206

European Central Bank (ECB), 87, 108, 109, 111, 116, 126, 138, 140, 141, 159, 165, 182, 208

European Economic Community (EEC), 18, 76

European Financial Stabilisation Mechanism (EFSM), 126

European integration, 28, 34, 35, 39, 100, 126, 130, 131, 143, 144, 149–151, 153, 156, 161, 166, 167, 179, 186

European Parliament, 61, 125, 142, 153, 157, 158, 172, 176, 186, 188

European Pillar of Social Rights (EPSR), 133, 173, 186, 188

European Single Market, 5, 10–12, 38, 151, 152

European Social Model, 13, 24, 28, 33, 172, 173, 184, 186, 187

European Stability Mechanism (ESM), 12, 110, 126, 136

European Union (EU), 4, 6, 12, 13, 17, 23, 34, 35, 73, 77, 90, 99, 113, 157, 172, 181, 190

Eurozone, 4, 9, 11, 40, 150, 159, 162, 174, 176, 183, 185, 206

Exchange Rate Mechanism (ERM), 21, 27, 30, 78, 80, 92

F

Finance, 2, 10, 11, 40, 45, 46, 61, 62, 64, 73, 78, 83, 91, 99, 100, 104, 115, 116, 118, 132, 133, 137, 141, 149, 151, 153, 159, 163, 177, 180

Financial integration, 111, 115, 149, 159, 161

Financial regulation, 12, 86, 99–101,
    104, 105, 116, 118, 134, 155
Financial services, 19, 22, 53, 59–62,
    66, 75–77, 79–81, 83, 85, 87–91,
    93, 102, 105, 112–117, 141,
    151, 153, 160, 163
Financial Transaction Tax, 101, 105,
    106
Fiscal Compact, 12, 87, 88, 127,
    131–136, 138, 143, 175
Foreign direct investment (FDI), 22,
    28, 52, 177, 179
Frankfurt, 61, 80, 113, 119

G
Globalisation, 1, 3, 36, 40, 44, 50–61,
    63–67, 162, 167, 188, 205

H
Hammond, Philip, 63
Hegemony, 43–45, 47, 51, 65, 67

I
IMF, 14, 126, 137–139, 144, 172,
    175, 176, 198, 200–203,
    207–214
Immigration, 7, 37
Industrial policy, 13, 49, 172–174,
    176–179, 184, 186, 189, 190
Inequality, 7–9, 13, 14, 37, 195, 196,
    198–201, 207–214

J
John Major, 23, 39
Juncker, Jean-Claude, 91, 112,
    114, 115, 132, 160, 172,
    177, 190

K
Keynes, J.M., 14, 204, 208
Keynesian, 2, 184, 196, 197, 203–
    207, 210, 213, 214
Keynesianism, 14, 196, 197, 203–205,
    207

L
Labour market, 4, 5, 7, 13, 39, 64,
    149–153, 156–158, 164, 166,
    173, 180–182, 184, 186, 206
Labour Party, 7, 50
Liberal Market Economy (LME), 2,
    6, 10

M
Maastricht Treaty, 101, 149
Macron, 178
Manufacturing, 3, 28, 31, 33, 35, 37,
    78, 79, 81–83, 85, 151, 152,
    172, 177–179, 185
Merkel, A., 132, 134, 141, 175, 178,
    180, 181, 189, 206

N
Neoliberal, 5, 13, 36, 64, 172–175,
    182, 188, 189, 210, 211
New Labour, 33, 35, 36, 156, 202

O
Obama, 85, 137
Osborne, G., 63, 81, 106, 139, 141,
    201, 203

P
Paris, 62, 88, 113, 119

R

Referendum, 6, 11, 17, 18, 60, 61, 63, 73–77, 86, 89–91, 93, 115, 118, 125, 131, 134, 144, 156, 158, 163, 164

Renminbi, 11, 83, 84, 93

S

Sarkozy, 86, 132, 134

Single Market, 60, 77, 80, 81, 87–89, 102, 115, 130, 141, 144, 150, 153, 157, 158, 161–164, 166

Social democracy, 10, 13, 14, 65, 171, 173, 178, 187, 190, 195–199, 203, 206, 207, 212–214

Social Europe, 174, 188, 206

Sovereign debt crisis, 4, 11, 99, 109, 110, 174

Stability and Growth Pact, 104, 131

Sterling, 11

T

Thatcher, Margaret, 20, 23

Theresa May, 6, 7, 63, 116, 142, 145

Third Way, 13, 171

Tony Blair, 23

Transatlantic Trade and Investment Partnership (TTIP), 102, 104

Treasury, 6, 11, 21, 44–46, 48, 49, 74, 78, 82, 84, 105, 106, 139, 144, 150, 151, 153, 155, 157, 158, 160, 161, 201

Two-level games, 12, 128, 129, 131, 136, 143–145

U

UKIP, 37, 40, 88

United States, 17, 20, 21, 34, 62, 79, 127

V

van Rompuy, H., 132, 134, 135

Varieties of Capitalism, 2

W

Welfare state, 2, 7, 30, 35, 65, 67, 172, 187, 197, 198

Printed by Printforce, the Netherlands